Immaterial Archives

D1714008

 FLASHPOINTS

The FlashPoints series is devoted to books that consider literature beyond strictly national and disciplinary frameworks, and that are distinguished both by their historical grounding and by their theoretical and conceptual strength. Our books engage theory without losing touch with history and work historically without falling into uncritical positivism. FlashPoints aims for a broad audience within the humanities and the social sciences concerned with moments of cultural emergence and transformation. In a Benjaminian mode, FlashPoints is interested in how literature contributes to forming new constellations of culture and history and in how such formations function critically and politically in the present. Series titles are available online at http://escholarship.org/uc/flashpoints.

SERIES EDITORS: Ali Behdad (Comparative Literature and English, UCLA), Editor Emeritus; Judith Butler (Rhetoric and Comparative Literature, UC Berkeley), Editor Emerita; Michelle Clayton (Hispanic Studies and Comparative Literature, Brown University); Edward Dimendberg (Film and Media Studies, Visual Studies, and European Languages and Studies, UC Irvine), Founding Editor; Catherine Gallagher (English, UC Berkeley), Editor Emerita; Nouri Gana (Comparative Literature and Near Eastern Languages and Cultures, UCLA); Susan Gillman (Literature, UC Santa Cruz), Coordinator; Jody Greene (Literature, UC Santa Cruz); Richard Terdiman (Literature, UC Santa Cruz), Founding Editor

A complete list of titles begins on p. 201.

Immaterial Archives

An African Diaspora Poetics of Loss

Jenny Sharpe

NORTHWESTERN UNIVERSITY PRESS | EVANSTON, ILLINOIS

Northwestern University Press
www.nupress.northwestern.edu

Copyright © 2020 by Northwestern University Press.
Published 2020. All rights reserved.

Edouard Duval-Carrié's *La vraie histoire des Ambaglos* (*The True History of the Under-water Spirits*), 2003, acrylic, sequins, collage, and resin on wood, 96 x 84 in. Collection of William D. and Norma Canelas Roth. Copyright © 2019 Artists Rights Society (ARS), New York / ADAGP, Paris. Edouard Duval-Carrié, *The Indigo Room or Is Memory Water Soluble?* 2004, NSU Art Museum Fort Lauderdale; acquired by exchange through the Dorothy A. Smith Bequest. Copyright © 2019 Artists Rights Society (ARS), New York / ADAGP, Paris. Frantz Zéphirin, *The Slave Ship Brooks,* 2007, Collection of Marcus Rediker. Kamau Brathwaite, *The Zea Mexican Diary.* Copyright © 1993 by the Board of Regents of the University of Wisconsin System. Reprinted by permission of The University of Wisconsin Press. Kamau Brathwaite, "Baptism Poem" from *the lazarus poems*. Copyright © 2017 by Kamau Brathwaite. Published by Wesleyan University Press and reprinted with permission. M. NourbeSe Philip, "Zong! #1," "Zong! #14," "Zong! #26," and "Zong! #" from *Zong!* Copyright © 2008 by M. NourbeSe Philip. Published by Wesleyan University Press and reprinted with permission. Sections of chapter 1 appeared as "The Archive and Affective Memory in M. NourbeSe Philip's *Zong!*" *Interventions* 16, no. 4 (2013): 465–82. Sections of chapter 3 appeared as "When Spirits Talk: Reading Erna Brodber's *Louisiana* for Affect." *Small Axe* 16, no. 3 (2012): 90–102.

Printed in the United States of America

10 9 8 7 6 5 4 3 2 1

Library of Congress Cataloging-in-Publication Data

Names: Sharpe, Jenny, author.
Title: Immaterial archives : an African diaspora poetics of loss / Jenny Sharpe.
Other titles: FlashPoints (Evanston, Ill.)
Description: Evanston, Illinois : Northwestern University Press, 2020. | Series: Flashpoints
Identifiers: LCCN 2019018290 | ISBN 9780810141575 (paper text : alk. paper) | ISBN 9780810141582 (cloth text : alk. paper) | ISBN 9780810141599 (e-book)
Subjects: LCSH: Caribbean literature (English)—Black authors—History and criticism. | Arts, Caribbean. | African diaspora in literature. | African diaspora in art.
Classification: LCC PR9210.5 .S473 2020 | DDC 810.99729—dc23
LC record available at https://lccn.loc.gov/2019018290

For Russel, in memoriam

Those who i hold most dear
are nvr dead

they become more than fixed
in song or stone or album

mixed with my sand and mortar
they walk in me with the world

—Kamau Brathwaite, **me/ong/**

Contents

Acknowledgments

The writing of a book is always a journey, and I have met so many remarkable people and been the recipient of several generous fellowships along the way that this book would have been a different one without them. NourbeSe Philip, thank you for such a moving performance of your *Zong!* poems on that autumn day following the once-in-a-lifetime alignment of earth, moon, and sun. Edouard Duval-Carrié, *merci* for talking to me in your Little Haiti studio about the centrality of Caribbean history and Haitian Vodou to your *métier*. Erna Brodber, after I expressed how much I loved your novel *Louisiana*, you said I had to visit the Jamaican Louisiana, and I did. Wandering through the lush tropical gardens of your Woodside home, visiting the nearby site of the Taíno petroglyph of Atabey, and engaging in long conversations over your home-cooked meals and ginger tea caused me to see your work in new light. During my travels across the Caribbean, I was planning on stopping off at Barbados to interview Kamau Brathwaite at his Cow-Pastor home but decided against it after hearing that his health was failing. Perhaps not so surprisingly, a tall, gregarious, and charismatic man I recognized to be the poet visited me in a dream, speaking at length in words that only made sense inside dreamspace. I hurried over to my laptop to find the questions I wished to ask, but by the time I returned, he was gone. His words may have been lost, but the sensation of the dream remained.

My understanding of Vodou would have been greatly diminished without the assistance of those whose expertise far exceeds what is accessible in books. *Oungans* Ti Edner in Port-au-Prince and Jean-Daniel Lafontant in Los Angeles patiently responded to my questions as I sought to understand the complexities of the religion, especially the sea *lwa*, Agwe and Lasirèn, and the geography of Ginen. Thanks also to Judith Bettelheim, Robin Derby, Lisa Paravisini-Gebert, Patrick Polk, and Kate Ramsey for pointing me in the right direction when I sought out their help to learn more about the sacred world of Vodou and Haitian art. Michel DeGraff and Kathy Smith translated the Kreyòl for me—*mèsi*! I'm also grateful to Kathy for relaying questions on my behalf to Frantz Zéphirin. *Mèsi, mèsi*! Marcus Rediker, Norma Canelas, and Bill Roth provided access to paintings in their private collections, and my conversations with them made their passion for Haitian art spill over into my world.

A second group of scholars helped me unravel archival sources on the *Zong* massacre. Michelle Faubert, Andrew Lyall, James Oldham, and James Walvin shared their working knowledge of the *Zong* archives with me as I attempted to pinpoint evidence concerning the lone African who climbed back onto the slaver after being thrown overboard. Velma Pollard was an invaluable resource for my understanding of Doris Brathwaite. Betty Wilson and Elaine Savory also shared stories of Doris with me, and these several female voices came together in a chorus to make the woman I had not met and did not know come to life.

The generous financial support of an American Council of Learned Societies Fellowship, a University of California President's Research Fellowship in the Humanities, and a Stuart Hall Foundation Fellowship afforded me the release time from teaching and service to hunker down and finish the book. UCLA Academic Senate grants provided funding for research assistance. The year I spent in residence at the W. E. B. Du Bois Research Institute at the Hutchins Center of Harvard University has left its indelible mark on my writing and being in the world. The scholarly space created by Henry Louis (Skip) Gates Jr., Krishna Lewis, and Abby Wolf went far in allowing me to test my ideas while providing community during these uneven and unpredictable times. A shout-out to my cohort of fellows, especially Zelalem Kibret Beza, David Bindman, Kurt Campbell, Myisha Cherry, Christa Clarke, JC Cloutier, Martha Diaz, Matheus Gato, Myles Osborne, Shenaz Patel, and Tef Poe. What a time we had!

My book has also benefited from an early testing of its ideas in my graduate seminars "Reading beyond Literary Narrative," "The Postcolonial Archive," and "The Archival Turn in Literature and Theory." The diverse and varied perspectives students brought to the classes allowed me to unpack the multifaceted aspects of the archive. Jen MacGregor and Arielle Stambler, my research assistants extraordinaire, tracked down books and obscure references, in addition to assisting me in preparing the manuscript for publication. My dissertation students have been involved in this project in one way or another, even as they have gone on to establish careers and scholarly reputations of their own. Dana Linda accompanied me to Orlando to view Duval-Carrié's *La vraie histoire des Ambaglos* when it was still in storage. The painting is now on display at the Orlando Museum of Art. Deb Doing was instrumental in bringing NourbeSe Philip to the UCLA campus and also translated sections of Freud's "Notiz über den Wunderblock" from German for me. Neetu Khanna's dissertation on revolutionary feelings (now a book) inspired my own exploration of affect. Sam Pinto turned her keen eye and exacting criticism to my manuscript for catching its leaps of faith and oversights. When a teacher can learn from her students, she knows that her mentoring work is done.

My own teacher, as always, is Gayatri Chakravorty Spivak, long after she has ceased to be my mentor, as I continue to learn from her work. This book is guided by the ethical imperative she invokes in *An Aesthetic Education in the Era of Globalization*, namely, that our writing respond to "the trivialization of the humanities and the privatization of the imagination" in the American academy today. Earlier versions of my chapters were presented at meetings of the Canadian Association for Commonwealth Literature, the Caribbean Studies Association, and the Caribbean Philosophical Association. Responses from unidentified members of the audience have found their way into my revisions, and I am grateful for their thoughtful engagements with the book's incipient ideas. I am also grateful to Sandra Gunning for inviting me to workshop the first chapter at the University of Michigan when the entire book project was still a sketch in my head. I also benefited from Anjali Arondekar presenting her work at UCLA and inviting me to present mine at UC Santa Cruz.

No one could ask for better interlocutors than the ones I have at UCLA. The intellectual community of Ali Behdad, King-Kok Cheung, Fred D'Aguiar, Liz DeLoughrey, Helen Deutsch, Yogita Goyal, Jonathan Grossman, Ursula Heise, Carrie Hyde, Françoise Lionnet, Arthur Little, Saree Makdisi, Kathleen McHugh, Uri McMillan, Harryette Mullen, Shu-mei Shih, Juliet Williams, and Richard Yarborough is surpassed by none other, and their collective scholarship has pushed me to do better. Michael Meranze was always ready to provide a historian's perspective when I needed one, and he, along with Ali Behdad, Helen Deutsch, and Yogita Goyal, read portions of the book at different stages of its writing, providing feedback along with their friendship. An extra expression of gratitude to Jonathan Grossman, who was always prepared on short notice to read and discuss the book's ideas, helping me make them accessible to non-Caribbeanists.

I am more than grateful to Susan Gillman, the point person for the Northwestern University Press FlashPoints series, for having the vision to see the book's potential at a time when, due to grief, I could not. A huge thanks goes out to the anonymous readers, whose identities I may have guessed, for catching errors and providing astute reviews that allowed me to make this a better book. Any outstanding errors are entirely my own. I could not have asked for a better production team than the one I had at Northwestern University Press. The collective expertise of Trevor Perri, Patrick Samuel, Anne Gendler, Tim Roberts, Marianne Jankowski, and JD Wilson made the process smooth, pleasurable, and anxiety-free.

This book especially would not have been possible without Jeff, my soulmate and partner in life—thanks for more than thirty years of intellectual and emotional support, as well as attending to family needs during my overseas research trips and yearlong residency in Cambridge. Our children, Maleka and Max, now adults, have lived with the writing of this book as much as I have and are probably happier than anyone else to see it finished. My younger siblings, Maxine and Steven, what can I say? You are my greatest fans and sole survivors of our vanishing and scattered tribe. The pale horse came for our brother in 2018—too early, too soon; there is never enough time. For seven months of the year, he and I were but a year apart in age, and memories of growing up together in London, Bombay, and Beirut sustained me when trying to find the right words for describing loss. His extraordinary storytelling skills and larger-than-life imagination fueled my childhood love of literature, as I sought out the adventures he described and which, for a girl at that time, were mostly available in books. It is to you, my dearest brother Russel, I now dedicate this book. I say good-bye to you who has left this earthly world with the same words you signed off your letters to me—*Banzai* Ten Thousand Years!

Immaterial Archives

Introduction

The Shape of Immateriality

Iles cicatrices des eaux
Iles évidences de blessures
Iles miettes
Iles informes
Iles mauvais papier déchiré sur les eaux

Islands scars of waters
Islands testimony of wounds
Islands crumbs
Islands without form
Islands waste paper shredded over the waters

—Aimé Césaire, *Cahier d'un retour au pays natal* (1956)

The immaterial archives of this book do not exist in a library or other repository; in fact, they are not an archive at all. The "immaterial" that qualifies the "archives" of my title refers to the intangible quality of affects, dreams, spirits, and visions that art and literature introduce into material archives. Are these phenomena something or nothing? Do they have substance or belong to the insubstantial and unsubstantiated realm of the imagination? *Immaterial Archives* addresses the paucity of documentary evidence concerning the lives of people who were immaterial to the archiving process, but not by treating contemporary art and literature as an alternative archive. In exploring intangible phenomena, it identifies a different relationship of the arts to written records than as imaginative reconstructions of archival silences and lost pasts. Through historically grounded readings that are also attentive to formal innovations, my book examines instead how Afro-Caribbean writers and artists disrupt, bend, and break the categories of archival knowledge and their accompanying notions of "the human." "Immaterial" refers to the degraded status of African-derived knowledge, languages, and cultures within colonial archives, as well as the diminished status of the humanities in an information-based society today. The term is also gendered as the book traces a female gendering and regendering of the elusive, silent, and invisible spaces of immateriality. Each chapter—"Silence," "The Invisible," "Word Holes," and "DreamStories"—centers on a different figurative form for reassessing the requirements of archival recovery and the meanings of loss. Together, the chapters reveal silences not to be absences, and the invisible as not the same as what cannot be seen, where words sit on top of large holes leading to a parallel world of spirits, and the gossamer of dreams paradoxically returns us to the repositories of material archives.

My study proceeds by way of transactions, exchanges, and conversations, both real and imagined, between history writing and the creative arts. The writers and artists of my study, residing in Canada, Jamaica, Barbados, Haiti, and the United States, were selected for their commitment to black histories—two are also historians. Tobagonian Canadian poet and writer M. NourbeSe Philip draws on her legal training for addressing the structured silences of British law. She was prompted to write her book of poems *Zong!* (2008) after chancing upon an account of the 1783 London trial during which underwriters contested liability for Africans thrown alive into the sea from the slave ship *Zong*. The poems attend to loss through the concrete imagery of Language poetry, but their words are so fragmented that they do not deliver meaning as such. I weave Philip's refusal of storytelling into histories of the massacre in order to explore the point at which creative and historical approaches to official records intersect but also where they part ways.

Jamaican fiction writer Erna Brodber and Barbadian poet Kamau Brathwaite, both trained historians, have been instrumental in a recovery of black histories. For her dissertation, "The Second Generation of Freemen in Jamaica, 1907–1944" (1984), Brodber conducted ninety interviews that are now archived on tape and in transcript at the University of the West Indies, Mona. Brathwaite is the author of several history books including the first (1977b) to offer documentary evidence of the existence of the Jamaican maroon leader Nanny, who was previously consigned to the realm of myth and legend.[1] For Brodber and Brathwaite, creative writing is one among several modalities for addressing archival gaps and silences, but not through a writing of straightforward narrative or historical fiction. Their contributions, along with the other creative enterprises of this study, are more on the plane of innovation and experimentation. Brodber is known for writing fiction that avoids direct storytelling in favor of puzzles, parables, and cryptic plots requiring an intimate knowledge of Jamaican vernacular culture. Brathwaite has reinvented himself as a poet, turning away from Standard English to writing in Nation language, to which he added the erratic punctuation, punning, and wordplay he calls Calibanisms and the computer-generated graphics of his Sycorax Video Style. The literary works selected for the purposes of this study thread archival materials through Afro-Caribbean sacred cosmologies, especially those belonging to Jamaican Revival religions and Haitian Vodou. But Brodber and Brathwaite do not simply include in their prose and poetry the sacred forms of these religions. They fuse them with modern machines for challenging a historicist temporality that locates the slave's world outside of industrial modernity.

Haitian American artist Edouard Duval-Carrié shares with Brathwaite the compulsion to collect that Walter Benjamin (1975, 29) identifies in one who senses the "pulse" of the past in the present. Over the years, Brathwaite has collected thousands of books, papers, and recordings pertaining to the cultural history of the Caribbean, particularly as it relates to his own poetic life. Duval-Carrié seeks out colonial-era European books in order to understand the circulation of ideas and people across the islands during the era of the Haitian Revolution. I have selected artworks in which he submerges images from these books and antislavery pamphlets within the vastness of a Vodou cosmology to make a European worldview and its perspective on slavery seem small by comparison. While Duval-Carrié's aesthetic style has been compared to the so-called "naïve" school of Haitian art, my chapter makes a case for how he combines European modernist and Haitian Vodou forms in a way that reconceives an early twentieth-century modernist appropriation of African sacred iconography.

My discussion of Vodou-inspired aesthetics includes a painting that is the product of an actual transaction between history writing and the creative arts. Stuart Hall calls interdisciplinarity one of the most challenging of practices due to two different skill sets or approaches not being transferable across lines that divide. But, he also says: "It's when these two begin to come together in a conversation that isn't organized by academic institutional lines of contact that something really happens" (1999). I identify a flash of creativity that jumps the line separating disciplinary from black vernacular knowledge in the course of a conversation between a university-trained historian and the self-trained Haitian artist Frantz Zépherin. The painting that my book addresses introduces Haitian oral histories into the written records the historian incorporated into his history book. The resulting image, in which the living memory of Vodou is superimposed onto a well-known antislavery drawing of a slave ship, opens the archival document's frame of reference to a Caribbean history that was previously ignored. By including Caribbean visual art and poetry in addition to fiction, my objective is to demonstrate that storytelling, which Literature and History share, is not the only form for working with archival materials.

Immaterial Archives enters a rich interdisciplinary field of inquiry about the nature of the archive: its silences, opacity, authority, form, and institutionalization.[2] Ann Laura Stoler (2009, 44–45) identifies the emergence of an archival turn within history, anthropology, and literary studies when the archive began to be treated as subject and not just as source. Yet, she also indicates that "the archive" is not necessarily the same object of scrutiny for historians and cultural theorists because for the former group it refers to a collection of documents in a building, whereas for the latter the term serves as a metaphor for what the archive represents. My book's discussion of archives traverses the division Stoler describes in its examination of different kinds of archival sources as well as the metaphors and literary imaginaries informing our approach to them. It works with an expanded understanding of what constitutes "the archive" in a movement from official records as the primary source in the first chapter to embodied memory forms, oral histories, and digitization in the subsequent ones. At the same time, my usage of "immaterial" rather than "nonmaterial" or even "embodied" archive signals a turning away from the recovery imperative that requires a continuous expansion of archival sources.

That conventional archives are material goes without saying. Anyone who has spent time in a repository of official records or special collections with their printed, typed, or neatly transcribed documents, handwritten drafts, and more personal papers like diaries and letters, knows that feeling of anticipation when a cardboard box, fragile manuscript, or leather-bound ledger is carried majestically into the reading room. Archives are as tactile as they are visual. To see writing on the page from the hand of a person who is long dead or to run one's fingers along the letters on parchment that was once living skin makes us feel as if we are actually touching the past. The description provided by Jules Michelet of history writing as an activity that liberates the dead from their entombment provokes Carolyn Steedman into calling the French National Archive a building of dreams. "To enter that place where the past lives," she declares in *Dust,* "where ink on parchment can be made to *speak,* remains still the social historian's dream, of bringing to life those who do not for the main part exist" (2002, 70). The tangible quality of archives as traditionally conceived licenses the conviction that the past is not dead. However, digitization increasingly places originals out of reach, locked up for safekeeping with only their images accessible on computer screens.

In "The Power of the Archive and Its Limits," Achille Mbembe (2002, 19–22) likens the archive, excepting digitization, to not only a tomb but also a temple: a sepulcher that buries the remains of the dead in order to save them from future destruction and a religious space where rituals are regularly enacted. The status and power of the archive, he explains, lies in the monumental stature of its building, with its columns, hallways, and labyrinth of rooms, and the tangible materiality of its records. The physical presence of the building offers proof that something happened, someone once lived, and serves as the basis for a storytelling that lies beyond its four walls. Since not all documents are destined for preservation, Mbembe also characterizes the status of the archive as imaginary due to the collection in one place of records considered worthy of safeguarding, giving an illusion of totality and coherence to "fragments of lives and pieces of time" (19).

For scholars of Atlantic slavery, the illusion of coherence is practically impossible to maintain when it comes to recovering lives that are irrelevant to the record-keeping process. This is why, in their introduction to the special issue of *History of the Present,* "From Archives of Slavery to Liberated Futures?," Brian Connolly and Marisa Fuentes assert that, at least in the Anglo-American context, "the history of slavery remains a field constructed around ideas of lack, absence, and silence" (2016, 112). The enslaved, particularly women, appear in documents for reasons having little to do with stories of their lives. Accompanying the feelings of anticipation over opening a plain unmarked box filled with documents or receiving a handwritten ledger is the disappointment at the end of the day when one leaves the building with few notes relative to the length of time spent. This is why Jennifer Morgan interjects into Steedman's dream of breathing life into inert documents her own experience of combing page after page for the appearance of the words "negro" and "woman" as "failure after failure to find the people you are looking for" (2015, 155). Yet, she does not resign herself to failure, seeing instead how archival lack fuels even more innovative approaches to reading the records and writing histories.

The propensity of recent studies to persist in recovering slave lives despite a recognition of the impossibility of the task has prompted the editors of a special issue of *Social Text* titled "The Question of Recovery" to describe the dual pull of recovery and its failure as a "generative tension" (Helton et al. 2015, 2). The tension they describe underlies the methodological approach Saidiya Hartman calls "critical fabulation," which involves imagining the lives of black women for whom little to no archival evidence exists. In her highly influential essay "Venus in Two Acts," she calls the archive a "death sentence, a tomb" (2008, 2) for the slave girls who appear only as satirical jokes, corpses, and violated bodies. Here, the metaphor of tomb is not the same as Mbembe's crypt, with its suggestion of embalming rituals and containment in a revered place. Rather, the archival burial site of slaves is closer to those unmarked graves whose bodies might never be recovered because they have already crumbled to dust. Hartman breathes life into the violated bodies of the two African girls who died on the slave ship *Recovery*, one flogged to death and the other of the pox, by imagining them forming a friendship and consoling each other. But she also pauses to contemplate whether the nonexistent evidence was conjured from a desire to free herself of the brutal image of their murdered bodies. Interrupting her imaginative re-creation with the stark reminder that the violent regime of the slave trade would not have permitted the social intimacy she imagines for the two girls, she concludes that her critical fabulation exists only as an "impossible story" (9–11).

The desire to tell stories of the sort Hartman provides represents the need to give a body, a materiality so to speak, to the lives that appear as the smallest of fragments within official records. In order to address this need, an archive that traditionally designated government documents, public records, newspapers, pamphlets, private letters, and other papers housed in official repositories has been expanded to include oral histories, myths, folk tales, novels, poems, murals, paintings, dance, songs, music, religious rituals, and other embodied forms. Yet, scholars also caution against addressing the problem of archival absences with an ever-expanding inventory of sources. Anjali Arondekar calls the project of filling archival gaps with missing stories an "additive model of subalternity" (2009, 6) that maintains a faith in archival recovery despite a mistrust of official archives. Lisa Lowe recommends that before moving too quickly to recuperating slave lives, we pay "productive attention to the scene of loss" (2015, 40–41). In *None Like Us,* Stephen Best is especially critical of "the recovery imperative" because he notes the same ethics at work in scholars who rise to the challenge of finding hidden histories as in those who resign themselves to the impossibility of recovery (2018, 84–85). Due to the recent emphasis within black Atlantic cultural studies on death, loss, and the traumatic afterlife of slavery, he identifies in this ethical demand the emergence of a philosophy of history he calls melancholic (63–80).[3] "Melancholy historicism," he explains, "provides for the view that history consists in the *taking possession* of such grievous experience and archival loss" (15).

Best traces the beginning of this "melancholic turn" to the 1987 publication of Toni Morrison's novel *Beloved* with its story of a fugitive slave mother's desperate act of infanticide to prevent her children from being reenslaved. The murdered baby, who returns fully grown to wreak havoc on her mother and the people who love her, serves as a metaphor for how the racial violence of slavery continues to affect the lives of African Americans long after Emancipation. *Beloved* had an enormous influence on black studies scholarship, promoting the idea that slavery, in its ghostly form, continues to exert its influence even today. Best, however, argues that not all answers to the existential condition of black people are to be found in a slave past. Drawing on the Freudian distinction between melancholia as a resolute holding onto a lost object and mourning as a process of detachment, he offers Morrison's uncoupling of race and slavery in *A Mercy* (2008) as a corrective to *Beloved.* In their introduction to *Loss: The Politics of Mourning,* David Eng and David Kazanjian derive more positive outcomes from Freud's description of melancholia than does Best, arguing that a "continuous engagement with loss and its remains . . . generates sites for memory and history, for the rewriting of the past as well as the reimagining of the future" (2003, 4). My book similarly recognizes a creative potential in an engagement with archival loss, but it takes a different approach than a Freudian one of divestment through mourning, as does Best, or depathologizing melancholia, as do Eng and Kazanjian. Instead, it locates *Beloved*'s ghost story within Afro-Caribbean spirit lore and sacred worlds for opening up its metaphor of haunting to African diaspora culture.

The felt reality of slavery as a ghostly presence alludes to a belief in the supernatural that Morrison describes as alternative ways of knowing and experiencing the world. She explains her fiction as drawing on a black vernacular culture that introduced into "practicality . . . what . . .

could be called superstition and magic, which is another way of knowing things" (2008, 61). Within the Caribbean, spirits assume a multiplicity of forms: some haunt like the spirit child of *Beloved,* others return so loved ones can move on with their lives, and still others empower the dispossessed through possession rituals. An attention to these diverse forms not only brings greater visibility to the ghost lore African Americans and Afro-Caribbeans share; it also allows us to see how former slaves reclaimed and transformed the terror-inducing strategies that remained in place during the post-Emancipation period. This critical move follows a different path than one of associating the haunting of Morrison's *Beloved* with the philosophy of hauntology Jacques Derrida introduces in *Specters of Marx* (1994) for describing the absence of a clean break between past and present belonging to a progressive narrative of history.[4] A Derridean hauntology deconstructs the pastness of a past belonging to a Western arrangement of time in order to show its persistence into the present. The spirits of Brodber's *Louisiana,* on the other hand, figure a different relationship of the present to the past than either a narrative of progress that leaves the past behind or a haunting indicating the ongoing trauma of slavery. A conjoining of the living and the dead through spirit possession in the plotting of Brodber's novel does not represent the return of a traumatic past that has been forgotten, which is the implication of the haunting in *Beloved,* but the remembrance of tactics for countering racism. A situating of Morrison's novel within circum-Caribbean culture allows me to introduce into its metaphor of haunting the heterogeneity of Afro-Creole spirits that do not all haunt in the same way as the murdered baby girl.

My chapters ask the question of what history might look like if we derive our understanding of the relationship between past and present from African diaspora cultures. In this regard, it embraces VèVè Clark's suggestion that we read black literatures through their own critical models.[5] Clark proposes a diaspora literacy she calls *Marasa* consciousness in allusion to the Vodou sign for the divine twins that appears to be a binary but is not. "*Marasa* consciousness," she explains, "invites us to imagine beyond the binary" due to its introduction of "movement and change" into binaries like creation/destruction, male/female, unity/difference, and stability/improvisation (2009, 43–44). This third principle does not assume the same form as Derrida's (1976) move of deconstructing a Western metaphysics of presence by introducing undecidability into binary systems of meaning. The divine twins sometimes appear as triplets known as *Marasa Trois* (Twa) with its sacred symbol being configured as the sign of three.[6] The introduction of an additional figure into the sign of twins represents a third principal or even a yet-to-be-born offspring who will be stronger and bring greater fortune than the first two (Clark 1991, 43; Houlberg 1995, 271; Michel 2012, 41–42). The futurity of the *Marasa Trois* is unmistakable.

A similar conceptual difference between deconstruction and African diaspora cosmologies exists in Brathwaite's "Dream Chad" (1994b), which incorporates Vodou states of dreaming and the future temporality of Rastafarian warning into a story of archival creation and destruction. A black female spirit warns of an impending devastation of his personal library in order to prevent it from happening. This is the opposite temporal movement to Derrida's presentation of archive fever as a desire to return to the beginning of things, which he bases on Freud's extensive analysis of German writer Wilhelm Jensen's *Gradiva: A Pompeian Fantasy* (1902). Freud sees in Jensen's novel a parable for how psychoanalysis can retrieve a traumatic event that has been forgotten, while Derrida's *Archive Fever* ([1996] 1998) derives from the story a counterparable for the nonoriginary status of the archive. I present Brathwaite's "Dream Chad" as a parable for archiving practices in the Caribbean in order to demonstrate how Derrida's explanation of the lure of the *arkhē* as a desire to return to the beginning of things speaks more to an enduring record of Western civilization—ancient Pompeii and all its artifacts preserved in stone—than to the precariousness of archives in the global South. The *arkhē* as the institutional place that Derrida (2) identifies with its Greek origins of *arkheion*, the residence of the superior magistrate that housed legal documents, is a place intimately related to the classical origins of the term.

Across the islands forming the archipelago of the Caribbean region, there are few magisterial buildings of the kind Derrida describes, except as the remains of Empire. These buildings, which contain the residual archives of the more important papers that were carried back to imperial centers, have suffered the ravages of earthquakes, hurricanes, and sheer neglect over a long period of time. Brathwaite himself has struggled to find a permanent home for his personal library, which since the late eighties has been in a steady state of decay after suffering water damage from the first of a series of megahurricanes to devastate the islands. I present the syncopated images and disrupting snippets of stories belonging to his Sycorax Video Style as an effort to salvage his wrecked archives by assembling its broken pieces into the virtual form of computer writing. Brathwaite does not restore his archives to their original wholeness but leaves the tattered edges of their damage exposed. The vision emerging from fragment and loss represents less a desire to return to the wholeness of a reconstructed past than a movement toward a salvaged future. I call Brathwaite's innovative poetry and prose writing a salvage poetics that figures the salvaging of Caribbean archives through the conversion of material records into a digitized virtual form. Unlike the dream sequence in Jensen's *Gradiva*, "Dream Chad" takes the archive further away from the *arkhē*.

In demonstrating how Caribbean art and literature defamiliarize the familiar codes of archival knowledge, I follow Jamaican writer and cultural theorist Sylvia Wynter's (2013, 495–97) suggestion that we treat "Latin Christian Europe" as a local culture rather than accede to the universal applicability of its terms. She particularly takes issue with secular definitions of "the human" due to the residual elements of Judeo-Christianity not being self-evident. For this reason, she prefers to call secularism a "degodding" of human history in order to identify the Judeo-Christian norms embedded in its language and narratives. Speaking from the perspective of Indian history, Dipesh Chakrabarty (2000, 72–90) notes that one of the major differences between the modernity of imperial centers and the kind that exists in its colonies is that the time of Europe's humanist history is disenchanted due to its disavowal of the agency of gods and spirits. He explains in *Provincializing Europe* that "the social scientist-historian" who follows the codes of humanist history produces a secular account that translates peasant religious beliefs into the universal language of enlightened modernity (72–90). Chakrabarty argues instead that subaltern groups who call on gods and spirits to come to their assistance do not exhibit a premodern mind-set. Since they are responding to the conditions of a new colonial order, their actions belong to the political modernity of *its* world (12–13). In *Wizards and Scientists*, Stephan Palmié (2002) makes a case for "Western modernity" and "Afro-Cuban tradition" belonging to the same interlinked system he calls Atlantic modernity by suggesting that they exist on a continuum rather than as dichotomies. This continuum is evident in the ritualized practices of Afro-Creole religions. The propensity of practitioners to call spiritual knowledge a "science" in the English-speaking islands and "*connaissance (konesans)*" in the French-speaking ones infuses the terms for secular disciplinary knowledge with African sacred meaning.

My study shifts the center of Atlantic modernity to the Caribbean by presenting art and literature that counters a Judeo-Christian logic of language and geography, attends to the agency of gods and spirits, and melds black vernacular culture with industrial technologies. I have selected works that distort and fragment official archives and, even when introducing alternative sites of memory, do not present them as external to Western forms of representation due to slavery breaking African cultures in a way that allowed no return to original wholeness. As Brathwaite has so movingly described and extensively theorized, the slave ship's hold was both a "wound" and "creative space" (1982, 3). "It is this broken human form of god, Ogotemmêli's smith, trans/formed as humble carpenter," he explains about the Yoruba divinity Ogun, "that growing up so many cemeteries west of the ancestors, I came to know and love" (4). The affective relationship the artists and writers of this study have with the African diaspora cultures they incorporate into their work shares in the intimacy and affection Brathwaite describes. Through an embrace of fragments and the veracity of affects, dreams, and visions, the arts of this book confront loss with forms indebted to the inventiveness with which slaves remade their shattered world. In view of Chakrabarty's observation that the project of provincializing Europe does not involve abandoning its philosophies so much as considering how they "may be renewed from and for the margins" (2000, 16), my study derives from African diaspora art and literature the positive value of silence, fragment, and loss.

Immaterial Archives begins with the infamous 1783 trial concerning the treatment of slaves as disposable cargo due to its prominence as an event in which death and archival silences converge. In 1781, the captain of the slave ship *Zong* ordered his crew to throw 132 sick Africans into the Atlantic so that the ship's owners could collect insurance for their loss. The horrific incident would have not have even entered the public record if not for the underwriters disputing a prior ruling of liability. Since the legal case concerned payment for destroyed property, its records are all but silent about the human status of the Africans being transported to Jamaican plantations where they were destined to labor—and die—as slaves. What is striking, when reading these records, is the degree to which the word "loss" pervades the legal arguments but not for describing a loss of lives, about which they are mostly silent. Philip's *Zong!*, rather than poetically reconstructing the lives of Africans aboard the *Zong*, disturbs the meaning of a public record that converts those lives into their monetary value. Her poetic commemoration of the dead comes the closest to a Freudian incitement of mourning for laying a traumatic past to rest. In the notes that follow her poems, Philip references Derrida's observation in *Specters of Marx* that one has to know where the body is buried in order to begin the mourning work (Philip 2008b, 201). Yet, her remembrance is not enacted through a recovery of the bodies and their accompanying stories that have been lost. By embracing what she calls a "poetics of fragmentation," she makes archival silences even larger.

Chapter 1, "Silence: The Archive and Affective Memory," contextualizes Philip's approach to archival gaps and absences with her theorization of silence as a diasporic black female space that is seen as nothing only within the logic of the master's language. In earlier writings, she explores silence as a linguistic wound graphically represented by the colonial edict that the slave's tongue be removed as punishment for speaking in his or her native language. Yet, she refuses to see this wound only as loss, exploring instead the poetic forms of expression that exist in silence. Her *Zong!* poems unleash the unruly potential of a silent language against the legal documents, forcing them to speak the African humanity that is immaterial to their arguments. Philip's fragmentation of an archival record destabilizes its meaning by exposing fissures in the classification of slaves as cargo in maritime law. The sounds of her poems constitute what I call an "affective memory" that elicits more visceral responses to the past than do thought and contemplation. The kind of affective memory that the poems introduce expresses the slave's experiences, thereby localizing empathy and sympathy, which are the affective modalities inherited from Euro-American antislavery discourse. The chapter moves from a legal case that was unconcerned with the humanity of enslaved Africans, through abolitionist arguments in which the value of these lives was paradoxically established through their negation in death, to Philip's poetic expression that affirms the humanity of those who drowned as well as those who survived. Her imaginative dismemberment of an archival record violates its sacred status by metaphorically moving it from the protected space of museums and libraries to the harsh environment of the Atlantic Ocean, where orders were given, words were translated into action, and the contested reasons for what happened entered the text of a legal case.

Chapter 2, "The Invisible: Haitian Art and a Vodou Archive of Slavery," examines Haitian art that introduces motion and movement into material records by viewing them through the iconography and cosmology of Vodou. The slave ship of Zépherin's painting *The Slave Ship Brooks* (2007) appears as the death ship depicted in antislavery pamphlets. But his painting also detours a Euro-American story of slavery and freedom to Haiti's revolutionary history and the sacred world of Vodou. Since Philip explains how her fragmentation of archival documents allows for small stories to emerge from its silences, I introduce her poetics into my reading of Zépherin's painting. One of the small stories I trace is that of slaves from neighboring islands stealing fishing boats to escape to the new black republic, which I present as an interisland account of slavery and freedom that is tangential to antislavery as a grand narrative of emancipation. Another small story concerns Haitian women who tell of their journeys underwater to the home of ancestral spirits from which they returned with psychic and healing powers. The unmappable underwater site of ancestral spirits known as Ginen belongs to an African diaspora geography that early anthropologists have defined as myth and one of its designated locations in the Haitian mountains as having no basis in reality. Yet cartographers, following the bread-crumb trail of Amerindian legends and European exploration stories, drew maps showing the exact location of El Dorado on the northeastern coast of South America. Did the legendary city of gold really exist for a brief moment in time due to its empirical verification on physical maps for almost two hundred years?

In his artwork, Duval-Carrié makes evident the Judeo-Christian frame of reference belonging to European maps when he presents the watery spaces of the Atlantic Ocean and Caribbean Sea from the perspective of a Vodou geography of Ginen as the underwater home of ancestral and familial spirits. By demonstrating how slaves and Haitian peasants embraced loss, but not as absence and deprivation, his artwork introduces a greater ambivalence into a seascape of death, drownings, and lost histories that appears in so many black Atlantic art and literary works. Duval-Carrié's painting *La vraie histoire des Ambaglos (The True History of the Underwater Spirits)* (2003), and art installation *The Indigo Room or Is Memory Water Soluble?* (2004), bring into visual representation the submarine home of ancestral spirits as well as slaves who died during the Middle Passage. It presents water as an element that is replete with diasporic memory because, within a creolized religion like Vodou, the Atlantic Ocean not only represents the loss of lives to the Middle Passage. It also provides an underwater passage for their spirits to return and empower the living. Duval-Carrié's placement of enduring records alongside the living archive of Vodou makes evident that a sentiment of loss is bound up with written documents and the meaning to be derived from them. His work positions the viewer to experience the Middle Passage, not from the distant and disinterested perch of a Judeo-Christian map in the heavenly skies but from a Vodou geography of Ginen as an island under the sea.

The Haitian artwork's reversal of the flow of knowledge is also to be detected in George Lamming's *Pleasures of Exile* ([1960] 1992), which draws on C. L. R. James's history of the Haitian Revolution for writing back to England on the cusp of decolonization. Lamming purposefully ascribes a universal significance to a Vodou ritual he witnessed in Port-au-Prince, where spirits of the recently deceased were summoned to settle differences with their family and loved ones. He invokes this ritual for describing the English propensity to listen attentively to radio broadcasts as a "tribal habit" of summoning the dead. Lamming explains that the parallels he establishes might be denounced as erroneous, but the lived reality of millions of people in the Caribbean form the basis to the truth of his words. His metaphoric presentation of the radio as an instrument through which the dead speak serves as a pivot on which the book turns to literary works that fuse modern technology with Afro-Caribbean sacred beliefs.

Chapter 3, "Word Holes: Spirit Voices in the Recording Machine," investigates Brodber's depiction of the anthropologist's field tool, the recording machine, as an instrument through which spirits enter the modern world to disrupt its historicist time. *Louisiana* brings greater visibility to a metaphoric relationship between American Spiritism and new sound technology that existed in the late nineteenth century but that became forgotten as scientific knowledge increasingly disengaged itself from superstitious thought, the natural from a supernatural world. My chapter also makes a case for Brodber's introduction of a local Jamaican frame of reference into the center of early twentieth-century American modernity as a fictional rather than a historical project. *Louisiana* retells Zora Neale Hurston's story as that of a Jamaican American anthopologist who does not give herself over to a North American perspective on hoodoo and voodoo as did the historical African American folklorist and ethnographer. While Brodber's history-writing projects license literary critics to identify her novel as introducing oral sources into archival records, I explain the spirit voices as evidence of the social scientist's inability to reconstruct the past. To regard the voices of the dead only as metaphors for missing oral histories is to overlook the reality the novel ascribes to spirits. Moreover, the spirit voices do not belong to a world of facts and information but one of vision and affect. In its inquiry of whether words spoken by spirits can be considered factual evidence that cannot be empirically verified, *Louisiana* reckons with the ability of the social sciences to transmit the stories of slavery and post-slavery. The stories the spirits tell the anthropologist remain as incomplete and partial as those that exist in written records, obliging her to shift her objective from filling in its blank spaces to explaining why her informants are either unable to recall the past or else refuse to tell their stories. In this way, Brodber provokes her readers into imagining an archive in which evidence is no longer the objective of scholarly work.

Like Brodber, Brathwaite conjoins African diaspora religions with modern technology through an account of how a new poetic style emerged from a female spirit in his Apple computer. Chapter 4, "Dream-Stories: The Virtuality of Archival Recovery," weaves Brathwaite's extensive writings—literary, theoretical, and historical—into the genre he calls dreamstories, a combination of myth, allegory, memories, and prophetic dreams written in innovative typography. The dreamstories exhibit his Sycorax Video Style, which pieces together scraps of poems, letters, and documents in computer-generated fonts and graphics. The chapter explains how this poetics is intimately bound up with the death of his wife, Doris, who was an early user of the home computer. Drawing on Philip's identification of black female agency in silence, the chapter locates a female-gendered space between orality and the poet's computer-generated writing that he presents as a visualization of speech. Behind the mythopoesis of Sycorax as the powerful spirit inside Brathwaite's computer is the small story of the woman who shared his creative life. Just as Brodber introduces black female agency into material archives by having the voices of deceased women magically appear on a recording machine, I introduce a once-living woman into the mythic dreamstorie of a spirit inside Brathwaite's writing machine. But this agency exists only in its immaterial form. Since Brodber also presents more creative approaches to accessing archival loss as the outcome of a husband assisting his anthropologist wife, I entertain the possibility, through a reassessment of women's traditional roles, of Brathwaite's expansive cultural work as the result of a similar partnership with his wife. The chapter reads the invisibility of the spirit in the machine as a figure for Doris's invisible labor, which went unrecognized until after her death. The woman, who in her lifetime maintained her husband's computer files and unruly personal library, returns in death as a powerful spirit who saves his archives, at least for a brief moment in time. If my book begins with one poet's metaphoric destruction of British legal records, it ends with another poet's gathering the pieces of his shattered archives for their assemblage into a new poetic form. In this way, it moves across shapes of immateriality from a creative fragmentation of an enduring European archive, scars of waters and testimony of wounds, to a disquieting re-creation of Caribbean archives, waste paper shredded over the waters.

CHAPTER I

Silence

The Archive and Affective Memory

in the beginning was
>   not
word
>   but Silence
>   and a future rampart
>   with possibility

—M. NourbeSe Philip, *Looking for Livingstone* (1991)

A narrator known only as The Traveller in M. NourbeSe Philip's mythic quest narrative arrives at a Museum of Silence, where all the silences of African peoples are stored. Once labeled, dated, classified, and publicly exhibited, silence assumes a tangible form she can "walk around, touch, feel, lick even" (1991, 57). Yet, the physical presence and visibility of silence comes at the price of dispossession. "At the very least," The Traveller tells the museum curators, "we should own our own silence" (58). Her characterization of the museum as a place that regulates and controls silences brings to mind Mbembe's description of the archive as a sepulcher that buries the debris of past lives in order "to establish an unquestionable authority over them and to tame the violence and cruelty of which the 'remains' are capable" (2002, 22). The narrator of *Looking for Livingstone* notices that the silence of one group of people she met on her travels is missing from the museum's "carefully regulated, climate-controlled rooms" (57). Known as the CESLIENS, they kept their silence to themselves, guarding it closely and even nurturing it. The Traveller learns from them "how wrong, how very wrong" (35) she had been in her perception of silence as an absence of language and self-expression. The Museum of Silence is a metaphor for government archives where a researcher like Philip has difficulty finding the voices of people of African descent. She learns that she has to rethink her approach to the archive's tangible form in which silence exists as an absence or empty space. As a self-identified Afrosporic writer who was born in Tobago and now resides in Toronto, Philip has devoted much of her creative work to defining silence as a black female space of expression rather than one of negation. This prior work informs her approach to the silences she encountered in official records on the transatlantic slave trade. In her book of poems *Zong! As Told to the Author by Setaey Adamu Boateng,* she mutilates a document that is silent about slave lives in order to release the violent potential of their irretrievable remains.

The poems are the result of Philip's search for a suitable form to tell the story of an infamous 1781 incident in which Africans aboard the slave ship *Zong* were thrown alive into the Atlantic Ocean so that the ship's owners could claim compensation for their loss. She explains in the afterword, called *Notanda,* that she was reading a novel about the massacre but found there was too much telling. As she repeats again and again in various and different ways, the story "cannot be told yet must be told, but only through its un-telling" (2008b, 207). Instead of filling archival gaps with stories, *Zong!* explores the meaning of the silences existing at the limits of those that have already been told. Consisting of ungrammatical arrangements of words and word fragments, the poems appear esoteric and even unreadable, particularly to those who are unfamiliar with experimental poetry. In this chapter, I argue that Philip's refusal of language and narrative breaks with the abstract logic of finance capital, on the one hand, and antislavery humanism, on the other. She calls the profit motive and the discarding of African lives "the material and nonmaterial" but then adds the following question about black lives—"Or is it the immaterial?" (2008b, 195). "Immaterial," as a word that traverses the binary logic of "the material and nonmaterial," introduces a third way to the binary of slavery, with its treatment of slaves as property, and antislavery, which falls short of addressing the complexities of African personhood. An abolitionist naming of the *Zong* killings as murder, while overturning the legal definition of slaves as insurable cargo, nonetheless elides the experience of the Africans aboard the ship due to their human status being figured through a negation of life in death, rather than what those lives were and might have been. The antislavery elision is repeated in subsequent English memorializations that include J. M. W. Turner's Romantic painting *Slave Ship (Slavers Throw-*

ing Overboard the Dead and Dying—Typhoon Coming On) (1840), and the 2007 Bicentenary of the Abolition of the Slave Trade Act.

My reading of the *Zong!* poems makes a case for a different kind of literary engagement with archival records than filling in the gaps of its silences with missing stories. Archives form the raw materials for creative expression but not for storytelling, because any effort to piece together their fragments into a story requires a prior narrative frame that is as likely to withhold signification as to deliver meaning. *Zong!* does not tell the stories that are missing from the archives so much as cause us to sense the presence of an unrepresented past within the very same documents that excludes them. Philip's poetic rendition conveys only the ghostly echoes of lost lives, but, in doing so, it makes an archival record speak the humanity about which it is silent. I characterize the book's commemorative form as "affective" due to its conveyance of black lives through patterns on the page and word fragments instead of the meaning of sentences. "Affect" has been explained in a variety of ways ranging from Arjun Appadurai's (1990) topographies of the self to Brian Massumi's bodily intensities (2002, 15) and Eve Kosofsky Sedgwick's intimacy of textures and feelings (2003, 13–21), to name a few. Although there is little consensus on its usage and meaning, my own interest in "affect" lies in its dislodging of the epistemological primacy of thought, reason, and "the individual" in theories of "the social." An attention to affective relations reminds us of how the dualism of mind and body belongs to a philosophical tradition that is not universal, being spread across the globe through European colonization. As Patricia Clough explains, "The affective turn throws thought back to the disavowals constitutive of Western industrial capitalist societies, bringing forth ghosted bodies and the traumatized remains of erased histories" (2007, 3). By traversing the division of mind and body, reason and passions, affect provides access to forms of representation that do not necessarily conform to the logic of European languages and their accompanying meanings. Writing against a metaphysical or universal concept of affect, Grenadian-born poet, playwright, and cultural critic Joan Anim-Addo identifies a gendered, creolized realm of affects that developed on Caribbean plantations. She explains that the slave woman's affects, like her silence, lie in a withholding of feelings and masking strategies but also in eruptions of a "disruptive performance" of laughter, shrieks, and cries as displaced expressions of fear and trepidation (2013, 7). In order to "give voice to the silenced and gendered Creole woman and to illustrate the workings of affect," Anim-Addo presents

Caribbean literary representation as a "neo-slavery text" that brings slave women's strategies into representation (2013, 11). Her characterization alludes to the neo–slave narrative as a literary genre closely identified with Toni Morrison's *Beloved* (1987), which has been theorized as a site of a countermemory to and critique of the historical documentation of slavery.[1] As Morrison famously declared, the novel's characters reflect the responsibility she feels for "these unburied, or at least unceremoniously buried, people made literate in art" (Morrison and Naylor 1985, 585).

Building on Clough's and Anim-Addo's descriptions, it is possible to say that *Zong!* creates an affective memory that conveys the traumatized remains of erased slave histories and the remnants of slave women's expressions consigned to silence. Through a rejection of narrative itself, Philip writes poems that do not conform to the affective modes of antislavery, which ranges from eyewitness testimonies like the slave narrative to English national commemorative forms. In Philip's poems, the disembodied sounds and voices a reader sees and hears—words that do not conform to the logic of language and sounds that evoke an intuitive response more than thought and contemplation—constitute a less tangible form of memory than storytelling or even the neo–slave narrative project of giving voice to the silent agents of history. This memory lacks the tactile and physical quality of material archives or the details of reconstructed lives because its power lies elsewhere. Due to its abstract and nonrepresentational quality, affect is not always self-evident, often requiring a reassessment of reading and listening practices. In order to identify this reassessment, my chapter circles back to the missing *Zong* story in the documents that served as evidence for the late eighteenth-century antislavery cause as well as current history writing, and that also became incorporated into memorializations belonging to the changing landscape of the English nation.

THE DESICCATED FACTS

Although we are by now familiar with the massacre that turned *Zong* into a proper name for Middle Passage terror, I want to begin by presenting the case distilled down to the archival evidence that constitutes the dry language of facts. The public record of what transpired on the open seas is a 1783 Court of King's Bench hearing, *Gregson v. Gilbert,* in which insurance underwriters appealed a prior ruling that they should compensate the ship's owners for their losses. The primary sources for the legal case are the sworn testimonies of Robert Stubbs, a passenger who commanded the ship when the ship's commander became ill, and the first mate, James Kelsall, who directed the crew to undertake the killings. The sequence of events to be derived from their testimonies is as follows: The Bristol privateer ship *Alert* captured the Dutch slaver *Zorgue,* which was docked at Cape Coast Castle in February 1781 with its prize cargo of 320 slaves. Renamed the *Zong,* the ship was subsequently sold to a syndicate of Liverpool merchants. It trawled the Guinea coast for additional slaves before leaving in August 1781 with nineteen crew and 442 slaves. The ship arrived at its final destination, the Black River in Jamaica, on December 22, 1781, with eleven of its crew and fewer than half of its slaves (Lewis 2007, 361–64). The *Zong's* transatlantic trip took sixteen instead of the usual six to eight weeks due to its commander, Luke Collingwood, mistaking Jamaica for the hostile Spanish territory of Hispaniola and setting off leeward from the island. The navigational error forced the ship to sail against powerful trade winds on its return. This mistake led to a water shortage, or so the commander claimed, that forced him to select 133 sick Africans to be thrown overboard in order to save the rest. On the evening of November 29, the crew pushed fifty-four women and children out of the cabin windows. A couple of days later, forty-two male slaves were thrown overboard from the deck. During the ensuing days, a final thirty-six to thirty-eight were selected for drowning, and from their numbers ten jumped into the water to avoid being shackled together and thrown into the ocean's choppy waters. One slave survived by using a rope to climb back on board. In addition to these slaves, sixty-two died during the voyage across the Atlantic and thirty-six on the journey back to Jamaica (Lewis 2007, 361–64). The court case concerned only the 122 slaves who were thrown into the water alive, a number slightly over half of the 242 Africans who died before reaching Jamaica. In accordance with marine insurance law at the time, the ten who jumped to avoid being thrown were determined to have died of natural causes.[2] Although the exact number selected to be killed varies in the eyewitness accounts, abolitionists seized on 132—the 122 in the insurance claim in addition to the ten who jumped—as the definitive number in their literature identifying the drownings as a massacre.

The *Zong* case was not the only instance of slaves being thrown overboard, especially since death by drowning was used as punishment for insurrections, but it was the one that was most widely publicized as illustrating a blatant disregard for African lives. Due to its historical prominence in giving a name to the transportation of people as cargo, the *Zong* stands for the estimated 1.8 million Africans who lost their lives on the journey from the West African coast to the Americas over a period of four hundred years. For Stephanie E. Smallwood, statistics alone cannot convey the total cost of the Middle Passage for Africans, because any single number of reported deaths aggregates individual lives, each of which endured the trauma of the journey (2007, 152). Vincent Brown compares the numerical data on the slave trade to "the chalk outline of a murder victim" (2008, 29) due to its inability to convey the cruel conditions aboard the slave ships. He supplements the statistical information about the *Zong* victims with the image of what Collingwood and his crew must have seen in the faces of the slaves they killed and the small piece of information about the survivor who used a rope to pull himself back aboard through the ship's porthole (159).

While archival records might not present the massacre from the perspectives of the slaves aboard the *Zong*, they do contain contradictions that provide openings to narrating histories "from below." Reading along the archival grain, as Ann Laura Stoler (2009) suggests we do, makes evident that the human status of enslaved Africans is not absent from transcripts of the legal case debating their insurable value. Stoler characterizes colonial archives as "records of uncertainty and doubt" displaying "deeply epistemic anxieties [that] stir affective tremors within them" (2009, 4, 19), and this characterization is evident in the *Zong* court proceedings, during which the word "murder" appears six times. Although the lawyers for the underwriters mention "Murther" (Lyall 2017, 244–90) as a means of avoiding payment, its mere utterance indicates a consensus about the personhood of the transported Africans outside of marine insurance law. As Anita Rupprecht explains, "Even if the underwriters' suggestion was purely instrumental, their recourse to the question of calculated murder in order to protect their interests unwittingly records the undisclosed conscience of the hearing" (2008, 274). The human status of slaves becomes erased and fixed as "goods & property" by the parameters of legal discourse because, as the solicitor general mockingly states during the trial, "I presume it would be perfectly ridiculous for a Man to insure so high upon human Creatures unless it was upon the Idea they are not only Property but of the Specific Value of 30£ a head" (Lyall 2017, 268). Statements of this sort epitomize for Ian Baucom in *Specters of the Atlantic* (2005) a conversion of the slave's personhood into the abstract value underpinning finance capital.

Antislavery activists seized on the callousness of the ship owners, crew, and underwriters for assembling their own evidence for a different kind of trial, a murder trial. Although the trial never materialized, historians now identify that moment as the beginning of the end of the slave trade. After reading a newspaper account about the March 6 hearing in which the jury ruled in favor of the owners, the former slave turned abolitionist Olaudah Equiano (then known as Gustavus Vassa), brought the case to the attention of the antislavery leader Granville Sharp, for whom it was a glaring instance of the immorality of the trade.[3] Sharp commissioned shorthand notes on the court minutes for the May 1783 hearing, which he had transcribed and labeled as "Voucher No 2." He filed a letter of petition with the Lords Commissioners of the Admiralty to investigate the case as one of murder but did not receive a response. He subsequently published his "Account of the Murder of One Hundred and Thirty-two Slaves on Board the Ship Zong" in newspapers, which allowed his campaign to gain widespread support (Hoare 1820, xvii–xxi). The captain's orders that the crew dispose of so many lives dramatically displayed the equation of slaves with their monetary value alone. "This contest of pecuniary interest," writes Sharp, "brought to light a scene of horrid brutality, which had been acted during the execution of a detestable plot" (Hoare 1820, 237). His use of the word "plot" denotes a calculated decision on the part of the commander because, as Sharp explains, owners would have to suffer the loss of any Africans who died of illness. He concludes that Collingwood's decision was self-interested since he was to receive a percentage of the sale price of the slaves and, by extension, also their insurance compensation (239). The evidence Sharp collected, which includes an authentic copy of Kelsall's testimony, identified as "Voucher No. 1," are filed under "Documents Related to the Case of the Zong of 1783" (MS REC/19) at the National Maritime Museum in Greenwich. A two-page summary, known as the Douglas version of Gregson v. Gilbert, was not entered into the public record of legal cases until 1831, which was just two years before passage of the Slavery Abolition Act. The summary is not as detailed as the manuscript notes but is the only public record of the case. When distilled to its essence, the brief summary of a two-day trial glosses over the epistemic anxieties running like an almost indiscernible thread through the documents labeled Vouchers number 1 and 2.

Philip recounts how she was so disturbed when learning about the drownings in James Walvin's *Black Ivory* (1992) that she was prompted to look up the case in the law library (Saunders 2008, 66). Yet, she rejected the idea of working with the language of full trial transcripts, choosing instead the Douglas version of *Gregson v. Gilbert*, due to its status as a public record. She declares it to be "the tombstone, the one public marker of the murder of those Africans on board the *Zong*, locating it in a specific time and place" (2008b, 194). The statement, coming from a poet with legal training, could be understood as expressing an attorney's faith in the precision of the language of the law. Yet, as a metaphoric tombstone, *Gregson v. Gilbert* does not contain the standard inscription—proper name and longevity (or shortness) of life, next of kin, and inscription of love, remembrance, and grief. The condensed trial notes present a conundrum: How to find the lives of slaves within a document that treats their humanity as immaterial? How to tell a story for which the evidence works against its telling? Or, as Philip herself asks: "How did they—the Africans on board the *Zong*—make meaning of what was happening to them?" (2008b, 194). She studies the document's words with the critical eye of a lawyer who "determines which facts should or should not become evidence; what is allowed into the record and what not" (2008b, 199). But, as a poet, she also uses its language to express an experience that is *obiter dicta*—beside the case or extraneous—to *ratio decidendi* or legal reasoning. By calling *Gregson v. Gilbert* the tombstone of the drowned Africans, she moves archival records from their museum sepulcher to the Atlantic Ocean containing the remains of the lives that might have been.

The *Zong* massacre has received greater scholarly attention in the late twentieth and early twenty-first centuries than it has ever before. Walvin, a historian who has been writing on slavery since the 1970s, says that his decision to make it the focus of an entire book entitled *The Zong: A Massacre, the Law and the End of Slavery* was due its "long shadow" that has been "impossible to escape" (2011, 10). The limitations placed on the historian who wants to recount the experience of the Africans selected for death is evident in his efforts to present their perspective on Collingwood's decision. Walvin provides detailed descriptions of the circuitous voyage from the island of São Tomé off the West African coast to the Black River in Jamaica, as well as the twists and turns in the case between owners and insurers. Based on the records at his disposal, he is able to provide biographies of the chief actors: Robert Stubbs, a passenger with interests in the slave trade who testified at the hearings; Lord Mansfield, who presided over the case; and the anti-slavery activists Olaudah Equiano and Granville Sharp, who brought the massacre to the public's attention. But there are no records that allow him to offer comparable biographies of the Africans aboard the ship. The only eyewitness accounts, the court testimony of Stubbs and sworn statement of Kelsall, are untrustworthy because they are from men who did not want to incriminate themselves in the deed for which they stood accused. Walvin is critical of how the testimony of Stubbs, a man he calls "an irrepressible liar" (2011, 210), has been presented as factual evidence. He provides a complex account of conflicting stories and missing information, all of which raises more questions for him than providing answers. In view of evidence that is "sparse," he invites his readers to imagine the "screaming terror" (2011, 98) of the Africans being drowned alive and the fear of their shipmates listening to the killings that happened over a period of three days. Drawing on "only a few dozen words" provided by Kelsall, which he characterizes as "little more than a throwaway line in a legal statement," he reconstructs a scene in which, as news spread in the hold about their compatriots being thrown overboard, an African spokesperson who knew English pleaded for their lives (2011, 157–58). But the story that the history book ultimately tells, as its title indicates, is the effect that "news of the *Zong* killings" (2011, 174) had on the English, whose numbers included those of African descent.

Philip, on the other hand, wants to tell the life stories of the Africans who were aboard the ship, which is not the same story as the role the massacre played in an abolition of the slave trade. She wants to know who the enslaved Africans were, where they came from, and how they prevented themselves from giving over to despair. She wants to know their thoughts and their feelings, their relationships to one another, and the nature of their familial ties. She especially wants to know their names. Since it was not standard practice to log slaves by name in the ship's ledger, the names of the dead are unknown. Nor is the exact location of the drownings known. The ship's log, where slaves would have been listed and the journey charted, is unrecoverable. It is presumed that Collingwood took it with him when he disembarked at Kingston, Jamaica. Since he died before he could return to England, the log went missing (Lewis 2007, 367).

The *Zong!* poems are the expression of the deep connection Philip feels with the millions of Africans crammed into thousands of ships' holds to be transported to the Americas as slaves. She characterizes her reaction as one of being "startled" to hear a Ghanaian Ewe elder inform her that her ancestors could not have possibly been among those who died (2008b, 202). Through the negation of kinship, he introduces the possibility of one, which takes Philip down the path of concluding that if one of their children had survived, he or she could have been her ancestor. Her train of thought is licensed by the small piece of evidence in the records that the ship "passed Tobago without touching, though she might have made that and other islands" (*Gregson v. Gilbert* 1783, 629). Since Tobago is her natal home, Philip recalls how the name jumped out at her when she first encountered it in the records (M. NourbeSe Philip, interview by the author, November 15, 2016). The closeness she feels to the dead is an intimacy based on a shared ancestry, which offers a way into understanding the poetic function of the African ancestor, Setaey Adamu Boateng. The book spine presents Philip and Boateng as coauthors, and Boateng is described on its jacket as "the voice of the ancestors revealing the submerged stories of all who were on board the *Zong*." The fictitious ancestor can be searched on the internet (and found!) as the book's "author." Is this a literary ruse of the same order as Daniel Defoe claiming that he was merely transmitting the true story of a shipwrecked sailor called Robinson Crusoe, or Charlotte Brontë's assumption of the pen name Currer Bell as the editor of an English governess's diaries "he" discovered? I would contend that *Zong!* works against the history-telling function of European realism as well as the empirical gesture of its invented worlds. Either a literal or metaphoric reading of Boateng as coauthor would subject the formally innovative book of poems to traditional codes of European realism. "The voice of the ancestors" alludes to those silent spaces of history, yes, but not as a space of "submerged stories" that can be located and identified. To see *Zong!* as a neo–slave text that recovers lost stories would be to make its ghosts reside within the house of archives.

FANTASIES, SPECULATION, FRAGMENTATION

The difficulty of telling the *Zong* story is not only one of too little archival evidence; it is also the outcome of too much narration, due to its memory being saturated with highly charged antislavery accounts and illustrations. In other words, the *Zong* as a discursive event comes to us already coded. Rupprecht makes a case for how antislavery advocates made the massacre into a representative image of the Middle Passage, providing "a kind of open space for the inscription of abolitionist fantasies" (2007, 341). Eighteenth-century accounts emphasized slaves as suffering victims due to their primary objective being one of motivating readers into calling for the end of the trade. The reason for describing the utterly devastating conditions of the Middle Passage was to provoke feelings of moral outrage, which is reflected in the language of the protest literature and pamphlets. Abolitionists described, in graphic detail, the physical conditions of the heat, stench, and filthy conditions of the slave ship's hold, as well as the torture and degradation of enslaved Africans. But when it came to expressing what it must have felt like to be crammed into the ship's dark hull, not knowing where one was going, or what future lay ahead, they did so only by denoting the failure of language to convey meaning. "Where shall I find words," writes Thomas Clarkson, a leading abolitionist, "to express properly their sorrow, as arising from the reflection of being parted for ever from their friends, their relatives, and their country? Where shall I find language to paint, in appropriate colours, the horror of mind brought on by thoughts of their future unknown destination, of which they can augur nothing but misery from all that they have yet seen?" (1839, 39). As a discursive move that invites readers to use their imagination and, in doing so, to imagine the worst, the professed failure to represent the slave's thoughts and feelings transfers the emotional force of suffering from the one who is experiencing the Middle Passage to the one who witnesses or hears stories about it. And the word used to describe the suffering of one who testifies to the horrors of the trade is "melancholy." I draw attention to the appearance of the sentiment of melancholy in antislavery writings in order to highlight its tropological effects that a melancholic historicism risks reproducing.

As one of the four humors recognized by ancient and medieval physiologists, "melancholy" was commonly used during the late eighteenth century to describe a situation that was "saddening, lamentable, deplorable" (OED). In his Essay on the Slavery and Commerce of the Human Species, Particularly the African, Clarkson describes the experience of being in the courtroom during the Zong hearings as one of listening to "the melancholy evidence with tears" (1788, 114). Quobna Ottobah Cugoano, a London-based African activist and former slave, called the massacre "a very melancholy instance" of the "vast carnage and murders" belonging to slavery in his Thoughts and Sentiments on the Evil of Slavery (1787, 111). The slave trader turned abolitionist John Newton also refers to the massacre as "a melancholy story" (1788, 18) with which readers of his *Thoughts upon the African Slave Trade* would be familiar. Even counsel for the owners called it a "melancholy event" (Lyall 2017, 273). An antislavery use of the term shifts the force of descriptions from "what happened" to the effect of its news on those who are sympathetic to the suffering slave's plight, which is an affective structure designed to prompt them into action.[4] Baucom considers Sharp's petition to the Lords Commissioners of the Admiralty to be "the first text to effect this reworking of history into sentimental fact and sentimental fact into melancholy evidence" (2005, 220). However, his presentation of the sentimental melancholy of abolitionism as a counternarrative to the speculative regime of Atlantic capital has come under criticism for eliding the perspective of slaves. Vincent Brown argues that "the effectiveness of his text depends on the silence of slaves" (2009, 1235), while Ramesh Mallipeddi explains that Baucom's account of sentimental melancholy overlooks evidence of the slaves' dejection and feelings of homesickness, which the records describe as a "fixed melancholy" (2016, 148–52). The slave's melancholic condition is external to both the melancholia of an abolitionist response *and* the legal definition of slaves as insurable cargo since insurance did not cover instances "when the captive destroys himself through despair, which often happens" (qtd. in Oldham 2007, 303). Their melancholic responses in song, action, and affect constitute utterances of despair even if what they were experiencing could not always be expressed in so many words or translated from their own languages into the European languages of the archives.

Although there are few first-person testimonies of what it felt like to be transported in a ship's hold, abolitionist accounts do attempt to describe the thoughts and feelings of African slaves.[5] Sharp reports the action of the ten *Zong* slaves who jumped into the water as an act of defiance and an effort to gain control over their impending demise. "The ten last victims," he writes, "sprang disdainfully from the grasp of their tyrants, defied their power, and, leaping into the sea, felt a momentary triumph in the embrace of death" (Hoare 1820, 238). While recognizing suicide as a form of escape and act of defiance, even if his suggestion of a "momentary triumph" in death is far too dramatic, Sharp also does not overlook the one who survived. Of the slaves selected for being thrown overboard, he mentions the sole survivor who managed to climb back aboard the ship, explaining that the man grabbed a rope "which hung from the ship into the water, and thereby, without being perceived, regained the ship, secreted himself, and was saved" (Hoare 1820, 243).

His account is based on Kelsall's sworn statement, which also credits the crew for saving the survivor by concealing him "amongst the remaining Cargo of Slaves" (Lyall 2017, 345). Cugoano's *Thoughts and Sentiments on the Evil of Slavery,* the first published pamphlet by a black abolitionist, embellishes the testimony in its report of how the rope was extended by "some in the ship" (1787, 111), thereby retelling Sharp's story of a miraculous escape into one of collective action. Cugoano's creative interpretation of how the rope happened to be hanging from a porthole speaks across the centuries to today's historians and fiction writers who are equally imaginative in speculative approaches to archival silences. Philip takes an even more creative approach to working with archival materials for her book of poems. Through wordless expressions, her *Zong!* poems introduce the slave's perspective into the dry language of legal deliberations.

Formally, the collection consists of six sections the poet calls "movements," a glossary, a parodic ship manifest, notes on the writing of her work, and the text of the Douglas version of *Gregson v. Gilbert.* Each section has a Latin name, since Philip considers Latin to be intimately connected to the language of law and also a father tongue of European languages (2008b, 209n). The first twenty-six poems in the section called *Os,* which is Latin for "bone," are constructed exclusively from the text of *Gregson v. Gilbert,* whose words Philip fragments and rearranges on the page. For each poem, there are more blank spaces than there are words, as if to suggest the vastness of what remains unsaid. The subsequent four sections—*Sal, Ventus, Ratio,* and *Ferrum*—displace the text of *Gregson v. Gilbert* with European and African words and phrases belonging to the transatlantic slave trade as well as its afterlife in plantation slavery. Philip characterizes these latter poems as "a translation of the opacity" of the first twenty-six (2008b, 206). The sixth and final movement, *Ebora,* consists of several pages of lightly printed superimposed words and word fragments. The poems work through their own logic of association, wordplay, and sliding signification, the meanings of which change with the insertion of a different letter or transference into another language or through alliteration. Words and letters join momentarily to create a sensation, touch off a memory, perhaps even an image, but they do not cohere into a story or sequence of events. The listener/reader—since Caribbean poetry is also performative—is able to hear/read partial stories spoken by a multiplicity of voices from the upper deck and lower hold that are not always easy to unravel into individual perspectives. Although Philip's original intention was to restrict her poetry writing to the language of *Gregson v. Gilbert,* she found that when she began to fragment its words, "these little stories are surfacing in the text" (Saunders 2008, 73). Despite the appearance of little stories, the poems maintain the broken words and sentences she calls a "poetics of fragmentation" (Philip 2008b, 202). When taken in its entirety, the book of poems draws attention to the silent spaces of history, while making silences in the master's language audible and visible.

Philip's poetic strategy is to "reintroduce those emotions and feelings that were removed" from the two-page reduction of the trial to "hard facts, this desiccated fact situation of *Gregson v. Gilbert*" (Saunders 2008, 66). In attempting to infuse its language with a poetic sensibility, she is aware of the limitations she faces. Since the hearings were intended to determine not whether a massacre had occurred but, rather, who should suffer the financial loss, she characterizes its language as "already contaminated, possibly irrevocably and fatally" (Philip 2008b, 199). *Gregson v. Gilbert* refers to the drowned Africans only collectively, as "negroes" and "slaves," and to the crew's action as "a throwing overboard of goods." Philip describes the ability of the law to convert a human being into chattel as approximating "the realm of magic and religion" (196) in its formal resemblance to the Christian doctrine of transubstantiation. By comparing the logic of insurance law to a theological dogma that became disputed with the rise of secularism, she draws attention to the almost religious faith in a legal definition of "the human." The delicate task confronting her involves using the trial's language for establishing the slave's humanity while refusing the sense of its meaning. In *Notanda,* she explains that her poems resist forming words into sentences because grammar adheres to the logic of reason and rationality, which is the same logic underpinning the law that sanctioned the killings (2008b, 198–99). Kate Eichhorn (2010) observes that the constraints Philip places on herself in working with the language of the legal text is the reverse action of other constraint-based poetry in which the aim of increased restrictions is to move closer toward linguistic freedom. For an Afrosporic woman like Philip, who is already a decentered subject, the search for freedom "is deceptive" (Eichhorn 2010, 36). Due to the race and gender exclusions embedded in a document that is constitutive of her past and structures her present, Philip demands from it something other than a greater freedom to use its words. This is one explanation to her repeated refrain that "this is a story that can only be told by not telling" (2008b, 191).

The other part of the "not telling" is to allow the story to tell itself. Since Philip sees grammar as an organization of language that also establishes limits on what can be said, she is suspicious of its logic, which is a logic that extends to narrative and storytelling. She likens her treatment of the legal summary of *Gregson v. Gilbert* to a sculptor who chips away at a block of stone until the figure locked within reveals itself. But she also admits that the analogy is flawed because language will divulge only "what is commonplace" (2008b, 198). Still, she chipped away at *Gregson v. Gilbert* for seven long years. During this time, she visited the site on the African coast from where the *Zong* set sail for Jamaica as well as the metropolitan center of London, where the legal battle between owners and insurers took place. She immersed herself in archival records, examining Sharp's letter to the Lords of the Admiralty and the account books of the Jamaican agent who purchased slaves from the owners of the *Zong* (Saunders 2008, 76–77). In the summer of 2006, she traveled to Ghana, where she conversed with an Ewe priest at a traditional shrine adjacent to a slave port. On her return trip, she stopped off at the port in Merseyside, Liverpool, where she poured a libation for the dead into the chilly, Atlantic waters (Philip 2008b, 202–3). After completing a draft of her *Zong!* manuscript, Philip returned to Liverpool and London in the summer of 2007 to visit several of the exhibits for the Bicentenary of the Abolition of the Slave Trade Act. Prominently featured was J. M. W. Turner's *Slave Ship*, which I consider to be a prior affective memory of the *Zong* massacre. The next section locates Philip's book of poems within the long history of formal commemorations that simultaneously enact a forgetting of the British involvement in West Indian slavery.

TRANSATLANTIC CURRENTS OF REMEMBERING AND FORGETTING

If slave women were obliged to mask their feelings or express them through seemingly unrelated emotions like laughter, Turner's *Slave Ship* enacts a grand affective scheme in which Nature's, God's, and Man's laws are all perfectly aligned. "Affect, here, is epistemology," writes Baucom about the painting; "imagination, sentiment, and melancholy *the* keys to a factual knowledge of an increasingly planetary (and hence increasingly invisible) European ordering of modern history" (2005, 222). The painting was exhibited at the Royal Academy in 1840, which was seven years after parliamentary passage of the Slavery Abolition Act and thirty-three years after Britain withdrew from the slave trade. Although the slave ship in the painting is not identified as the *Zong*, art historians believe it to have been inspired by Clarkson's account of the murders in his *History of the Rise, Progress, and Accomplishment of the Abolition of the African Slave-Trade*, which was republished the previous year. Visually, Turner's painting is a confusion of light and dark, motion and stillness. The Africans who have been thrown overboard are aestheticized in a manner that makes them one with the sea: the outstretched hands emerging from the water appear like so many waves, while a shackled leg follows the line and symmetry of a leaping fish besides it. *Slave Ship* is a study in light and shadow, with thick daubs of white and red paint contributing to its impressionistic quality. The viewer's eyes are drawn to the center of the scene, where the sea is split by the light of the setting sun, illuminating the only portion that is devoid of drowning bodies. The dead and dying of the painting's title are rendered imperceptible by the flash and fury of the storm; they are, both visually and metaphorically, in its shadows. The slave ship in the distance appears small against the backdrop of the storm. Like the abolitionist writings on which the painting was based, *Slave Ship* depicts a melancholy scene of guilt, horror, and sorrow. The terror of the slave trade is displaced into nature, conveyed less through the slave's nightmarish journey than "embodied in a sky made of blood and a sea convulsed with pain," which is how art historian Marcus Wood describes the metaphoric interpretation provided by the Victorian art critic John Ruskin (2000, 62).

Victorian spectators found Turner's *Slave Ship* to be incomprehensible and its execution of a horrific scene somewhat absurd as indicated by William Thackeray's sardonic question—"Is the picture sublime or ridiculous?"—which is probably not the response Turner was seeking. Thackeray's preference for the genteel sentimentalism of François Biard's *The Slave Trade,* which was exhibited the same year, indicates his displeasure with Turner's visual rendition of a "hell-and-brimstone sermon" (Boime 1990, 42). Ruskin alone expressed admiration for *Slave Ship* by identifying the painting as testimony to Turner's "immortality" as an artist (1903, 572). However, for him, its subject is "the power, majesty, and deathfulness of the open, deep, illimitable sea" with its Middle Passage reference being relegated, as so many scholars have noted, to a footnote identifying "the guilty ship" as "a slaver, throwing her slaves overboard" (572–73). Since Ruskin was an unapologetic defender of

Empire, his assessment of the slaver as guilty could have been an allusion to nations that continued to participate in the trade. After all, it was an era when British abolitionists began to direct their attention to ending the human trafficking that was interfering with their missionary and civilizing work in Africa. Still, he claimed that he sold the painting after owning it for twenty-eight years because he could no longer live with its painful subject (1903, lv), which is a statement some have interpreted to mean the lingering stain of slavery on the English nation.

Scholars disagree on whether Turner's *Slave Ship* was consigning slavery to the past, since England had already emancipated its slaves, or addressing a vital and ongoing issue indicated by the first World Anti-Slavery Convention being held in London that same year. Baucom argues that the effect of Turner's painting is to bury its violence in the past (2005, 282). Mark Frost, a Ruskin scholar, makes the reverse case, which is, in the context of a slavery that continued to exist in the Americas, "Turner was responding to horrors that were not past, but continuing, and not British, but global" (2010, 376). Art historian Albert Boime introduces yet a third interpretation through his contextualization of the painting with the aesthetics of Turner's other works and the poem "Fallacies of Hope" that accompanied its exhibition. He argues that the death ship represents the rapacious destructiveness of industrialization (1990, 41–42). Despite these diverse interpretations, what is indisputable is that *Slave Ship* was displayed at a time when the heroic ethos of Empire was replacing the moral outrage of abolitionism. Tennyson's dramatic monologue "Ulysses" (1842), which ends with the speaker urging his mariners "to strive, to seek, to find, and not to yield," embodies the spirit of adventure belonging to a Victorian maritime age more than Turner's frail ship tossed about by a furious storm or divine retribution.

The significance of the painting to the English nation would be seized upon by black British writers and artists during the 1990s, which was an era when they were carving out a space for themselves within it. In "Art of Darkness," Paul Gilroy considers the painting to be implicated in questions of national belonging facing black Britons because it brings into visual representation an image of race relations that "is not the *other* story . . . but *the* story of England in the modern world" (1990, 52). For him, the painting is especially relevant to black Britain due to Turner's and Ruskin's "special status" in an English cultural history (1990, 49).[6] Gilroy's observation belongs to period in which black British artists, writers, filmmakers, and intellectuals were addressing the nation's amnesia about its participation in slavery and not only its role in the emancipation of slaves. Part of the effort in demonstrating a much longer history of complex race relations in Britain involved reconfiguring the privileged place of Turner and Ruskin in definitions of Englishness by foregrounding what *Slave Ship,* as well as Ruskin's interpretation, marginalize. David Dabydeen's long narrative poem *Turner* (1994) creates a life for the painting's submerged head in the dark turbulent waters, giving voice to an African who speaks back to Eurocentric misrepresentations and racist fantasies. Lubiana Himid's painting *Study for a Memorial to Zong* (1991), is a close study of what is obscured by Turner's brushstrokes and color that make the extended hands of the dying blend in with the waves. The painting focuses on a single hand rising from the waves except that by using contrasting colors, Himid allows viewers to see that the extended hand is making the gesture of one who is struggling to live. Fred D'Aguiar's *Feeding the Ghosts* (1999), which combines historical fiction with self-conscious literary devices about the documenting of history, does not explicitly reference Turner's *Slave Ship*. However, the prologue's presentation of the Atlantic as haunted by the spirits of those who died during the *Zong* massacre moves the affective response of its seascape from European guilt to African trauma. D'Aguiar imagines the lone survivor of those who were thrown overboard to be a woman named Mintah, inventing for her a written testimony that contradicts eyewitness reports in the archival records. This narrative strategy allows the dead to speak. When presented as evidence during the novel's re-creation of the trial, the survivor's journal is declared by the insurers' counsel to have been "penned by a ghost" (169).

It was not the ghosts of the drowned Africans that appeared in March 2007 from the mist of a gray and drizzly London morning but a ghost ship sailing down the River Thames with the strains of John Newton's "Amazing Grace" floating from its upper deck. The ship was a replica of the *Zong* procured for the national commemoration of the Abolition of the Slave Trade Act.[7] Turner's *Slave Ship* was also reproduced for a glossy government brochure claiming the painting to have "immortalised" the *Zong* murders, a language that suggests the singularity of its image in memorializing the massacre for posterity. The debate over whether the painting was recalling the slave trade in order to relegate it to the past or to make visible the ongoing story of slavery during the Victorian era is laid to rest by the 2007 Bicentenary of the Abolition of the Slave Trade Act. The *Zong* ship replica docked at the Tower Pier for a public viewing of an onboard exhibition of the deplorable conditions under which slaves were transported, while an accompanying exhibition at the Tower church told the story of the abolitionist struggle to end the trade. Rupprecht observes that the commemoration's focus on an anti-slavery archive "tells us far more about how the abolitionists imagined themselves and their mission than it does about a trade deemed to be so 'unspeakable' as to be well nigh unrepresentable" (2008, 266). Wood sees such sanitized efforts at realistic re-creations of a Middle Passage experience as encouraging a forgetting of what the actual experience might have been like (2000, 300). And Barnor Hesse calls "Western styles of remembering slavery" a form of empirical memory that is bound up with empirical forgetting due to the re-creations and replicas acting in the place of a historical past. The forgetting that he identifies in empirical forms of memory is the relationship of Atlantic slavery to race and racism, the plantation in its modern incarnations, and the Haitian Revolution as a successful slave revolt (2002, 163–64). By virtue of living in a nation that continues to script its own participation in slavery as a story of emancipation, black Britons are positioned by the invisible structures of West Indian plantations. The recently discovered records of compensation paid to absentee English plantation owners for their emancipated slaves reveal the long reach of the financial tendrils of slavery into England's modern industrialized cities, its prominent families, and the great houses of its pastoral countryside (C. Hall et al. 2014).

The affective memory of the *Zong!* poems works against the forgetting embedded in the empirical reality belonging to national commemorations of the abolition of the slave trade. The exhibits that Philip visited all screamed out to her: "It didn't happen here! It didn't happen here! It didn't happen here!" (2008a, 14). The commemoration not only presented an abolitionist archive of the slave trade but also extended a Victorian vision of Empire into the present through the Royal Navy frigate that escorted the *Zong* down the Thames. The exhibition aboard the frigate instructed the public about the Royal Navy's continued efforts to eradicate modern-day piracy and illegal trafficking (Gold 2007). Since today's pirates and human traffickers are African, the story of the enormous profits earned through Britain's participation in the slave trade, and acts of piracy through which ships like the *Zong* were obtained, is overwritten by the story of the nation as a global emancipator. Published a year after the 2007 commemoration, *Zong!* introduces a temporality that shifts between the Middle Passage, West Indian plantation life, and a present in which the violence of slavery is repeated

(Philip 2008b). For Philip, the total disregard of black lives exhibited by the *Zong* captain's decision and the ensuing legal dispute has an afterlife in the indiscriminate killing of black people today. She generated the portmanteau "Ferguzong" for placing the 2014 Ferguson, Missouri, police shooting of Michael Brown, as well as the repetition of its violence in cities across the United States, within the memory of the *Zong*. The slave regime sanctioning the *Zong* killings also speaks to a Caribbean present in which tourism preserves a benign version of plantation life that "equalled death for the African" (Philip 1997, 170).

While alluding to the death and racial terror that continues to be repeated even after slavery has ended, Philip's *Zong!* poems disrupt this cycle of repetition through an incorporation of African cultural forms. The exclamation point added to the slave ship in the book's title emphasizes its poetic expression as a chant or song, since West Africans sing on the occasions of births and deaths, to express both sorrow and joy. "Why the exclamation mark after *Zong!?*," asks Philip in anticipation of the reader's query. "*Zong!* is chant! Shout! And ululation! *Zong!* is moan! Mutter! Howl! And shriek! *Zong!* is 'pure utterance.' *Zong!* is Song!" (2008b, 207). As song, Philip's book recalls the African women who sang laments aboard the slave ships. By creating songs to remember the families they left behind and to express their condition of exile, the women served as griots for the shiploads of displaced Africans journeying toward an unknown destination (Walvin 2011, 40; Rediker 2007, 284). The sounds of their laments are not to be heard in any of the records submitted for the *Zong* trial. However, their wails, if not the stories of their songs, are evoked in the lilting rhythm of Philip's poems. These nonverbal but not insignificant sounds are where history writing bleeds into experimental poetry to unusual and even startling effects. Philip's poetic fragmentation of *Gregson v. Gilbert* delivers a slave experience through emotive sounds, tone, and mood, as language progressively breaks down in each of the collection's sections. By summoning the Africans caught between life and death, filled with humanity and also drowning in its negation, the experimental poems convey the ghostly presence of lives within a document that treats those lives as inconsequential.

Philip mentions how her rereading of Jacques Derrida's *Specters of Marx* (1994) allowed her to see that her book is "a wake of sorts" for mourning the dead and performing the burial rites that were denied them. However, she is confronted with her inability to recover the bodies as tangible evidence of their lives. "I, too, want the bones," she declares, alluding to the need for a body to mourn the dead (2008b, 201). In the absence of a physical body, she conjures the dead as breath or air, in their spectral rather than their embodied forms. Referencing Derrida's idea of haunting as both an absence and presence, Philip characterizes her poems as hauntological. "The one who has disappeared appears still to be *there*, and his apparition is not nothing," writes Derrida (1994, 120). Philip proceeds to use the word "tidal" to evoke the spectral quality of the *Zong*'s elusive memory because she sees water as a metaphoric conduit to the past. Like Derrida's ghostly event that appears for the first time but only as a repetition, each wave that washes ashore appears to be the first but follows the one that has gone before. "As the ocean appears to be the same yet is constantly in motion, affected by tidal movements," explains Philip, "so too this memory appears stationary yet is shifting always" (201).

The idea of a memory that is tidal—appearing to be stationary but always shifting—unsettles the presumed stability of an archival memory suggested through the fixity and solidity of its temple-like building or an empirical memory that resuscitates a material past through artifacts and historical re-creations. Building on Philip's characterization of *Zong!* as a wake, Christina Sharpe's *In the Wake* (2016) introduces into the tidal flow of the ocean's movement an image of the waves created by the forward motion of the slave ship. Sharpe indicates how the design of a ship like the *Zong,* in which the shape of its bow was intended to minimize the turbulence of the waves, has the effect of creating in its wake ever-expanding transverse waves as the arc of one wave circles outward to create another in a movement maximizing their flow. She visualizes the geometrical patterns of these waves as being broken by the smaller waves created by the people who were thrown overboard, bobbing in the water before being swept underwater by the transverse waves. These multiple and increasing surges figure for her the trauma of the Africans aboard the ship and the ensuing waves that touch subsequent generations in the diaspora (2016, 40–41).

The difference between minimized waves at the ship's bow and heightened turbulence in its wake represents the amplified effects of hauntological time on diasporic Africans, which explains the metaphoric relationship Philip establishes between her poetry writing and the treatment of slaves. Calling the legal document a "word store," she says that she "would lock [herself] in this text in the same way men, women, and children were locked in the holds of the slave ship *Zong*" (2008b, 191). She performs a "random selection [of words] that parallels the random selection of Africans" (192) and speaks of murdering and mutilating the text, just as captured Africans were murdered and their bodies mutilated. In this way, Philip metaphorically attacks the body of a legal record. As a poetic form of expression, *Zong!* is a metaphoric assault on the empirical presence of a document that treats African lives as inconsequential. However, by refusing the logic of language and narrative, the poems present a problem for the reader: How are we to interpret the words and letters on the page? Do we read them from left to right, top to bottom, or even diagonally? Perhaps we should read them as concrete poems by seeing pictures in their layouts on the page. Water appears to be an overriding theme. The words of one poem spiral downward as if caught in a liquid vortex (94), while others bob up and down like waves on the open sea (106–7). Still others sink to the bottom of the page under the weight of their signification (19). Each poem is a picture to be viewed but also a series of sounds and words to be heard.

Philip's poetic style exhibits the concrete imagery and epistemological inquiry into the meaning of language belonging to Language poetry. Yet, she describes her poems, which also address the traumatic afterlife of slavery, as starting from a different place than that of other Language poets. It is a place she characterizes as "the wasteland between the terror of language and the horror of silence" (2003, 198). Her description of language and silence alludes to the plantation process known as "seasoning" for making Africans into a manageable work force by forcibly stripping them of their languages, cultures, and memories of their homeland. The *Zong!* poems move between the terror of a language that classifies African people as property and the horror of its silence about their lives. In fragmenting the text of a document that designates slaves as cargo to be disposed of at will, Philip opens up wide spaces between words and even the letters of words to suggest that silence is not emptied of meaning even if it does not deliver language as such. How does turning away from the logic of language force one to confront its underside, namely silence?

VOCALIZING THE SILENT SPACES OF HISTORY

Philip has long been interested in exploring silence, particularly as it relates to herself as an Afrosporic woman. Silence is the site of a linguistic wound due to the violent uprooting of African people and active suppression of their native tongues as a means of social control. In

"Discourse on the Logic of Language" from the collection *She Tries Her Tongue, Her Silence Softly Breaks* (1989), the edict for mixing different linguistic groups of slaves to prevent them from plotting rebellions appears alongside a meditation on the English language. The poet shuttles between the father tongue and mother tongue, which, for her, is also the father tongue because both are English. However, there is another reference to the mother tongue that runs vertically along the margins of her poem. This mother tongue does not consist of words that form into meaning. Rather, it exists in the sensation of a mother's tongue passing over her baby's skin, touching her tongue, and forcing her breath into her mouth:

THE MOTHER THEN PUT HER FINGERS INTO HER CHILD'S MOUTH—GENTLY FORCING IT OPEN; SHE TOUCHES HER TONGUE TO THE CHILD'S TONGUE, AND HOLDING THE TINY MOUTH OPEN, SHE BLOWS INTO IT—HARD. SHE WAS BLOWING WORDS—HER WORDS, HER MOTHER'S WORDS, THOSE OF HER MOTHER'S MOTHER, AND ALL THEIR MOTHERS BEFORE—INTO HER DAUGHTER'S MOUTH. (56–58)

The words that appear in the margins of the book but are also capitalized are alongside a second edict recommending the removal of a slave's tongue as punishment for speaking in his (or her) native language. It suggests that the mother tongue exists as a linguistic memory transmitted across generations even if language itself is not. As Patricia Saunders explains about these lines, linguistic agency does not overturn the edict relegating the mother tongue to a place of silence (2001, 147). At the same time, the mother tongue is not a space of loss when it exists as a space of affect: the sensation of touch and a silent breath that passes from one mouth to another. Inasmuch as linguistic memory is transmitted from mother to daughter, an affective language that is coded as silence is also female-gendered.

To accept silence as a missing text or absence begins from the premise that black women who do not appear in the archives are not present in other ways. In "Dis Place—The Space Between," Philip calls *ratio decidendi*, the reason for a decision, as a sentencing of black women to silence (1997, 75). The dual implication of "sentencing" as the punishment that is the outcome of a legal decision and the meaning that is the outcome of putting words together draws attention to the intersection of the rules of law with the grammar of language. This is why Philip begins from a different place, which is that "women have, in fact, left their mark on the many silences that surround language" (85), and the problem is more one of learning to read them. To enable this reading she draws attention to silence as sounds between words and temporal pauses that enable meaning. In this manner, she moves black women's linguistic absence from the margins to the body of the text:

> silence is
> silence is
> silence is
> the sound, the very sound; between the words,
> in the interstices of time divided by the word
> between
> outer and inner
> space /silence
> is
> the boundary (85)

Without the pauses in time and empty space between words, we would have a cacophony of noise and gibberish. Silence is as much a part of language as words. While the grammar of language establishes boundaries between sound and silence, ghosts, whose spectral form gives them the ability to traverse boundaries, enable us to see that the spaces of silence are not nothing even if they lack the materiality of words. "If we talk of silence and assign to it a validity equal to the word, is it then right to talk of a 'missing text,' since the text of silence is already embedded in the word?" inquires Philip in "Dis Place" (1997, 85–86). These prior meditations on silence offer a way to understand how *Zong!* makes visible—and audible—silences when she fragments the language of marine insurance law in the first movement of poems she calls *Os*.

"Zong! #1" (figure 1.1), as the first poem in the collection and *Os*, sets the tone for Philip's dismemberment of *Gregson v. Gilbert* by transforming its silences into spaces of affect. The poem forces apart the letters in words belonging to the statement that there was not enough good water for the extra days at sea. "This was an action on a policy of insurance," begins *Gregson v. Gilbert*, "to recover the value of certain slaves thrown overboard for want of water." The counterargument during the hearings was that "there were three butts of good water, and two and a half of sour water, on board" (1783, 629). In the poem, water appears as an overriding theme because, not only is the ocean the watery grave of the Africans who were thrown overboard, but also a shortage of fresh water was the alleged justification for that action. Visually, the words appear as a series of letters bobbing up and down on the page like so many waves or driftwood in a sea of monosyllabic utterances. But hearing the poem read aloud elicits the uncanny sounds of the voices of those who were lost at sea. Listening to Philip's performance of "Zong! #1," when compared to seeing it on the page, is to hear the silences in the legal case filled with ghostly sounds from the past: first the sounds of the thirst from which all slaves were suffering and then of drowning, which was the condition of the ones selected to be thrown overboard. The experience the voices convey, which is at the heart of the legal case but about which it is silent, is of life being cut short through an unexpected and unwarranted death. When vocalized, a breaking up of the words—water was sour water good water one day of want—creates a linguistic stutter that becomes a plea, a gurgle, and a chatter.

Language falls apart as the spaces between letters open up, fragmenting the words to expose blank spaces on the page as spaces of sensations. The utterance of this poem evokes a visceral response in listeners, more like goose bumps on the skin than an image in the mind's eye. Calling "the taken-for-grantedness of the emotionally contained subject . . . a residual bastion of Eurocentrism in critical thinking," Teresa Brennan characterizes affect as emotions and energies that are transmitted across and between individuals through a relationship of affecting and being affected (2004, 24). "Zong! #1" causes listeners to receive the sensations of slaves dying from thirst or swallowing salt water as their bodies sink to the ocean floor. This affective response is not the same as the silence of the mother being transmitted to the child that Philip describes in "Discourse on the Logic of Language." It is the uncanny sensation of a listener hearing voices issuing from the master document that has excluded them. We hear the gasp for water in "w w w," the chatter in response to cold water on the skin in "d d d," and the choking and shudder of water filling the lungs in "g g go o o o" (Philip 2008b, 3–4). The sounds that emerge from "Zong! #1" are to be distinguished from literal re-creations of slave ship sounds, complete with the moans and groans of slaves, to be found in slavery museums like the Wilberforce House in Hull or the National Museums and Galleries at Merseyside. Liverpool's black community has refused to visit the Merseyside museum in protest of not being consulted in the planning of its slave ship

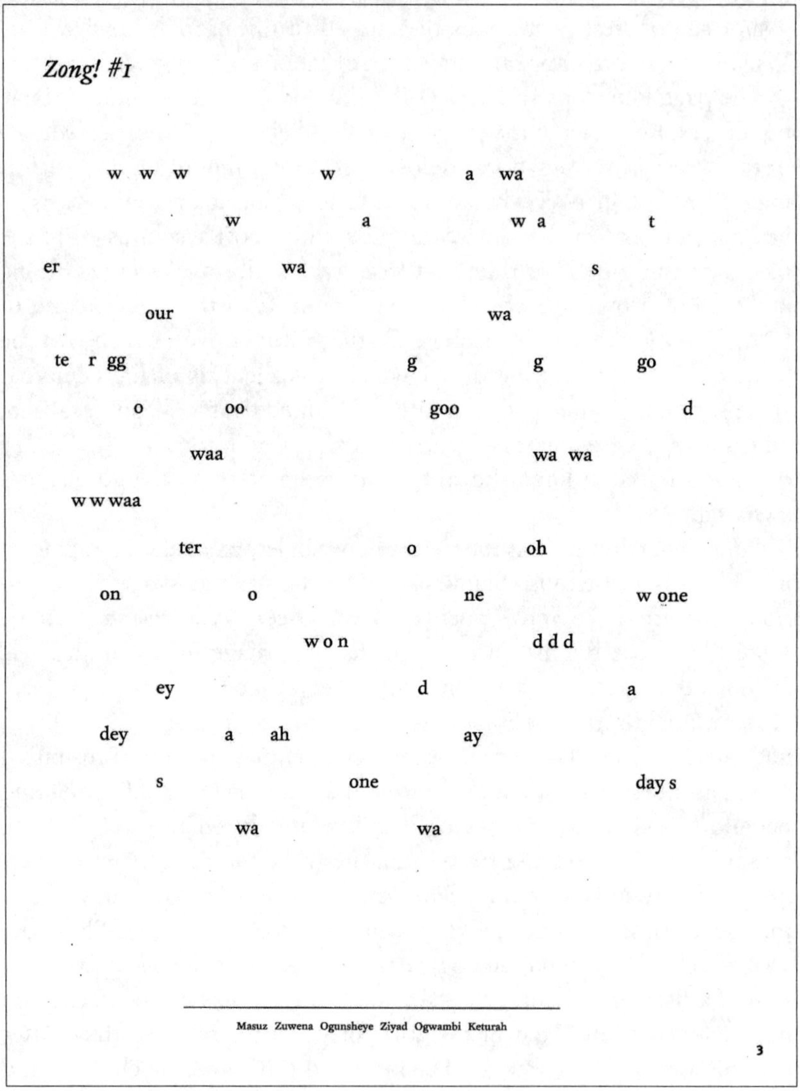

Zong! #1

w w w w a wa

w a w a t

er wa s

our wa

te r gg g g go

o oo goo d

waa wa wa

w w waa

ter o oh

on o ne w one

w o n d d d

ey d a

dey a ah ay

s one day s

wa wa

Masuz Zuwena Ogunsheye Ziyad Ogwambi Keturah

3

Figure 1.1. Zong! #1

galleries (Wood 2000, 295–301). Unlike national museums that often turn a Middle Passage experience into spectacle, Philip's poetic memorial avoids filling a silence with slave voices because it simultaneously wants us to remember why those voices are absent. Although a poem is not a monument, the form of "Zong! #1" resembles those memorials James E. Young identifies as countermonuments, which he distinguishes from commemorative forms that encourage forgetfulness by doing "our memory work for us" (1999, 3).[8]

It is not simply the case that the words from the legal hearing are being fragmented; rather, through the repetition of syllables that prolong their utterance, the smooth progression of language is being slowed to a halt. A stalling of the rhythmic flow of language draws attention to the silence that exists at the margins of its meaning: "*When a language is so strained* that it starts to stutter, or to murmur or stammer . . . *then language in its entirety reaches the limit* that marks its outside and makes it confront silence" (Deleuze 1997, 113; italics and ellipses in the original). The language of *Gregson v. Gilbert* "trembles from head to toe" (109), to use Gilles Deleuze's characterization of a linguistic stammer, when the smooth operation and normative function of legal discourse is slowed down to the breaking point. The trembling of English law is interrupted by the names of the dead as a verbal litany that inserts a different kind of order into the poem's linguistic breakdown. When she reads "Zong #1," Philip moves from the fragmented words of *Gregson v. Gilbert* to the list of African names at the bottom of the page before returning to the words of the document and the continuation of the list of names on the next page. In this way, the names introduce individual identities to the African voices being released from the blank spaces in the public record of the trial. As a text that exists outside the language of *Gregson v. Gilbert*, appearing in an unbroken single row of small lettering separated by a thin line, the names are the closest Philip comes to a creative act of recovery in *Os*, although the names are not only from the African regions involved in the slave trade but also reflect the diversity of African people missing from archives in which they appear simply as members of the "Negro race." The proper names of the dead in Kiswahili, Arabic, Akan, Shona, Yoruba, Tiv, Ngoni, and Luganda, among other languages belonging to the diverse peoples of the African continent, interject their linguistic intonations into the formal language of the court minutes.

A positioning of the African names as footnotes below a black line separating them from the rest of the text indicates a personhood that lies outside both the legal document and a European definition of "the human." In *Notanda,* Philip describes this personhood in terms of communal ties established through language, kinship, culture, and ancestors (2008b, 196). Alluding to African religions in which the spirit of a person survives the death of the physical body, Myriam Moïse suggests that the list of names alludes to a "spiritual survival despite their physical murder" (2010, 26). Based on their position on the page, African American poet and critic Evie Shockley calls the footnotes "underwriters" that shift the injury of "the loss" from English insurers to the African kin and ancestors of the people in the hold (2011, 814–15). And Sarah Dowling (2011) draws attention to how the lines without any names beneath them continue into the next section, *Dicta,* as if to indicate the power of English law to erase these complex identities. Her observation indicates that, by restoring individual identities but not to their wholeness, the poems make evident the stripping away of visible evidence of their languages, ethnicities, and kinship. These diverse readings show that the pull to read *Zong!* as a neo–slave text that restores African voices and identities exists in tension with a counterpull of its failure, which is the objective of Philip's poetics of fragmentation.

As a way of undermining the power of English law to define the boundaries of African personhood, Philip cuts up the words and sentences of *Gregson v. Gilbert* and rearranges them seemingly at random on the page. The document itself begins to crumble as the equilibrium of its words—which is achieved through a balance between language and silence—is set in motion.[9] Michel Foucault reminds us that the archive is not simply a document housed in an official building but also the "law of what can be said" (1972, 129). In the effort to determine who was liable for the loss—owners or underwriters—*Gregson v. Gilbert* lays out the rules and regulations that constitute the condition of possibility for the drownings to take place. What happened aboard the *Zong* was not unique despite Lord Mansfield and a solicitor for the underwriters avowing the singularity of the case (*Gregson v. Gilbert* 1783, 630). Since African slaves were transported as property, they could be thrown overboard, much like the jettisoning of goods during a storm, if the action was deemed necessary for saving the ship. This is one of the legal arguments that is considered in the *Zong* trial and, as such, belongs to the rationale of insurance law. "It has been decided," argues counsel for the owners, "whether wisely or unwisely is not now the question, that a portion of our fellow-creatures may become the subject

Zong! #14

the truth was

the ship sailed

the rains came

the loss arose

the truth is

the ship sailed

the rains came

the loss arose

the negroes is

the truth was

Nkrumah Ato Nobanzi Oduneye Opa Fagbulu

24

Figure 1.2. Zong! #14

of property. This, therefore, was a throwing overboard of goods, and of part to save the residue" (*Gregson v. Gilbert* 1783, 630).

By postponing the question of their humanity ("whether wisely or unwisely is not now the question"), *Gregson v. Gilbert* contains the Africans' "thingness" but not their personhood; an ontological state of being that denotes the facts—*what* is or was—but not identity, *who* is or was. In the alternating columns of words in "Zong! #14" (figure 1.2), there is symmetry to factual evidence both in the past and present (Philip 2008b, 24). The facts of the legal arguments do not change: the ship sailed, the rains came, the loss arose. But the symmetry of the stanzas is disturbed by the singularity of "the negroes is," an ungrammatical phrase that is not intended to demonstrate the ontological being of "the negroes" so much as to introduce that absence as a haunting presence of what is left unsaid. "Zong! #26" (figure 1.3) provides, in a single run-on sentence, the arguments presented by the lawyers for each side (45). The poem opens with "was the cause was the remedy was the record was the argument was the delay was the evidence was overboard was the not was the cause was the was" and ends with "was the therefore was the this was the that was the negroes was the cause." Philip's snippets of reasons provided by counsel for owners and underwriters reveal a logic of legal argument in which murder is unrepresented. In the court hearings, the "cause" or premise with which the poem ends, "the negroes," is irrelevant to the case.

Six additional poems constructed from the language of *Gregson v. Gilbert* follow "Zong! #26" in a subsection called *Dicta,* the title of which alludes to judicial opinion that does not carry the weight of legal precedent. These poems, which have no numbers, appear on the page as columns of words mimicking the neatly written ledgers recording Africans as commodities. "Through their graphic simplicity and economy," writes Smallwood about slave records, "invoices and ledgers effaced the personal histories that fueled the slaving economy" (2007, 98). An effacement of unique identities is evident in the slave ledgers, where the movement down the column from one individual to the next is marked only by a slight shift in term: "negro man," "negro woman," "negro girl," "negro girl meager" (Philip 2008b, 194). Imitating the layout of these documents, the last poem of *Dicta,* "Zong! #" (figure 1.4), lines up in three columns with diverse combinations of the phrases—"uncommon case," "great weight," and "new trial"— used by Lord Mansfield to describe the unprecedented nature of the legal case:

Zong! #26

was the cause was the remedy was the record was the argument
was the delay was the evidence was overboard was the not was the
cause was the was was the need was the case was the perils was the
want was the particular circumstance was the seas was the costs
was the could was the would was the policy was the loss was the
vessel was the rains was the order was the that was the this was the
necessity was the mistake was the captain was the crew was the
result was justified was the voyage was the water was the maps
was the weeks was the winds was the calms was the captain was
the seas was the rains was uncommon was the declaration was the
apprehension was the voyage was destroyed was thrown was the
question was the therefore was the this was the that was the
negroes was the cause

Omolara Chimaneya Adekemi Oke Mowunmi Iliola

Figure 1.3. Zong! #26

This is a very *uncommon case,* and deserves a reconsideration. There is *great weight* in the objection, that the evidence does not support the statement of the loss made in the declaration. There is no evidence of the ship being foul and leaky, and that certainly was not the cause of the delay. There is weight, also, in the circumstance of the throwing

> overboard of the negroes after the rain (if the fact be so), for
> which, upon the evidence, there appears to have been no ne-
> cessity. There should, on the ground of reconsideration only,
> be a *new trial,* on the payment of costs. (*Gregson v. Gilbert*
> 1783, 630; emphasis added)

The poem's shifting of terms follows the logic of the slave ship's ledger: "uncommon case" becomes "uncommon weight" becomes "great
weight" becomes "new weight" becomes "new trial," and so on (Philip
2008b, 55–56). When applied to the language of law, the ledger form
used for recording slaves appears pointless or meaningless. The poem
reveals that the logic for one system of classification does not translate
or carry over into another. The missing text of the lost ship's ledger,
which itself acts in the place of the absent African names, is the silence
behind the *ratio decidendi* of Lord Mansfield's testament to the singularity of the legal case for an action that was more commonplace. Philip's poems recode the silences in *Gregson v. Gilbert* not as an absence
so much as the boundary of a signification indelibly marked by the
master-slave relationship.

   Zong! is a poetic expression of archival silences belonging to the
traumatic history of slavery. Those who have attended multiple readings have noticed changes in Philip's approach as well as the effect of
the readings on diverse audiences. Eichhorn describes how the readings
changed after the book went into press, when the poet ceased to provide
an explanation of her process and "began to honor the silences marking
the text" (2010, 38). The differences that she observed between Philip's
reading to the background of a Toronto snowstorm blowing outside
and at a historic site on a Tobago beach led her to identify what she calls
"multiple registers of silence" in the poems (2010, 38–39). Eichhorn
also describes the mixed response of an audience of writers, artists, and
literary critics at one of the several Toronto readings she attended, some
of whom were appreciative while others felt uneasy with being obliged
to be silent and still during Philip's performance. A mixed response of
this kind was not entirely evident at the reading I attended when Philip
visited the UCLA campus in the second week of November 2016. It
might have been due to Donald Trump having just won the U.S. pres-
idential election since feelings of despondency weighed heavily in the
room. Members of the audience sat completely still and in silence as
the sensations of affecting and being affected ran like an electric current
through the room, bringing us closer together as a community—not

Zong! #

uncommon case

great weight   new trial

great weight

new trial   uncommon case

new trial

uncommon case   great weight

uncommon weight

great trial   new case

great trial

new case   uncommon weight

————————————————

Figure 1.4. Zong! #

through feelings of a shared history, due to the audience being as diverse as is the city of Los Angeles, but through a shared rejection of the misogyny, racism, and homophobia that fueled Trump's campaign and election.

The diverse responses reported for readings at different times and in different locations point to how the transmission of affect is not direct but rather, channeled through received codes and historical frames of reference. The invisible power of received codes—particularly those belonging to antislavery—is evident in Veronica J. Austen's description of readers who saw a resemblance between their disorientation and becoming unmoored while reading Philip's poems and the experience of slaves in the ship's hold (2011, 75–76). The historical antecedent to these readerly responses is the antislavery trope of empathy with which Saidiya Hartman opens her *Scenes of Subjection*. "In making the other's suffering one's own," she explains, "this suffering is occluded by the other's obliteration" (1997, 19). Not all expressions of empathy operate in this way, as literature does have the potential to communicate an experience without a reader being obliged to make it his or her own. Citing Judith Butler's writings on how conveying someone else's trauma necessitates not only failing to depict the experience but also signposting that failure, Austen concludes her essay with the statement that disorientation in the reader is not the desired outcome of Philip's poetic style (2011, 79). To phrase it differently, a seamless identification of the cerebral process of reading poetry with the physical, psychological, and emotional state of Africans aboard a slave ship sutures over all of the ways that the poet signposts her failure to represent a Middle Passage experience. Yet, Philip does not abdicate her responsibility to transmit that experience to her readers, because she evokes a spectral past in which slave lives are both present and absent. An archive of affect holds the political potential for overturning antislavery codes of sympathy and empathy, but only if coupled with uncovering the hidden structures through which they continue to operate.

SMALL STORIES IN THE FLOTSAM AND JETSAM

Small stories begin to emerge from the fragmented words in the last movement of *Zong!* entitled *Ferrum*, which is Latin for "iron." In an interview, Philip mentions the small stories of Wale, Sade, and their child Ade, but these stories are so disjointed that they are not self-evident and difficult for the reader to reconstruct. She describes how Wale dictates a letter to his wife, Sade, before swallowing it and jumping overboard (Saunders 2008, 74–75). His action is symbolic of how any archive presenting an African perspective drowned with the slaves who jumped or were thrown overboard. Wale, Sade, and Ade are the last three names in the list of twenty-two African names with which *Ferrum* concludes. Unlike the litany of names at the beginning of *Zong!*, these are in the same script as the book's title, thereby suggesting a transformation of loss into song. One of the small stories that appears in the section, but is missing from the African names in the list, concerns Dido Elizabeth Belle Lindsay. She was the mixed-race daughter of Lord Mansfield's nephew, John Lindsay, who was a captain in the Royal Navy, and a slave woman about whom little is known other than her name, Maria Belle, and that she was taken from a Spanish ship during the British 1762 siege of Havana. Lindsay brought his illegitimate child to live with his uncle, who called her Dido after the famous queen of Carthage. The chief justice not only presided over the *Zong* case but also the prominent 1772 Somerset case, wherein he ruled that slaves who escaped from their West Indian owners in Britain could not be returned to the colonies against their will. Despite a ruling that circumvented the thorny question of the existence of slavery in Britain, it is commonly believed that Mansfield's familial relationship to and affection for the mixed-race Dido influenced his decision. He similarly avoided addressing the status of slaves as property in the *Zong* trial by deferring the legal decision to a future trial for which no record exists.[10] Philip explains how her legal training left her unprepared to learn that Mansfield presided over the *Zong* case since she studied most of his decisions in law school but not this one (M. NourbeSe Philip, interview by the author, November 15, 2016). She presents the reader with an inexplicable event that occurred in the course of writing her book of poems, which was the arrangement of letters in the name of Dido, a name that she consciously associated with the queen of Carthage (2008b, 206). A few years later, while leafing through the pages of a book on the slave trade, she came across Dido's name again. Then, on the first day of September 2007, she saw a painting that was the centerpiece of an art exhibit in Lord Mansfield's Kenwood House as part of the Bicentenary of the Abolition of the Slave Trade Act (2008a, 2).

Dido comes to us as a visible presence, like so many eighteenth-century black British slaves and servants, as a result of her appearance in a painting.[11] The portrait shows her standing next to her cousin Lady

Elizabeth Murray in a pose that introduces movement into its staged scene.[12] Philip describes Dido's unusual posture as an attempted flight from the painting's frame, the movement and motion of which belongs to a black aesthetic: "While her cousin is stationary, facing the artist and viewer straight on, Dido is moving off to the left, away from her white cousin, almost as if she is moving out of the 'frame' of the story. Whether consciously or not, the artist has captured a quality of kinesis which I have identified as an aspect the African aesthetic which crosses all disciplines" (2008a, 26). *Ferrum* raises a series of questions about the nature of Dido's flight from the scene followed with the response that "did o flees to afric a seeks a place to re st" (2008b, 142). The final phrase claims Dido for her African mother, whose slave status is hidden in the portrait of an elegantly dressed yet exoticized mulatress with her index finger playfully placed on her cheek. By returning Dido to Africa, Philip reverses the deracialization of a lineage that ends with the mixed-race free woman's great-great-grandson identifying himself as white in South Africa (2008a, 26). Formally, however, the words are so fragmented—with large empty space between "afric" and "a" and the "st" of "rest" appearing on the next line—that the answer to the question of "wh ere does di do f lee" does little to lay her story to rest. Like the woman in the portrait, her story is in motion. In my discussion of affective memory as not only the traces of the absent personhood of slaves but also the archival process of absenting them, I am equally interested in how Philip introduces her African aesthetic of kinesis into the *ratio decidendi,* or reason for a decision, by making the legal language speak what it, by the rules of law, cannot say. Just as the small story of Dido fleeing to Africa does not reconstruct her life but reveals the hidden African mother in the great-great-grandson's claim to whiteness, an African aesthetic of kinesis introduces a hidden mother tongue into the English language.

It is only after breaking open legal discourse that Philip feels as though she has come into a language of her own in *Ferrum,* although unlike the metallic solidity suggested by iron, she calls it a "language of the limp and the wound" that has been "broken by history" (2008b, 205). This characterization points to how her poetics of fragmentation through which she shreds the language of the law extends even to her own form of expression. The section begins with comprehensible phrases but increasingly becomes incomprehensible as broken English words and sentences stagger across the page to meet the words of other languages, also broken. When the English language becomes fragmented and interspersed with African words, the sound of what Philip calls the Caribbean demotic emerges from its interstices:

from omi   *ìyè we be*   *ẹbọra àkì*   ash
   es and sa   lt for the bo   die s   of kin un
     der the sk   in of s   ea whe
                                                  (168)

In these lines, the English words "ashes," "salt," "bodies," and "sea"—but not "kin" which establishes continuity with the present—are fragmented, but the Yoruba words *omi, ìyè, ebora,* and *àkì* are not. In the context of a transatlantic slavery, Caribbean patois or creolized speech is a linguistic process of the enslaved, but one that, like Philip's poetic sword, breaks apart the master's language by mixing it with different European and African languages and grammar. Philip refers to the process by which African slaves remade language in the Americas as "transforming the leavings and detritus of a language and infusing it with their own remembered linguist traditions" (1989, 85). The linguistic memory of their native tongues is silently embedded in the master's language. Creolized speech does not appear among the diverse languages listed in the book's glossary as "words and phrases overheard on board the *Zong*" (Philip 2008b, 183) because it belongs to the afterlife of the Middle Passage—namely, the arrival of transported Africans in the Americas. Yet, what transpired in the open seas with no historical marker or material evidence from which to re-create its story has left its unacknowledged, because silent, imprint on both sides of the Atlantic: Europe, the Americas, and, yes, even West Africa.

In moving from bones to flesh, the poems have transitioned from a Middle Passage death scene to arrival on the other side. But this is not the end to the book's poetic movements; there is a coda. *Ebora,* the section following *Ferrum,* can be considered a short refrain after the five preceding movements, to invoke Philip's musical metaphor. The first word of *Ebora* is "seas," and its last is "reason," but for the most part the letters appear as a faint shadow and ghostly script, whose words are rendered illegible under an increasing density of superimposed text. These pages are the result of Philip's efforts to print the initial draft of her manuscript on a laser printer. The first two or three pages for each section came off the printer superimposed while the rest of the pages printed as they should. Philip decided to include these pages less as poems to be read or heard and more as a visualization or, to use her phrasing, "a dense landscape of text" (2008b, 206). *Ebora* appears in the glossary as Yoruba for "underwater spirits," which suggests the spirits of the drowned in the water. The glossary also lists *omi* as Yoruba for "water" and *omi ebora* as "water in which spirits reside" (184). In *Ferrum, omi* accompanies the chanting/singing voices of "*oh ye ye oh ye ye oh*" that fragments the proper names of the Atlantic and Caribbean:

ẹyọ   aro orun   oh ye ye oh ye ye oh
      lantic oh   ca ri be eh oh   oh omi ero
                                                              (168)

African words wash over the Atlantic and Caribbean, breaking the proper names into small pieces in the same way the currents churned the drowned slaves' bones. The song, with its accompanying reference to *omi ebora*, moves the reader outside the frame of the slave trade, and its accompanying signification of property, insurance, death, and drowning, to an African-derived meaning of water as the place where spirits reside. This movement represents another difference between Philip's poetics and that of other Language poets; namely, that her poems participate in what Shockley (2013) calls "ritual enactments of spirituality" belonging to Caribbean cultures. The spirits that are unnoticed in the cacophony of sound and motion surface at different moments of the book's movements.

What I am calling an affective memory does not involve unearthing new historical data so much as seeing silence as a limit of what was recorded. In exploring a nonverbal language in the silence that factual evidence leaves behind, Philip's poems force us to rethink the presumed stability of archives as records of the past. *Zong!* not only questions the ability of language to deliver the meaning of "the ineffable," scenes of massacre, terror, displacement, and dislocation; it also constitutes the search for a new and different kind of speech/language for speaking/writing the memory that silence holds. Its poems destabilize written records by fragmenting their words, sending them spiraling across the page to expose their missing text as spaces of affect. They open wide gaps between words and even the letters of words to suggest that silence and emptiness can elicit a verbal expression if not language. The empty spaces unleash the emotive force of thirst, sickness, hunger, and drowning that are immaterial to the deliberations of *Gregson v. Gilbert.* Seen/heard in this way, silence can also be a form of expression rather than a puzzle of history to be solved.

CHAPTER 2

The Invisible

Haitian Art and a Vodou Archive of Slavery

but this Caribbean so choke with the dead
that when I would melt in emerald water,
whose ceiling rippled like a silk tent,
I saw them corals: brain, fire, sea fans,
dead-men's-fingers, and then, the dead men.
I saw that the powdery sand was their bones
ground white from Senegal to San Salvador

—Derek Walcott, "The Schooner *Flight*" (1979)

Due to the loss of millions of lives to the Middle Passage, the sea some-times appears in Caribbean literature as a morbid space of death and drownings. Jamaica Kincaid reminds the American tourist who sees its crystal-clear waters as warm and inviting that the Caribbean washes into the Atlantic Ocean. "It would amaze even you," she continues, "to know the number of black slaves this ocean has swallowed up" (1988, 14). In his much-cited poem "The Sea Is History," Derek Wal-cott provides a more vivid picture of bone fragments crushed into tiny mosaic pieces that become set in living coral. "Bone soldered by coral to bone," the poem proclaims; "mosaics / mantled by the benediction of the shark's shadow" (1986, 364). Édouard Glissant sees in Kamau Brathwaite's phrase "the unity is submarine" the image of "all those Af-ricans weighed down with ball and chain and thrown overboard when-ever a slave ship was pursued by enemy vessels and felt too weak to put up a fight" (1989, 66–67). Descriptions of this kind lead Ian Baucom in his *Specters of the Atlantic* to identify in the writings of Walcott, Glis-sant, and Brathwaite, along with NourbeSe Philip, Fred D'Aguiar, Da-vid Dabydeen, Paul Gilroy, and Kobena Mercer, "the circular exchange of images, figures and epigraphs" that forms a "collective gaze on this image of the drowning grounds" of the Atlantic Ocean (2005, 329–30). One can add to his list the artwork of Lubiana Himid, mentioned in the previous chapter, along with that of Keith Piper, Howardena Pindell, Betye Saar, and María Magdalena Campos-Pons in their creation of seascapes that foreground the failure of the written records to record the traumatic experiences of Africans transported as slaves. But these works also produce countermemories to slavery's racial terror in their depictions of black resistance and survival, because dwelling on death and loss risks reproducing the narrative one seeks to overturn. Although Baucom identifies through his reading of D'Aguiar's *Feeding the Ghosts* the hopeful sentiment of "diasporic survival" despite the Atlantic's submarine burial ground, the philosophy of history his book articulates is "the repeating event" of the *Zong* drownings (2005, 329–30). Through the disjointed time of Derrida's *Specters of Marx* and Benjamin's image of the debris of the past piling up before the angel of history, Baucom professes the elegiac idea of the accumulated time of slavery weighing heavily on the present (2005, 462–64). Stephen Best sees this perspective as a prime example of the melancholic historicism he identifies in *None Like Us* and takes Baucom to task for endorsing "the notion that the past simply is our present" (2018, 70). The connection Best establishes between the melancholic turn of black Atlantic studies and the publication of Morrison's *Beloved* is evident in last line of Baucom's book—"all of it is now, it is always now, even for you who never was there" (Baucom 2005, 333)—which repeats words uttered by Morrison's characters. While the phrase "all of it is now" alludes to the persistence of a racial trauma that does not end with slavery, it is also the case that scholars who dwell on the terrors of slavery lock history into a repetitious pattern from which there appears to be no escape. This is why Best proposes a history of discontinuity in which the slave past being recovered does not serve as a point of origin for black selfhood (21–22).

Although I agree with Best's assessment of a melancholic historicism, I nonetheless see a need to address contending versions of a slave past, especially today when benign images continue to circulate. Slavery reverberates and resonates in sites and sights where its traces are not always self-evident or visible. A silencing of the slave's story manifests itself in monuments and memorializations like the Great Houses that were restored for Caribbean tourism and Britain's 2007 commemoration of its abolition of the slave trade, both of which I have already discussed in chapter 1. Still, Best's identification of the melancholic turn in black Atlantic cultural studies makes evident how emphasizing the traumas of slavery risks foreclosing alternative futures to its racist regime. "The history of the black Atlantic," he explains, "comes into existence only through loss and, in turn, can be sustained only through more tales of its loss" (2018, 67). In order to disrupt a temporality in which slavery weighs heavily on the present as a tale of loss, this chapter proposes that we change the way we view the past, much of which is derived from official records. To this end, it examines Haitian art that introduces a sacred Vodou cosmology into those archives in which slaves appear overwhelmingly as tortured, dead, and dying bodies. The artwork introduces greater ambivalence into familiar scenes of black trauma, thereby disrupting the totalizing effect of the vastness of the Atlantic Ocean as a graveyard. Instead of depicting the weight of accumulated time, they offer combined images of different historical moments for revealing the racial violence of slavery to be only a small part of the story.

The Vodou-inspired artworks of Haitian painter Frantz Zéphirin and Haitian-born, Miami-based painter, sculptor, and mixed-media artist Edouard Duval-Carrié complicate the image of the sea as the burial ground of unrealized lives and lost histories. The ship of Zéphirin's painting *The Slave Ship Brooks* (2007) is a mobile space of death and torture as it exists in antislavery pamphlets and eyewitness accounts, but it is also a pathway to other futures than the one charted by the Atlantic slave trade's nautical routes. By rerouting an iconic antislavery image through Haitian history, the painting brings a British and American story of bondage and freedom into the geographical space of the first black republic. It also introduces into antislavery Christianity the Vodou sea *lwa*, or ancestral spirits, whose presence disrupts an image of the slaver as a harbinger of death. Duval-Carrié's painting *La vraie histoire des Ambaglos (The True History of the Underwater Spirits)* (2003) and installation *The Indigo Room or Is Memory Water Soluble?* (2004) depict through the sacred world of Vodou a different kind of seascape than the one that appears in the Caribbean literature with which I opened this chapter. The underwater scenes of these works are not littered with bones turned to coral, as in Walcott's iconic poems, nor do they depict salt water washing the wounds of shackled slaves in the often-cited opening scene of D'Aguiar's *Feeding the Ghosts*. Rather, they drown archival images within a Haitian cosmology of water as a sacred element. Whether inhabited by spirits rising from the ocean floor as in *La vraie histoire des Ambaglos* or replete with cultural artifacts and the stuff of memories that overflow *The Indigo Room*, water exists in these two artworks as a space of drowning and forgetting but also of remembrance and return. Although Zéphirin and Duval-Carrié have unique aesthetic styles and approaches, their works are connected by their introduction of the living archive of Vodou into enduring archival materials. In this way, both artists provide counterimaginaries of the sea than what is to be derived from the enduring records as well as Anglophone Caribbean literature.

Granted official recognition as a religion of Haiti only as recently as 2003, Vodou combines the sacred beliefs of the Fon (Benin), Yoruba (Nigeria), and Kongo (Angola and Bas-Zaire) peoples who were transported to the Caribbean with the Catholicism and Freemasonry of the French planter class (McCarthy Brown 2006, 1–9; Ramsey 2011, 13). Its ritual drawings, *vèvè* and *pwen,* are considered some of the earliest nonindigenous art forms and, as such, contain sacred memories passed from one generation of *oungans* and *manbos* (Vodou priests and priestesses) to the next.[1] *Vèvès* are abstract or figurative line patterns drawn from memory on the floors of Vodou temples, or *ounfòs*. They are the gateways through which the *lwa*—the divine principles of the most powerful ancestors—enter the human world, which is why they have been likened to maps (Beaubrun 2013, 279). *Pwen,* or "points," drawn on the outer edges of the *vèvè* consist of stars, crosses, and other symbols signifying a concentration of power and energy (McCarthy Brown 1976, 242–43).[2] These ritualistic signs and symbols, as well as the images accompanying them, have made their way into Haitian art and onto the cover of at least one Anglophone Caribbean literary work. The original edition of Brathwaite's *Islands* (1969), the third book of *The Arrivants* trilogy, displayed an exquisite *vèvè* drawn by the Haitian artist Neamy Jean (Walmsley 1992, 209; Jones 1995, 92).

When Brathwaite declared "the unity is submarine" in *Contradictory Omens* (1974, 64) to describe creolized Caribbean cultures linking the islands to each other and collectively to the African continent, he was referring to the pleasurable shock of recognition he experienced during a 1968–69 visit to Haiti. The nation that had its beginnings in the first successful slave revolt bore such a strong resemblance to the Ghana he knew and remembered that it allowed him to recognize a hidden West African culture. "Parts of Kingston could be Kajebi or Kibi; parts of Port-au-Prince, Ibadan," he explains; "and in the Haitian countryside, the resemblance is quite astonishing—even the West African villages are there" (43). The impression Haiti left on Braithwaite during his visit was "strongly visual," as he was struck not only by the resemblance of its countryside to African villages but also by the vibrancy of its colorful paintings and wall murals (Jones 1995, 92). The connection between Brathwaite's phrase and Haitian art licenses me to take his phrase "the unity is submarine" in a different direction than Glissant's interpretation of slave bodies lining the ocean floor. That direction is a living archive of slavery that is cited, reproduced, and reinterpreted in Haitian art.

Twentieth-century Haitian art is commonly identified with the masters of the Centre d'Art, which was established in Port-au-Prince in 1944. However, the Centre was more responsible for introducing the outside world to Haitian art than for introducing art into Haiti, due to the nation having a much longer tradition of modernist paintings and popular art connected to Vodou (Lerebours 1989; Alexis 2007; Asquith 2012). The Centre's establishment also coincided with the Catholic Church's antisuperstition campaign involving the destruction of Vodou compounds, which forced artists and artisans to seek out new commercial markets (L. Gordon 2018, 131). Michel Philippe Lerebours distinguishes commercial from sacred forms of Vodou art, saying that those artists who claim to be visited by the *lwa* or receive their inspiration in dreams and visions are catering to an overseas clientele craving the fantastic and mysterious (1989, 75–76, 269–70). While this distinction is a cautionary tale against conflating the Vodou of commercial art with its religious forms, it is also the case, as Katherine Smith observes, that American consumption "does not necessarily stifle the creative potential of the artist" and commercial art has been reappropriated for the *ounfò* (2012, 36). The beaded and sequined Vodou flags, or *drapos*, that serve a ritualistic function during religious ceremonies now display scenes of everyday life and, more recently, catastrophic events like the 2010 earthquake. Even when made for commercial markets, they are sewn with the same attention to the ritualistic four cardinal points required in the making of flags sewn for ceremonial purposes (Wexler 2000, 70–71). An aesthetic repurposing of *drapos* is but one instance of the blending of the sacred and secular in Haitian visual culture. In addition to these canvases, there are brightly colored wall murals, metal sculptures from recycled oil drums and found objects, papier-mâché masks for Jacmel's Kanaval, and the brightly painted *tap-taps*, or buses. Although it might appear contradictory for me to call a chapter on visual culture "The Invisible," this contradiction belongs to a knowledge system that transgresses the boundaries of a dualistic worldview. For its practitioners, Vodou is more than a religion as it pervades every aspect of their lives, connecting them to their extended families, ancestors, and history. Claudine Michel explains that, "as a comprehensive religious system, it ties together the visible and invisible, material and spiritual, secular and sacred" (1996, 282). As a metaphor for the method of reading belonging to this chapter, "the invisible" refers to that which is not seen as a critical oversight rather than the opposite of what can be seen.

The *lwa* may be known as *envizib, les invisibles*, or the invisible ones, but they appear in a multiplicity of places and a myriad of forms, as do symbolic forms of slavery integrated into Vodou rituals.[3] Karen McCarthy Brown identifies an "iconography of slavery" in the blowing of police whistles and cracking of whips during the service of *Petwo* or hot-tempered *lwa* (1991, 101). Andrew Apter and Lauren Derby call the African American dancer Katherine Dunham's description of an initiation ceremony in which she participated during the 1930s a "ritualized palimpsest of the transshipment of slaves" (2010, xv–xvi). In *Island Possessed*, an ethnographic memoir of her stay in Haiti, Dunham describes how she and other initiates were made to lie down on their sides, pressed closely together on the damp ground of the temple floor for three days. They were instructed to turn over from their left to right sides every few hours. When a spirit takes possession of the trembling body of one of the initiates whose body was pressed into her own, she became soaked in the woman's urine. Apter and Derby remark how Dunham herself notices the resemblance between the ceremony and a Middle Passage experience as is evident in the analogy she draws: "There we lay, scarcely breathing, waiting, listening, senses alert, packed like sardines much as the slaves who crossed the Atlantic, motionless as though chained, some of us afraid" (qtd. in Apter and Derby 2010, xxviii). They explain the ceremony involving a ritual washing of the head (*lave tête*) to prepare the body to be mounted by the *lwa* as a transformation of Middle Passage dispossession into possession. The act of remembering slavery in order to gain power over a traumatic past would explain the incongruous and inexplicable presence of an instrument of terror—the same vicious tool Glissant identifies as being attached to slaves who sank to the ocean floor—within the sacred space of an *ounfò*. Colin Dayan expresses being frightened as a child at the sight of a ball and chain in a temple and wondering how "the relic of a horrible past" was passed down from one generation of *oungans* to the next and what its relationship to all of the objects on the altar might have been (1995, xii). Its presence leads her to conclude that "Vodou practices must be viewed as ritual reenactments of Haiti's colonial past, even more than as retentions of Africa" (xvii).

The dual meaning of Vodou rituals—as connection to Africa and re-enactment of a colonial past—exists in the iconography Zéphirin and Duval-Carrié incorporate into their art. Their work features embodied memories that Diana Taylor in *The Archive and the Repertoire* (2003) calls "the repertoire." She introduces "the repertoire" for distinguishing those ephemeral forms of living memory from enduring records of the past. The social knowledge transmitted through singing, dancing, gestures, oral storytelling, and other embodied forms, she explains, "allows for an alternative perspective on historical processes of transnational contact and invites a remapping of the Americas" (2003, 20). But Taylor also insists that the distinction between the archive as enduring and the repertoire as ephemeral is a conceptual one based on the assumption that archival materials, among which she includes archaeological ruins, maps, literary works, and even bones, are immutable. This is why she debunks what she calls several "myths" about the archive—namely, that it is unmediated, resistant to change, or does not involve interpretation, selection, classification, and political manipulation (19). Her description suggests how viewing material records through the repertoire holds the potential for disrupting and even changing their meaning. The artworks I have chosen compel the viewer to see enduring archives through the iconography and sacred rituals of Vodou. Duval-Carrié's painting, in particular, demonstrates the smallness of those pictures that have been preserved in European art museums and libraries, whose stately edifices endow the documents they contain with the authority of depicting the slave's world. Looking at textual evidence through the cosmology of Vodou disturbs the fixity of their meaning by introducing movement where before there was none.

If the prior chapter demonstrated how Philip destabilizes a historical document through a poetics of fragmentation, this chapter explores the visual effects of the kinesis she identifies in Dido's flight from the staged scene of a formal portrait painting. I turn to Haitian visual culture for developing VèVè Clark's idea of *Marasa* consciousness as "another norm of creativity" based on the divine twins of Vodou, who sometimes are two and other times three and represent for her a third principle beyond the binary. She goes on to explain that "*Marasa* denotes movement and change and may serve as a metaphor representing the profound differences in environment, social organization, and language encountered by slaves in the Americas" (1991, 44). Her explanation indicates how

Marasa, when used as a metaphor for black diasporic cultures, extends beyond Haiti and Vodou, speaking to the particularities of the experiences of Africans in the Americas. The chapter explores the characteristics of an African-derived cosmology in Vodou, which Zéphirin and Duval-Carrié seize for making their political statements. Zéphirin's painting *The Slave Ship Brooks* superimposes Vodou iconography and Haitian oral history onto a late eighteenth-century antislavery illustration so as to introduce motion and movement into a picture of the complete and total immobilization of African slaves. Duval-Carrié's *La vraie histoire des Ambaglos* displays a double image of the earlier Middle Passage crossing behind the more recent history of Windward Passage drownings of Haitian migrants attempting to reach Florida in makeshift boats. The more contemporary scene of death and loss might suggest a pattern of history as repetition, but only if we understand the artwork's visual aesthetics as hauntological. The message of the *Marasa* is not simply one of the racial terror of slavery being repeated today because Duval-Carrié interjects into a Middle Passage scenario the Vodou signification of water as a medium through which ancestral spirits return to communicate with the living. And then there is the third member of the divine twins when depicted as triplets—the stronger child that is yet to be born. For Duval-Carrié, a potentially hopeful future is represented in the birth of a *dyaspora* that is emotionally and politically connected to its Haitian homeland.[4]

AFRICAN KINESIS IN AN ANTISLAVERY ARCHIVE

Zéphirin is a self-taught artist and member of the famed Obin family of artists in the northern port city of Cap-Haïtien. Philomé Obin (1892–1986), who along with Hector Hyppolite (1894–1948), is the most acclaimed of Port-au-Prince's Centre d'Art artists, started his own school in Cap-Haïtien, where he trained local artists, including his sons, Antoine (Zéphirin's uncle) and Télémaque. Zéphirin began painting early in life, selling his work to cruise ship tourists and by the age of thirteen to galleries. He was initiated as an *oungan* during the late 1980s and moved to Mariani on the outskirts of Port-au-Prince (Cosentino 2016). Having painted thousands of underwater scenes, he sees himself as having an intimate relationship with marine life and spirits, the "oceanic realities" that come to him in "visions" and "dreams" (Zéphirin 2012). Zéphirin has developed a unique style he calls "historic animalist" for its merging of spirits, humans, and animals, often in historical settings. His brightly colored canvases display the detailed intricacies and attentiveness to geometric forms belonging to sacred Vodou drawings. Based on his painting of the 1919 and 1994 invasions of Haiti by the U.S. Marines and his commemoration of the 2,500 victims of Hurricane Jeanne, which struck northwestern Haiti in 2004, Donald Cosentino calls Zéphirin "a chronicler of Haiti's history" (2016). The appearance of his 2007 hurricane painting *The Resurrection of the Dead*—with its wall of faces of those who were killed—on the cover of the *New Yorker* magazine just three days after the 2010 earthquake, made the work seem almost prescient. Zéphirin's Mariani home and studio was at the earthquake's epicenter, and when he stepped outside and into the street, he began to paint the destruction he witnessed around him (Eskin).

As the outcome of a conversation between Zéphirin and Marcus Rediker, author of numerous seafaring histories, *The Slave Ship Brooks* (figure 2.1) combines the perspective of a self-taught Haitian artist with that of a university-trained American historian. Having spent thirty years in the maritime archives, Rediker was drawn to Haitian art, explaining how his passion as an art collector was driven by a desire "to understand how Haitian folk artists have recorded, remembered, and disseminated their history through art" (2014). Although he already owned several of Zéphirin's paintings, he met the artist for the first time in 2017, when they were introduced by Bill Bollendorf, owner of the Galerie Macondo in Pittsburgh.[5] Zéphirin and Rediker talked extensively about their shared interest in Haitian history and also discussed the Atlantic slave trade, since Rediker had just finished writing his history book *The Slave Ship: A Human History* (2007). When Rediker visited Zéphirin in his makeshift studio a couple of days later, he saw him putting the final touches on a new painting, which he subsequently purchased (Rediker 2018). It depicts his book's characterization of the slave ship as a "floating dungeon" and the crew's use of sharks as instruments of terror for rebellious slaves, while introducing into its scene the Vodou sea *lwa*, Agwe and Lasirèn, oral histories of the punishment of rebellious slaves, and two of Haiti's revolutionary leaders. But Zéphirin does not simply bring a textual description of the slave ship into a painting steeped in Haitian history and Vodou culture. By calling his ship *Brooks,* which is a name Rediker suggested to him (2018), he opens up an iconic abolitionist image to a history that is not self-evident in the late eighteenth-century drawing.

The 1788 antislavery broadside of the slave ship *Brooks,* with its tightly packed cargo of slaves, is an image with which we are all too

Figure 2.1. Frantz Zéphirin, *The Slave Ship Brooks* (2007)

familiar.[6] The line drawing was based on the notes of a Royal Navy captain who had been sent to Liverpool to measure the dimensions of several slavers. The *Brooks*, among the ships with the least amount of space allocated to each slave, had air holes for ventilating the lower decks since it was specifically built for the trade. The 1789 London version of the drawing called *Description of a Slave Ship* displays how, in order to carry the 482 slaves that were permitted by law (prior to the Regulation Act, the ship carried as many as 740), they had to be packed lying down side by side on a series of platforms resembling shelves (Rediker 2007, 310–17). As Clarkson explains in his history of the abolitionist movement, the drawing was intended "to give the spectator an idea of the Africans in the middle passage, and this so familiarly, that he might instantly pronounce upon the miseries experienced there" (1839, 377). The drawing shows tiny black men, women, and children lined up in neat rows and stacked one above the other, a detail so macabre that it incited wonder and fascination.[7] The slaves are segregated by sex and age, but the men alone are shackled. The textual description explains that the wrist and ankle chains were necessary due to the constant threat of insurrections. Despite this small piece of information, the overall presentation of the slaves is one of complete and total immobility due to the drawing's objective of arousing shock and horror at the sight of the degrading and dehumanizing conditions of the ship's hold. As a diagram intended to show the brutality of transporting people as cargo, the woodcut also has the unintended visual effect of reproducing their "thingness."

African, black British, Caribbean Canadian, and African American artists have incorporated the iconic image of the *Brooks* into creative works that question its depiction of slaves as nameless, faceless, and inanimate cargo (Francis 2009; Bernier 2014; Finley 2018). Several of these artworks were purchased or commissioned for the 2007 Bicentenary of the Abolition of the Slave Trade Act, since the *Brooks* diagram was one of the antislavery images featured. These works constitute the multiple and heterogeneous sites of what Huey Copeland and Krista Thompson call "afrotropes," which are recurring images in black diasporic culture that give "a fresh consideration of what is repressed or absented within the visual archive" (2017, 7).[8] While the slave ship in Zéphirin's painting does not assume the iconic form of the *Brooks* diagram that would permit Copeland and Thompson to identify it as an afrotrope, I include his *Slave Ship Brooks* in the African diaspora culture they describe because it resituates and reframes the visual archive. Like other black Atlantic art, Zéphirin's restores the humanity of the Africans portrayed as cargo in the antislavery diagram.[9] Although the slaves are squeezed together within the ship's hold, they are not in a prone position in his painting. Their faces, peering from the air holes along the side and through the hold's trap doors, force the spectator to confront them eye to eye. Their human status is all the more apparent when viewed alongside the animal forms of the ship's crew. The absent crew in the abolitionist drawing is visualized in *The Slave Ship Brooks* as anthropomorphized animal creatures bearing instruments of oppression: a land deed, telescope, sword, musket, whip, and bayonet. "An imperial alligator captain held a deed to the land on which the enslaved would be working" explains Rediker, while the first mate, depicted as a skeleton, is "Death incarnate" (2018). As in Turner's *Slave Ship,* dark and stormy clouds appear on the horizon; however, unlike the Romantic painting that makes the drowning secondary to the emotional turmoil of the sea storm, the slaves who are half-submerged in the water are the focal point of Zéphirin's *Slave Ship Brooks.*

Instead of the male slaves being shackled in a prone position on platforms inside the ship, they are chained to its exterior and also to one another, their body size disproportionally large in relation to the ship. Each one bears a nameplate on his neck iron denoting the different nations of the *lwa* pantheon—Yoruba, Dahomey, Ghédé, Savi, Sakpata, Agasou, Nago, Ibo, Congo, Rada, Alada, Guinée, Petro—to suggest the strong connections between the spirit world and a Haitian spirit of rebelliousness. Their faces and bodily extremities are covered with white dots or *pwen* as the sign of their power and energy. Some of the slaves, both within the hold and on the ship's exterior, have red eyes (*gé-rouge*), signifying their fierce and fiery tempers, as ravenous sharks baring sharp white teeth swim toward them. This particular scene does not appear in written records, which depict rebellious slaves as being "variously flogged, pricked, cut, razored, stretched, broken, unlimbed, and beheaded, all according to the overheated imagination of the slave-ship captain" (Rediker 2007, 217). Having the rebels chained to each other on the ship's exterior, even if the approaching sharks suggests that they are about to be devoured, restores to them the courage and communal resistance that the sadistic forms of punishment by dismemberment were intended to repudiate. The image alludes to Haitian oral histories about the punishment of rebellious slaves, which Zéphirin shared with Rediker and has incorporated into the painting (Rediker 2018). Since the rebels are all men, the painting reproduces the male-gendering of

heroic narratives of slave resistance and, in this sense, adheres to a nationalist vision of a revolutionary past. Two of the men have broken
free of their wrist chains and are holding up one arm in a gesture of
liberation. They are Dutty Boukman and Toussaint Louverture, well-
known leaders of the Haitian Revolution, and their eyes are fixed on
some distant point in space and time beyond the frame of the painting.
By anachronistically including these leaders among the Africans aboard
the *Brooks,* Zéphirin introduces an alternate future than the one of immobility in the abolitionist drawing. The painting also brings the British
and American story of the antislavery movement into the geographical
space of the French colony of Saint-Domingue and the Haitian Revolution as an earth-shattering event that Michel-Rolph Trouillot characterizes as "unthinkable" outside of Haiti for more than a century after it
took place (1995, 95).[10]

The Saint-Domingue rebellion, which was initiated at the Bois
Caïman in 1791, was occurring at the same time that the *Brooks* diagram was being disseminated in pamphlets, newspapers, and posters in
Britain and the United States. Planters and proslavery advocates seized
the opportunity to blame abolitionists for the violence that was unfolding in the wealthiest of the West Indian sugar colonies. Clarkson
responded with a short pamphlet, *The True State of the Case Respecting the Insurrection at St. Domingo* (1792), which offers the numerous
revolts before the formation of the antislavery association as evidence
of freedom as an inalienable right rather than proof of a causal relationship between abolitionism and slave rebellions (1792, 8). Although
they presented insurgency as proof of slaves' assertion of their rights,
abolitionists did not go so far as to condone it. The few exceptions
were individuals who were marginal to the antislavery movement. For
instance, Percival Stockdale's call for slaves to "rush with resistless fury
on their foes" was widely ridiculed in the press (Geggus 1982, 124–27).
There was also the more radical African abolitionist, Cugoano, who
considered it the moral duty of slaves to resist and even "lawful" to
enslave their masters if the only way "to deliver a man from slavery"
(1787, 73–74). As a way of addressing the changing antislavery landscape, abolitionists added the sketch of a slave insurrection aboard a
ship to the *Brooks* drawing in 1794 (Rediker 2007, 330–31). But they
were silent on the involvement of British troops in assisting the French
in their suppression of the Saint-Domingue rebellion prior to 1798,
when a French withdrawal from the island left the black Jacobin leader
Toussaint Louverture in complete control (Geggus 1982, 127–28).

Once the French were defeated and Haiti was declared a self-governing republic in 1804, British public opinion and the mainstream abolitionist position underwent a radical change. In December of that same year, the *London Gazette* reported that the British had assisted Louverture in the "happy revolution," words that denote a seismic shift in public opinion, not least of which due to the revolution being directed against France as Britain's longtime rival and enemy (Geggus 1982, 127–30).[11] Across the Atlantic, as news of black freedom leapfrogged from one island to the next, slave revolts occurred in greater frequency, as did attempts to escape. One Jamaican colonialist warned that he was "convinced the Ideas of Liberty have sunk so deep in the minds of *all* Negroes that whenever the greatest precautions are not taken they will rise" (qtd. in Geggus 2014, 186). During the years leading up to the 1834 Emancipation Act, black seamen, both enslaved and free, deserted their ships when docked at Haitian ports (Bolster 1998, 144–53). Hundreds of slaves from the neighboring Turks and Caicos Islands stole sloops from their owners to set sail southward for Haiti, which is an interisland story of slavery and freedom that remains largely untold (Turks and Caicos Museum 2016). The almost thirty-six thousand voyages catalogued in the Trans-Atlantic Slave Trade Database have generated still, animated, and interactive mappings as visualizations of the transportation of millions of African slaves to the Americas, the largest number of whom were brought to the Caribbean. While a valuable resource in its own right, the voyages database tells only the slave ship story.

SMALL STORIES OF THE FISHING SLOOP

The sea voyage of the small sailboat or fishing sloop tells a more local and less spectacular story than that of slavers like the *Brooks,* but that does not mean that it is any less important. This humble boat has made its way into Vodou iconography. Behind the large ship in Zéphirin's *The Slave Ship Brooks,* most of which lies outside the frame of the painting, is a small boat with *IMMAMHOU Lahdé* written on its side and its sail bearing the words "Agoué Taroyo nou mélé." Agoué Taroyo, or Agwe, is the *lwa* of fishermen and seafarers, to whom Haitians pray for protection before setting out to sea or leaving on long trips. Sometimes depicted as an admiral, Agwe rules over the sea and all of the plant and animal life that lives within it. Agwe's *vèvè* is a figurative drawing of a steamship or

Figure 2.2. Agwe's *vèvè*, Port-au-Prince, Haiti, 2016

sailboat with an anchor and flags and the word "Immamou" inscribed on its side (figure 2.2). The origin of "Imamou," which is the name of Agwe's boat, cannot be established with any certainty. The word is generally taken to reference Imam, which is Arabic for prayer leader, and there are historical indications that some Haitian slaves were Muslim. François Makandal was known to have come from a high-ranking African Muslim family, and, having attended a *madrasa,* he could read and write Arabic. Other Vodou leaders, like Dutty Boukman, whose name means "man of the book," and Cécile Fatiman, whose name could be a variant of Fatimah, were also believed to have been Muslim (Gomez 2005, 88–90; Benson 2006; Diouf 2013, 217–20).[12] Dunham describes the high-pitched tone of a Vodou liturgy she heard in Haiti as resembling the Muslim call to prayers she had heard in Dakar ([1969] 1994, 126). Despite its suggestion of an Arabic origin, linguist Pierre Anglade describes "Imamou" as etymologically belonging to the West African Fongbe language, as does the word "Vodou" (1998, 111). He identifies "Ague" as the name of a fishing village in southwest Benin, and the sea *lwa*'s title of respect, Awoyo, as meaning "the immensity of the sea that is sacred" in Fongbe (43). The dual etymologies would suggest that "Imamou" is a hybrid word and, as such, is the product of Caribbean creolization. It potentially belongs to the Vodou archive of the Middle Passage I am tracing, although, as with any living memory, the historical moment of emergence cannot be determined with any certainty, and there are likely multiple origins occurring at different moments in time.

In Zéphirin's painting, *Agwe's* boat is not depicted as the steamship that sometimes appears in his *vèvè* but as the smaller and not always seaworthy vessel called a *kannot,* used by fishermen, Haitians fleeing the political instability of their country, and before them, slaves escaping to freedom. In the *vèvè* on which Zéphirin bases his drawing, the boat is devoid of human forms but often surrounded with stars and other *pwen* as signs of the Agwe's power. Haitian seafarers sing the following prayer in times of danger for the *lwa* to steer their boats to safety.

Mèt Agwé kòté ou yé?	Maitre Agwé where are you?
U pa wè mwê nâ résif?	Don't you see I'm on the reef?
Agwé taroyo, kòté ou yé?	Master Agwé where are you?
U pa wè mwè su lâ mè	Don't you see, I'm on the reef?
M'gê z'avirô nâ mê mwê	Don't you see, I'm on the sea?
M'pa sa tunê déyé	I've a rudder in my hand
M'duvâ déja	I can't go back
M'pa sa tunê déyé	I'm already going forwards
Mèt Agwé-woyo kòté u yé nu	I can't turn back.
U pa wè mwê nâ résif.	Agwé-taroyo, where are you?
	Don't you see I'm on the reef?

(Métraux [ca. 1959] 1972, 103)

The cry of *nou mélé,* or "we are in trouble," that appears on the sail of Agwe's boat in Zéphirin's painting can be read as a version of this prayer. Since we already know the story of slave ships like the *Brooks,* the words predict the disastrous outcome of an Atlantic passage during which there was no turning back. Indeed, the ship's captain is carrying the deed to the land on which the slaves will be worked to death. And there are other signs of death in the painting. Late eighteenth- and early nineteenth-century European and American observers noted the resemblance of the shape of the *Brooks* in the abolitionist diagram to a coffin, which is highlighted in Zéphirin's rendition of the ship due to the color contrast in the wood texture of the hold containing the slaves.[13] The two crosses standing upright in the rear of Agwe's vessel suggest impending death if read according to Christian iconography of the crucifix. In Vodou, however, the Christian cross, introduced into the Congo by Portuguese traders, is also used to represent a Dahomean cosmology of the four cardinal points and crossroads as joining the worlds of the living and the dead (Desmangles 2006; Benson 2008, 154n2).

The presence of Dutty Boukman, Toussaint Louverture, and Agwe—all belonging to Haitian history and Vodou culture—introduces a greater ambivalence into the meaning of the *Brooks* as a death ship. The exclamation *"nou mélé,"* like the prayer "Don't you see I'm on the reef?,", is less a prediction of impending disaster than a plea for safe passage. Does the prayer contain a Middle Passage memory in its reference to a danger that lies ahead but that cannot be avoided? It is difficult to say. However, there are Haitian oral stories recounting Agwe's protection of slaves during the Middle Passage and other ones of slaves returning to Africa on the backs of fish, which is one of the *lwa*'s several sea life forms (Marcelin 1949, 104). A Vodou archive of the Middle Passage is not only detectable in stories of fish rescuing slaves but also in the mermaid *lwa* who is the consort of Agwe. The two sea *lwa* are popular subjects in Haitian folk art, the tradition of which is evident in Zéphirin's painting.

Lasirèn, whose Kreyòl name is from the French *la sirène* for mermaid, appears in *The Slave Ship Brooks* as she does in *drapos* and murals: displaying a colorfully textured fish tail and long, flowing hair, while carrying an *asson*, or sacred rattle.[14] Lasirèn resembles the West African deity of Mami Wata, who also appears as a woman with a fish tail, long, flowing hair, and carrying a mirror and comb (Houlberg 1996). Some consider Mami Wata to have Hindu origins, but LeGrace Benson also traces her to the Brittany mermaid Arhes, a figure she identifies as appearing in West African lore only after the arrival of European traders (2006, 168). McCarthy Brown reminds us that mermaid figureheads decorated the prows of slave ships, a piece of information suggesting that her form could potentially have been witnessed by transported Africans (1995, 46). Like Agwe, Lasirèn is a creolized *lwa* having complex origins and recognizable as the Brittany mermaid perhaps only in her half-woman, half-fish form. Whether introduced on the African continent or at sea, the mermaid is implicated in a history of colonial encounters and Atlantic slavery. Or, to use Dayan's characterization of the *lwa* in general, the sea *lwa* can be seen as "deposits of history and as remnants of feelings that cannot be put to rest" (Dayan 1995, xviii). In Zéphirin's painting, Lasirèn is announcing the arrival of the *Brooks* and its cargo of new slaves by blowing a horn and ringing a bell. She appears in front of slave ship if not exactly on its bow, where a mermaid figurehead would have been located. Although she is leading the slave ship, it does not mean that the *lwa* is simply a harbinger of death due to her shifting signification within Vodou.

Also known as Ezili of the Sea, Lasirèn belongs to the Ezili assemblage of *lwa* that includes Ezili Dantò, Ezili Freda, Ezili-je-wouj, and Marinèt

(McCarthy Brown 1991, 220–57; Dayan 1994, 58). Lasirèn can also transform into Labalenn the whale, at times black and at other times white, a female who changes into a male and back again into female.[15] Queer studies scholars observe that the absence of a male-female dualism in Vodou allows for its practitioners to express taboo sexualities particularly through the multiple forms of Ezili (Strongman 2008, 4–5; Tinsley 2018, 19–20). McCarthy Brown similarly explains that, as a heterosexual woman, the Brooklyn *manbo* Mama Lola, with whom she studied and interviewed, was elusive in her own description of the gender fluidity of the mermaid and the whale (222–23). Although in this particular painting Zéphirin does not depict Lasirèn in all of her multiple forms, he has other paintings of androgynous sea spirits. The fluidity of meaning in Vodou also explains how the home of the sea *lwa* is sometimes identified with Ginen as the place where all the *lwa* reside.

The home of Lasirèn, Labalenn, and Agwe is an island below the sea called Z'ile Minfort, which is often related to Ginen as *zilet anba dlo*, the island under water (McCarthy Brown 1976, 124; Deren 1953, 338). Inhabited by the spirits of the recently deceased, ancestors, and the *lwa*, Ginen as a land under the water shares the same name with Ginen signifying "Africa" as a land across the water (McCarthy Brown 2006, 9; Dayan 2000, 17; Ramsey 2011, 7).[16] I mention the dual meaning of Ginen, as the continent of Africa and its spiritual manifestation as an underwater island in order to move the invisibility of the slave's perspective in the written archives to a Vodou conception of "the invisible," which defies the logic of established scholarly patterns for thinking about archival forms as either seen or unseen, material or ephemeral, silent or spoken. In like manner, drowning does not only signify death and loss. Some of the stories McCarthy Brown heard about Lasirèn pulling her victims down into the depths of the sea concern tragic deaths by drowning or suicides. But other stories, often involving women unable to afford expensive initiation rites, tell of how they disappeared for three days, three months, or three years to return from *anba dlo* with the power of divination. The sea as the watery grave of slaves who jumped or were thrown overboard is not only a space of loss and trauma within Vodou. For women, drowning can even be a mode of acquiring a sacred knowledge to heal. "Thus the Vodou *lwa* Lasyrenn," explains McCarthy Brown, "may have roots that connect, like nerves to the deepest and most painful parts of the loss of homeland and the trauma of slavery. It is therefore fitting that she also reconnects people to Africa and its wisdom" (1991, 224).

Due to an absence of religious orthodoxy, regional differences, and requirements of secrecy when Vodou was outlawed, there is no single explanation for or agreement on the exact location of Ginen. It can be high up in the mountains of north Haiti in a town called La Ville-aux-Camps, on an island in the depths of the water, or under a riverbed (McCarthy Brown 1976, 122–23; Courlander 1973, 19; Métraux [ca. 1959] 1972, 91–92; Desmangles 1992, 69). In describing the *vèvè* as "doorways to Ginen," McCarthy Brown explains that the *lwa* are summoned from the "waters that surround Haiti" (1995, 14).[17] Ginen *anba dlo* paradoxically exists under the water but is not *underwater* because it is spoken of as "dry and airy, like the countryside of Haiti" (Courlander 1973, 69). Some Vodouisants call the place under the water's surface "the back of the mirror" due to water being a reflecting surface and describe the world of the spirits as a mirror reality to the world of the living (McCarthy Brown 1991, 223). Although a mirror reality, Ginen is not a parallel universe but one that intersects with the human world, as suggested in the geography of the crossroads, where the vertical and horizontal planes meet to provide an access point for *les invisibles* to enter the human world (Deren 1953, 35–36). McCarthy Brown notices that all the different locations of Ginen share one quality, which is that it is at a great distance involving a difficult journey to reach. Yet, the *oungan* or *manbo* who visits the *lwa* in Ginen can return with spiritual knowledge, or *konesans,* a psychic power and ability to heal (1976, 130–37).

Ginen does not appear on colonial maps of the island of Hispaniola or nautical charts used by slavers for navigating the journey from West Africa to the Americas. The reason, one might say, is because it is an imaginary place. And yet, European cartographers *did* map a place that was entirely imaginary. In the late sixteenth century, the English explorer Sir Walter Raleigh, following the bread-crumb trail of Amerindian myths, legends, and eyewitness accounts, drew on a map of South America's Guiana coast the exact location of the fabled city the Spaniards called El Dorado. He dreamed of the riches he would bestow on his queen and also imagined himself a savior of the Amerindian people. V. S. Naipaul observes that with each generation of explorers who returned with a handful of beautifully wrought gold figurines accompanied by even more carefully crafted stories of the wealth that was left behind, "the legend of El Dorado, narrative within narrative, witness within witness, had become like the finest fiction, indistinguishable from truth" (1973, 38). The presence of the city of gold on Raleigh's map was sufficient proof of its existence, and El Dorado was identified and located on subsequent European maps. It was not until Alexander von Humboldt's expedition at the end of the eighteenth century that El Dorado was declared to be a mirage. Since its presence on maps endowed the invisible city with a reality for the good part of two centuries, it is possible to say that Raleigh dreamed El Dorado into existence.

A dream reality transubstantiates into the empirical one once it appears on a physical map. The same cannot be said for Ginen as a place that is meaningful to the descendants of slaves. Writing in the late 1950s, the Swiss anthropologist Alfred Métraux called La Ville-aux-Camps, one of sites for Ginen in the mountains surrounding St-Louis-du-Nord, "an entirely mythical city" ([ca. 1959] 1972, 91–92). Some twenty years later, the American anthropologist McCarthy Brown would dispute Métraux's claim, saying that her Haitian informant reassured her that La Ville-aux-Camps is "quite real" (1976, 123). In a later work, she characterizes the place as "an actual town with a mythic function" which is a phrasing that reconciles Métraux's dismissal of its empirical existence with the physical geography of a Vodou sacred space (1991, 285). Whereas El Dorado was an illusion sustained by early explorers' insatiable greed for gold, Ginen is the reconstitution of a homeland nourished by slaves' sustained sense of loss. Like Agwe and Lasirèn, the sacred geography of Ginen was born of the Middle Passage because it speaks to how displaced Africans did not have to be stranded in a hostile land even if their enslavement was a one-way journey. As a place that can be located but that is also unlocatable, Ginen speaks to Katherine McKittrick's observation that black geographies are not about mappings in the traditional sense. "Black is in the break," she writes, "it is fantastic, it is an absented presence, it is a ghost, a mirror, it is water, air" (2017, 97). Duval-Carrié incorporates the watery and airy invisibility of Ginen into his painting *La vraie histoire des Ambaglos* and installation *The Indigo Room,* two artworks that are the subject of the next section.

DROWNING THE MATERIAL ARCHIVES

Although Duval-Carrié's relationship to Vodou is not from within the religion as it is for Zéphirin, he incorporates its sacred design, affect, and iconography into his artwork to make political statements, often with an ironic take on history.[18] Having fled the François Duvalier regime for Puerto Rico with his family at the age of nine, he returned to Haiti briefly as a teenager before leaving for a university education in Canada and France, eventually settling in the United States in 1993. Duval-Carrié recalls frequenting the Centre d'Art, where he saw the works of Haitian masters like Hyppolite, Georges Liautaud (1899–1991), Rigaud Benoit (1911–1986), and Préfète Duffaut (1923–2012), which he admired and emulated (2013,

17). Despite this influence, Jerry Philogene warns against understanding his art strictly through a "Vodou lens" or the so-called "naïve" style of self-taught artists, due to the formal training he shares with a prior generation of Haitian artists like Georges (Géo) Remponneau (1916–2012) and Pétion Savain (1906–1973), coupled with his diasporic perspective on Haitian culture and history (2008, 144–45).[19] Duval-Carrié was trained at the École nationale supérieure des Beaux-Arts and began to embrace a Vodou aesthetics more fully on his return to Paris in 1989 to exhibit his work for an art show, *La Révolution Française sous les tropiques* (The French Revolution in the tropics) at the Musée des Arts Africains et Océaniens.[20] During the late nineties, the period leading up to his installation, he created a series of artworks on the theme of migration, beginning with his installation for the Paris exhibition. Duval-Carrié describes how a trove of archival documents representing the influence of the French Revolution on Haiti was made available to him for executing his work. Instead, he was inspired by the Africans he encountered in Paris, which caused him to see resemblances between Haitian and African Vodou (Duval-Carrié 2016). Reminiscent of the galleries of saints and sacred icons in Catholic churches, his installation for the Paris exhibition, *Rétable des neuf esclaves (Altar to Nine Slaves),* is a memorial to the slaves who survived the Middle Passage and whose unpaid labor went into the accumulation of French wealth. Framed by a painting of nine Africans being led through jungles on one side and slaving in cane fields on the other, the central painting shows them cramped into a small boat. Their bodies may be restrained with shackles, but they carry their cultures on their faces and in their hands. Due to his creation of an altar honoring the "millions of nameless slaves" for the exhibit, Carl Hermann Middelanis identifies it as a defining moment in the artist's life because it represents the beginning of "a journey to his roots" (2005, 111). *Rétable des neuf esclaves* was followed by a series of installations on the theme of migration, beginning with the tetraptych *Milocan ou La migration des esprits (Migration of the Spirits)* (1996) and the triptych *Migrations* (1997), which depicts the migration of the *lwa* from West Africa to Haiti and from Haiti to the United States.

Duval-Carrié's large mixed-media painting *La vraie histoire des Ambaglos (The True History of the Underwater Spirits)* takes a slightly different approach to the theme of migration by depicting the spirits of the dead rising from the depths of the ocean floor. Since the work was undertaken at the height of the exodus following the September 1991 military coup against President Jean-Bertrand Aristide, it harnesses a Middle Passage iconography for the Haitian boat people, or *botpippel*, as they became known.

Tens of thousands of Haiti's poor, rural people crammed into small, unseaworthy vessels to make the perilous 728-mile sea journey to Florida. Thousands—the precise number remains unknown—were lost at sea when their boats capsized. Lizabeth Paravisini-Gebert and Martha Daisy Kelehan (2008) survey what they call *botpippel* art as a genre that developed during this period and resumed in the period following Aristide's second deposition in 2004, when the U.S. Coast Guard became more aggressive in its interception of Haitian boats. Consisting of paintings and murals, several of the artworks depict Haitians in shark-infested waters. In Zéphirin's *M'ap cherche la vie* (1998), for instance, two large rocky outcrops that the *botpippel* believe to be Miami destroy their small boat and, with it, their dreams of a new life. But there are also paintings and murals that depict Lasirèn escorting their boats through dangerous waters. Paravisini-Gebert and Kelehan characterize *botpippel* art as providing a "visual language" for an experience that Haitian writers, with a few exceptions, were unable to narrate (2008, 159).[21]

Duval-Carrié describes his rendition of the simultaneity of the two journeys—the original Atlantic crossing and the modern Windward Passage one of the *botpippel*—as "a resonance from the past and an accusation of the present" (2007, 566). Like the first-generation Haitian American multimedia artist Rejin Leys's *Boat People: Three Passages* (1993) and *The Ties That Bind* series (1994), his paintings and installations suggest that, although the sea the modern migrants cross is not as vast as the Atlantic Ocean, their voyages are filled with the danger and uncertainty of the ones slaves made centuries before.[22] Both sets of work also suggest a racial violence that is repeated in the U.S. government's designation of Haitians as economic refugees, in contrast to the mostly white Cuban boat people, who were designated as political asylum seekers, a distinction that allowed the Coast Guard to return Haitians to the political instability they were escaping. While both artists incorporate records and documents into their creations—Leys through mixed-media collages—my interest in Duval-Carrié's artworks lies in their contestation of a Judeo-Christian geography of the Atlantic Ocean and Caribbean Sea.

The eight water spirits, or *Ambaglos*, of the painting's title float upward, with outstretched arms, through an entanglement of vines, leaves, and flowers (figure 2.3). The scene is peaceful, and their faces, some with closed eyes, are serene. Only their upper torsos are visible emerging from the water. The two central female spirits with their beckoning gestures suggest Lasirèn, who brings luck and money to her worshippers but who can also lure those who cause offense to death by drowning. Using an innovative technique in which he applies resin between the layers of paint, Duval-Carrié creates a sense of depth to the seascape. He explains that the painting could be used on the floor or even at the bottom of a pool since "everything in the African cosmography happens in the water" (2007, 563). Due to his use of yellow and orange pigment for the water, aqua-green for plant leaves, and white for its lotus-like flowers, the sea is a place of mournful beauty that contrasts with Turner's melancholic blood-stained water. Duval-Carrié explains that he intended *La vraie histoire des Ambaglos* to be a meditation piece, adding that he was inspired by Rajasthani cloth paintings, or *pichwai*. He says that he travels far for inspiration because "the Caribbean has everything dropped into it, so one cannot claim that this place is autonomous or authentic" (2007, 565). *Pichwai* means "that which is hung at the back," because the cloth paintings are generally hung on the wall behind the shrine of Hindu temples and intended to capture particular moods of Lord Krishna. Whereas *pichwai* tend to be small, Duval-Carrié's painting is expansive, approximately eight by twelve feet and consisting of twelve smaller panels, which means that it is difficult to grasp its totality even though it works through a repetition of patterns. His integration of a Rajasthani sacred form into a painting memorializing slaves who drowned in the Caribbean Sea is a reminder that Vodou is a syncretic religion that incorporates, and continues to borrow, elements from different religions from around the world. Duval-Carrié mentioned an acquaintance who sought out ancient Peruvian ceremonial cups called *qirus* in *ounfòs*, and he wonders how they were acquired because "they were not brought over the other day" (2007, 565). There exists such a long history of *oungans* bartering and trading for objects and drawing from a wide array of sacred signs that Benson characterizes them as "cosmopolitans" (2006, 156).

Since Duval-Carrié is an artist and not an *oungan,* his painting pays homage to the creativity with which Haitian slaves and peasants reconstructed their religion out of loss and deprivation, while expressing his own vision of the Caribbean Sea. "To me it's the middle passage," he explains about the subject of *La vraie histoire des Ambaglos*. "In that particular piece, it's more like the Sargasso Sea, where things were thrown overboard during bad weather. The first ones to go were the slaves" (Duval-Carrié 2007, 564). His description alludes to both the fearful image of the Sargasso Sea for sailors and brutal slave-trading history for which the *Zong* has come to serve as a proper name. The Sargasso Sea, a place dead center in the Atlantic Ocean without any land boundaries like other seas, was believed to trap ships within its tangled mass of sargassum weeds. Yet, as Rachel L. Carson explains in *The Sea around Us,* "the dense fields of

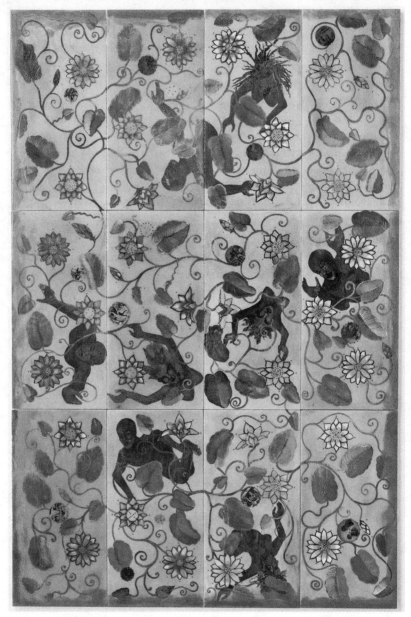

Figure 2.3. Edouard Duval Carrié, *La vraie historie des Ambaglos*

weeds waiting to entrap a vessel never existed except in the imaginations of sailors, and the gloomy hulks of vessels doomed to endless drifting in the clinging weed are only the ghosts of things that never were" (1989, 27). In Duval-Carrié's rendition of the Sargasso Sea there are no imaginary ghost ships or sunken galleys with their hidden treasures and coral bones. *La vraie histoire des Ambaglos* presents the sea through an imaginary in which the spirits of ancestors and slaves rise up from the depths of the water to its surface. In this way, the sea as a space of death is transformed into a medium through which spirits return to commune with the living. Eighteenth- and nineteenth-century Middle Passage records and eyewitness accounts do not show the world of *anba dlo* because it existed outside of their Judeo-Christian frame of reference. The closest approximation is Clarkson's description of slaves who believed that in death, "they shall immediately be wafted back to their native plains, there to exist again, to enjoy the sight of their beloved countrymen, and to spend the whole of their new existence in scenes of tranquility and delight" (1788, 155). But even this description does not capture the metonymic relationship of Ginen as a spiritual Africa to the physical Africa to which there was no return, or the significance of water in the passage from life to death in African cosmologies.[23]

Duval-Carrié's execution of Ginen in his painting reverses the flow of knowledge by presenting abolitionist ideas about slavery as fragments of information, which is how African beliefs appear in antislavery manifestos like Clarkson's. Scattered across the painting are small circles containing eighteenth- and nineteenth-century European drawings of masters and slaves. Each circle is outlined with indigo-blue resin dots that aesthetically resemble the sequin power points or *pwen* of *drapos* and suggest the historical power of these images.[24] The semi-translucent circles contain pictures gathered from the pages of abolitionist pamphlets and colonial history books, among them Thomas Branagan's *The Penitential Tyrant; or, Slave Trader Reformed* (1807), Marcus Rainsford's *An Historical Account of the Black Empire of Hayti* (1805), and Isaac Cruikshank's satirical print *The Abolition of the Slave Trade, Or the Inhumanity of Dealers in Human Flesh Exemplified in Captn. Kimber's Treatment of a Young Negro Girl of 15 for Her Virjen Modesty* (1792), the latter being one of the murdered slave girls whose life Hartman attempts to imagine (2008, 7–9). The pictures Duval-Carrié incorporates into his painting belong to the most common images in abolitionist literature: women and men being viciously whipped, runaways with iron masks to immobilize them, women and children attacked by the bloodhounds used for tracking rebels and runaway slaves. While intended to show the brutal and dehumanizing treatment of slaves, the historical illustrations enact a violence of their own through their fetishistic focus on the slave's abject and violated body, particularly in scenes showing slave women being tortured and killed. Belonging to what Hartman calls the "scandal and excess" of the archive (5), the pictures represent an indulgence that is even more excessive than textual descriptions due to the immediacy and shock value of visual records.

The recognizable scenes of slavery are from the artist's personal collection of history books, whose pictures he incorporates into his work. Edward J. Sullivan characterizes Duval-Carrié as an "*artiste philosophe*" who is captivated with the past and describes how this obsession manifests itself in the artist as collector: "He combs secondhand shops, rare-book stores, and flea markets for things that relate to the past of Saint Domingue, the Haitian revolution, the individuals involved in the 'heroic' phase of Haiti's separation from France, especially Toussaint Louverture" (2008, 170). In *La vraie histoire des Ambaglos,* European images of the cruelty enacted against slaves join the spirits in an entanglement of vines. In this way, the two contrasting imaginaries—Haitian and European—are shown to be intertwined with each other. But the painting also diminishes the power of the more familiar scenes of slavery by rendering them almost unrecognizable. The historical pictures, and the late eighteenth- and early nineteenth-century European consciousness to which they belong, are dwarfed by the much larger, floating bodies of the underwater spirits (figure 2.4). The tearing of these pages from antislavery pamphlets and history books and surrounding them with a Vodou cosmology makes the grand narratives of slavery and antislavery appear smaller than they are in the material archives or at least positions them as only small pieces of what belongs to the known world. Like Philip, Duval-Carrié fragments material records, but he does so to create the effect of drowning them in a Haitian sacred worldview.

PLUMBING THE DEPTHS OF MEMORY WATER

Some of the same antislavery images of *La vraie histoire des Ambaglos* are reproduced in an even larger project that claims a small corner of American public space for Haitian culture and history. *The Indigo Room or Is Memory Water Soluble?*, a room-size mixed-media installation Duval-Carrié undertook while an artist-in-residence at Fort Lauderdale's Museum of Art, is located in the elevator lobby for galleries on the upper floor. The darkened room, with its deep indigo-blue walls, is bathed in a blue-green light emanating from illuminated blocks and the ceiling to create the illusion of

Figure 2.4: Detail from *La vraie histoire des Ambaglos*

being underwater.[25] Every museum visitor has to pass through the room, and while some do just that with scarcely a glance, others linger in wonderment. For a brief moment in time, visitors are transported to an underwater world with its own sensual appeal and beauty. Duval-Carrié speaks of his artistic vision as borrowing the approach of Haitian people who, out of necessity, create "from dribs and drabs of things" (1995, 75), and this characterization most certainly applies to his Fort Lauderdale installation. *The Indigo Room* consists of a translucent grid of ninety plexiglass and cast acrylic blocks filled with pictures, found objects, and memorabilia, a translucent ceiling, and a glowing Vodou statue surrounded by disembodied hands nestled in an alcove. Several of the acrylic blocks contain reproductions of Duval-Carrié's own paintings, including one of Lasirèn. In *Sirene rouge* (2004), the mermaid *lwa* appears in a magically luminous underwater scene framed by shells embedded in resin. Her presence in the room, along with all the flora and fauna of the sea such as lobsters, manta rays, crawfish, crabs, water snakes, starfish, sharks, sea horses, seaweeds, and shells, suggest the riches of the sea *lwa's* underwater kingdom. Agwe's colors are blue, white, and green, while his emblems are miniature boats, including steamboats, oars, eels, small metal fish, and shells. Lasirèn's colors are pink, light blue, and blue-green, and her symbols are shells, combs, and mirrors. The myriad of symbols for the sea *lwa*, particularly Agwe's anchor, are featured in the acrylic blocks.

The Indigo Room, which fills an oceanic space of loss with the richness of a Vodou cosmology, channels the feelings associated with a ritual honoring Agwe. Known as the *barque* or boat ceremony, the ritual involves placing offerings that include liquor, champagne, sweet cakes, soft fruits, and sacrificial animals on a decorated wooden raft that is floated across the water toward Agwe's island under the sea. Maya Deren, the dancer and experimental filmmaker whom Dunham hired as her personal assistant, describes the surge of worshippers' emotions at the exact instant the boat sinks into the sea, which is the sign of Agwe having accepted their offering. The joyous singing is so infectious that it brings tears to her eyes. "It was at this moment," she declares, alluding to stories she heard about water *lwa* weeping out of compassion for humans, "that I understood why the gods, who loved these men, would weep" (1953, 130). The *lwa* share an affective space with the living, and in that shared space, people experience the power of community and belonging. "If all of these religions can be said to coincide perfectly in one area," remark Margarite Fernández-Olmos and Lizabeth Paravisini-Gebert about Afro-Creole religions of the Caribbean, "it is in their promotion of a ritualized union of the people with the spirit world, in the reciprocity of the link between the spirits and the community" (2000, 3). The place of spirits in the affected and affecting relationship of community building prompts a revision of "the social" in affect theory. This revised idea of "the social," one that is mediated through the spirit world, belongs to the memory form Hartman identifies as redress, a counterpart to the body in pain. She explains how black memory does not take the form of recalling Africa in its wholeness but as loss through which the "dis-membered body of the slave" is countered by a "re-membering [that] takes the form of attending to the body as a site of pleasure, eros, and sociality and articulating its violated condition" (1997, 77). Hartman qualifies such forms of redress under slavery as being incomplete in view of the enormity of the violation of the black body and extreme conditions of domination. A critical attention to the black body as a site of pleasure, eros, and sociality, particularly as it exists today, is nonetheless crucial in overturning a dominant imaginary in which Haiti exists as the poorest (and by implication the most miserable) nation in the Western Hemisphere and "voodoo" is perceived as evil black magic.

Duval-Carrié's installation disputes the one-dimensional picture of Haiti as a place of mass poverty and human misery, on the one hand, and black magic and soulless zombies, on the other. Visitors to the Florida museum space of *The Indigo Room* would most certainly not have the same affective experience as Haitians who participate in a sacred ritual like the *barque* ceremony, especially since his installation includes reminders of Haiti's violent history. A reviewer for the *Broward/Palm Beach New Times* was disturbed by the contradiction between drawings of slaves and despots and the calming sensation of being enveloped by the soft glow of the panels in the darkened room (Mills 2004). Art critic Joel Weinstein explains his own experience as a mixed sensation of floating and drowning: "Standing in The Indigo Room's subaqueous glow, some of us might feel the ordinary titillation of the underwater swimmer—a sense of weightlessness, an enveloping coolness, the hint of impending asphyxiation" (2007, 58). But the contradictory feelings of danger and delight are not so strange or unusual to the underwater realm of the sea *lwa*. Lasirèn can pull people underwater to their death, or she can shower them with wealth, be it riches or the power of divination. Duval-Carrié introduces the sensibilities of this submarine world into the most public of a museum's space, its lobby, to show the rich and multidimensional quality of Haitian history and culture.

With the reflecting ceiling as the water's surface, the installation embraces a Vodou geography of the crossroads, involving fluidity and movement across the human and spirit worlds. As spectators, we are immersed within the depths of the water looking up, which reverses the perspective of European maps that gaze down on the Caribbean from above. But Duval-Carrié is doing more than simply reversing perspectives; he is also making us aware of how a view of the planet and its geography from the perspective of the global North is replete with its own cultural and religious history. As he further explains about his propensity to represent underwater worlds, "In African culture everything moves under water contrary to the Western culture in which (everything) goes in the cosmos" (qtd. in Cosentino 2004, 40). His words indicate how a Judeo-Christianity cosmography influences our sense of space and place even in a secular and scientifically verifiable world, since maps are drawn from the omniscient perspective of the heavenly skies or today's modern satellites. European maps became universalized by "suppressing non-European conceptualization of space and spreading European 'cartographic literacy'" (Mignolo 1992, 59). In filling the museum lobby with the worlds of the sea *lwa* and Ginen *anba dlo*, Duval-Carrié's installation is a reminder that as Western art became secularized, the museum itself became a sacred space. "In the increasingly de-sacralized space of the nineteenth century," writes art theorist Rosalind Krauss, "art had become the refuge for religious emotion; it became, as it has remained, a secular form of belief" (1979, 54).

Duval-Carrié's incorporation of Christian religious art forms such as triptychs and altars into his work alludes to the sacred origins of Western art. A reproduction of the central painting of his *Rétable des neuf esclaves* appears in a top panel of *The Indigo Room* as an extension of its theme of migration—except that its Middle Passage scene of transported Africans wearing the symbols of their cultures is now underwater alongside archival images of slavery. Like Zépherin, who incorporates Haitian oral stories of rebels chained to the exterior of slave ships into his painting, Duval-Carrié brings visual representation to the repertoire of Haitian history. But he also considers art museums to be the cathedrals of a modern secular world, and by honoring the Vodou *lwa* he hopes to "re-sacramentalize" the museum or gallery space (cited in Sullivan 2007, 22). Yet, the fact that an installation depicting the sacred world of *an bas dlo* is adjacent to the elevators and even restrooms reflects how often, out of necessity, the sacred and profane mingle in Vodou. As McCarthy Brown explains, "Vodou, largely a religion of people without money or social power . . . has adapted whatever relevant sacred sites, images, and objects were ready-to-hand" (1995, 22).[26] *The Indigo Room* is not a self-contained room where the viewer can sit quietly and meditate; rooms of this kind do exist on the museum's upper gallery floor. Rather, it inhabits a busy space with doors opening and closing and people coming and going. The installation is at home with the irreverent, particularly through reproductions of the artist's own work, since copies undermine the idea of originality on which the sacred status of Western art historically relied. As Glissant notes about the difficulty of distinguishing the work of the Haitian masters from their apprentices and imitation of their styles in tourist art, "Haitian painting challenges the magical notion of 'authenticity' in art" (1992, 157).

The centerpiece of *The Indigo Room* contains miniaturized reproductions of Duval-Carrié's *Migrations* series (1997), the original paintings of which belong to the permanent collection of the Bass Museum of Art in

Miami (figure 2.5). The three backlit reproductions—*Embarquement pour la Floride (Embarcation for Florida), La calebasse magique (The Magic Calabash)*, and *Débarquement à Miami Beach (The Landing)*—show the migration of the *lwa* from Haiti to the United States. In the brightly colored triptych scenes that stand out from the blue hue of the room, the vibrant figures are both the *lwa* and the Haitian people, as is evident in their all-too-human demeanor. The migration paintings offer powerful social commentary on Haitian history through their doubling of space and time: the originary Middle Passage crossing and the more contemporary sea journeys of Haitian people. By endowing the *lwa* with human attributes, Duval-Carrié simultaneously tells the *botpippel*'s story. The first painting shows the *lwa* leaving Haiti in a small boat under the cover of night; in the second, they are holding up a magical calabash to ward off an approaching U.S. Coast Guard cutter; and in the third, they are standing on a causeway attired in their fineries, with the Miami skyline visible across the water. As Duval-Carrié observes about their indeterminate location between sea and land, the migrants have nonetheless arrived: "They're there on your causeway. And you pass by and you see them" (2007, 567).

Unlike *La vraie histoire des Ambaglos, The Indigo Room* makes an explicit statement about the Haitian *dyaspora* through its suggestion of the Caribbean Sea as water that both joins and separates the islands from the mainland. Each picture of the three central images offers a small segment of a migration story, but their combined effect is to raise questions about diasporic identities in relationship to Haitian ones instead of providing easy answers. Similar questions are provoked through the form of the *lwa* of motherhood presiding over the underwater scene. Resembling a stained-glass window with its grid of translucent panels, the ceiling displays an enormous Ezili Dantò looking down on the underwater scene (figure 2.6).[27] Blue is her symbolic color, and she appears in the installation as a majestic indigo-blue woman with her blue halo resembling an Afro due to the absence of color contrast. Her headdress, eyes, and earlobes contain tiny dark-skinned babies, echoing the black Kewpie dolls often placed on Vodou altars, while her hands are extended, palms facing outward on either side of her face. Her presence in the room suggests the birth of a new diaspora. In this way, *The Indigo Room* literalizes a Haitian usage of the phrase *lòt bò dlo,* the other side of the water, both for deceased relatives under the water and those living across the water in the United States.[28] However, with the exception of her symbolic color, Duval-Carrié's Ezili bears little resemblance to the chromolithograph of the Black Madonna of Częstochowa that is used to represent the *lwa* of motherhood. The Cath-

Figure 2.5: Edouard Duval-Carrié, *The Indigo Room or Is Memory Water Soluble?* (2004)

olic holy picture was introduced into Haiti by Polish soldiers who were sent to subdue the Saint-Domingue rebellion but some of whom deserted to join the rebels (Dayan 1995, 295–96n120; Dubois 2004, 294–95). The Black Madonna has a double-line scar on her right cheek as the sign of her strength, and she shares with Lasirèn long, shiny hair (McCarthy Brown 1991, 229). The Ezili of *The Indigo Room* bears scars on her hands, forehead, and chin but not on her cheek. They take the shape of arrow and star symbols, which, while alluding to *pwen* and *vèvès,* appear as indecipherable hieroglyphs belonging to another place and time. Their message is that Haitians living in the diaspora may not know how to read the signs of their own culture. It is not just the illegibility of the hieroglyphs but the entire installation that raises questions about knowledge of Haitian history and culture within the United States, beyond even what Haitian Americans can or cannot recall. This is why the second half of the room's title—*Is Memory Water Soluble?*—appears as a question more than a definitive statement.

The Indigo Room reveals both the Haitian influence on American art and culture and an invisibility within the United States of the two nations' intertwined histories at least since the migration of Haitians during the early nineteenth century and the U.S. occupation of Haiti in the early twentieth century. Each of the ninety blocks presents a miniature portrait assembled from pictures, memorabilia, and found objects. Through its allusion to water as an element that is flooded with memory, the installation unlocks the sea's "gray vault" of Walcott's poem. Here, the sea is overflowing with history and culture, and we, the museum visitors, are swimming within it. Since the installation opened the same year as the bicentennial of Haitian Independence, its history centers on the world the French colonialists made for themselves and which their slaves burned to the ground. The blocks contain abolitionist images, including the ones showing the cruelty of iron masks, whippings, and brandings, but also pictures of slaves being freed and supplicant slaves giving thanks. There are ethnographic drawings of Saint-Domingue's stratified society from colonial history books like Médéric Moreau de Saint-Méry's *Recueil de vues des lieux principaux de la Colonie Françoise de Saint-Domingue* (1791) and Bryan Edwards's *The History, Civil and Commercial, of the British Colonies in the West Indies* (1793): half-naked slaves in idyllic settings, turbaned mixed-race *affranchis* or free women of color, and the opulence of white Creole life.

If Zépherin's painting celebrates the revolutionary heroism of Haiti's past, Duval-Carrié's artistic execution of that same history exhibits a greater ambivalence. The blocks contain pictures of the most famous revolutionary leaders, Toussaint Louverture (figure 2.7), in particular, but oth-

Figure 2.6: Ceiling of *The Indigo Room* showing Ezili Dantò, the Vodou *lwa* of motherhood

ers like Alexandre Pétion and Jean-Pierre Boyer, as well as Jean-Jacques Dessalines, Henri Christophe, and Faustin Soulouque (figure 2.8), who betrayed the revolution's ideals by declaring themselves emperors and kings. The installation's subtitle is posed as a question: What do Americans know about Haitian history and culture? Duval-Carrié asked that same question of the Dillard High School students with whom he collaborated in creating *The Indigo Room*. Dillard, with its prestigious Center for the Arts, has the distinction of being the first public school in Fort Lauderdale for people of African descent and is in an area with a particularly high concentration of Haitian and Jamaican immigrants. Duval-Carrié charged students with the task of collecting information, photographs, and personal objects from the local immigrant community (Duval-Carrié 2004, 37). The team integrated into the installation more personal memories through family photographs of wedding couples and children, as well as icons from American popular culture such as small statues of the characters from Disney's *Snow White and the Seven Dwarfs* and Florida's famous pink flamingos. The coming together of the familial with the popular points to an identity that is both Haitian and American. The family photographs are arranged collage-style as cutouts in each acrylic box as an affirmation of *anba dlo* being inhabited not only by the *lwa* and spirits of revolutionary heroes (figure 2.9) but also loved ones who are recently deceased (figure 2.10). By placing these memory objects underwater, the installation foregrounds the centrality of water to a Vodou conception of ancestral and familial ties.

The remaining blocks of *The Indigo Room* are an eclectic mix of art reproductions and *objets trouvés*. The installation includes a reproduction of Los Angeles–based artist Alison Saar's *drapo*-influenced *Mamba Mambo* (1985) to show the wider diffusion of Haitian aesthetics. Conversely, a copy of Haitian artist Célestin Faustin's *Ezili Dantò* (1977), depicting the appearance of the *lwa* to tell his *manbo* grandmother that he would serve Ezili Dantò, shows the influence of surrealism on Haitian art. Philogene describes the function of these cross-cultural references as "culling together ethnically diverse black diasporic communities while traversing generation lines through the assistance of first-generation Haitians whose knowledge of and connection to Haiti is *not* limited to Vodou" (2008, 148). Several of the blocks contain a single anchor, which is associated with Agwe's boat. However, the framing of an anchor with two sabers in one of the blocks makes it more likely to be interpreted as a reference to Caribbean pirates, which shows the difficulty of deriving a story or meaning from a collaborative assemblage of pictures, symbols, and signs. In addition to anchors, *vèvès*, and crosses, there are more common shapes from popular culture,

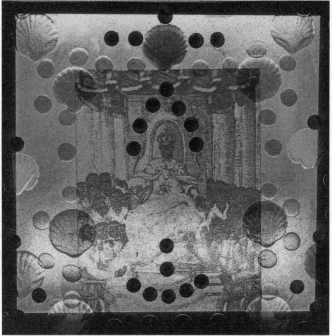

Figures 2.7 and 2.8. Detail from *The Indigo Room* showing
Toussaint Louverture (*top*) and Faustin Soulouque (*bottom*)

such as plastic hearts, stars, lips, strawberries, and watermelons. The under-water scenes also depict land flora and fauna—palm trees, flowers, ferns, animals, reptiles, and insects—and combine land with sea life so that we are uncertain as to whether the birds are swimming or the stingrays are in flight. The arrangements of objects in each block are more artful than meaningful—fan shells descending onto a hand fan, an airplane flying alongside dragonflies, spiders crawling across a whipping scene. Some of the blocks are so cluttered that it is difficult to identify their contents. We are reminded that a collaborative project is not entirely within the artist's control, as Duval-Carrié expressed surprise when I mentioned the Disney characters to him.

Unlike the three center paintings, which can be read as a story of Haitian migration, the surrounding blocks with their thick black borders invoke a modernist grid that Krauss describes as working against literature, dis-course, and narrative. "Whereas grids are not only spatial to start with," she explains, "they are visual structures that explicitly reject a narrative or sequential reading of any kind" (1979, 55). Like the word fragments of the poems in Philip's *Zong!*, there is no hierarchical or linear relation-ship across the individual blocks of Duval-Carrié's installation. Moreover, their straight geometric lines emphatically resist giving the impression of the fluidity of water as a natural element. Each block is compartmentalized as a self-contained box surrounded by thick black lines of equal length forming a square. The squares are then lined up around the three central pictures as a grid. But the blocks are also three-dimensional, which means the installation lacks the flatness of the minimalist form belonging to the modernist grid. By filling each block with a multiplicity of pictures and ob-jects, Duval-Carrié introduces into the clean lines of European modernism the visual overload of Vodou altars, which display *drapos*, sacred statues, rosaries, crucifixes, and Catholic chromolithographs alongside decorated empty perfume and liquor bottles, fine china, and dressed-up black dolls, in addition to an array of food and beverages for the *lwa*. "The accumulated waste," explains Dayan, "is not revised out of the sacred. . . .What appears as randomness is actually a tough commitment to the facts of *this* world" (2000, 18). An aesthetics of accumulation prompts a perception of hap-hazardness, but a closer look at an assemblage of the detritus of modern culture reveals it to be a commentary on modern life itself.

The visual overload of Vodou altars would appear to be incompatible with the minimalist style of the modernist grid, but only if we see the two aesthetic traditions as unrelated. Early twentieth-century modernists broke the hegemony of European realism through their appropriation of Afri-

Figures 2.9 and 2.10. Detail from *The Indigo Room* showing *anba dlo* as the dwelling place of not only the *lwa* and revolutionary heroes (*top*) but also family members and loved ones (*bottom*). The *vèvè* in the top block is for Papa Legba, guardian of the crossroads.

can and Oceanic art forms, but they did so through an abstraction and selectiveness that made African and Oceanic sacred objects conform to "a familiar European grammar of form and symmetry" (Gikandi 2006, 53). European modernists, particularly the cubists, who preferred African over Oceanic art, appropriated the shape and lines of African masks and sculptures by filtering out incongruous details and avoiding less tidy sculptures like nail-fetish power figures. By introducing the busy aesthetics of Vodou altars into modernism's clean lines, Duval-Carrié takes back from the modernists what they appropriated from African sacred arts.

TO REMOVE THE DEAD FROM WATER

Zéphirin's and Duval-Carrié's artworks exist as metacommentaries on European archives by shifting definitions of "the human" away from their Christian frame of reference toward Vodou and a Haitian revolutionary past. Whereas Zéphirin's *The Slave Ship Brooks* and Duval-Carrié's *La vraie histoire des Ambaglos* bring these archives into a Haitian worldview, *The Indigo Room* makes visible the Haitian culture and history existing within the United States. In this way, they shift the center of Atlantic modernity. Yet there was a time in the not too distant past when moving the center of European history to the Caribbean would be treated as "blasphemous," to use George Lamming's term in *The Pleasures of Exile* for how his suggestion that knowledge from the colonies could inform the metropolis might be received. He counters a universalization of Western history with a declaration of "the universal significance" of a religious ritual he witnessed in "one corner of the Caribbean cradle" ([1960] 1992, 9). The ritual he calls a ceremony of Souls involves a retrieval of spirits from water so they could converse "through the medium of the Priest" with close friends and family members about unresolved issues from the past (10). We now know that the ceremony Lamming witnessed in the suburbs of Port-au-Prince is called *wete mò nan dlo,* which means "to remove the dead from water." A year and a day after a loved one's death, but often much longer if a family cannot afford the expensive ritual, an *oungan* is called to summon the spirits of loved ones from Ginen. As Karen E. Richman explains, the ceremony is an occasion for "the ancestor to settle personal accounts as his or her spirit individually addresses each relative and close friend he or she left behind" (2007, 380). Lamming concludes that the futures of both the living, who can now proceed with their lives after settling unfinished business, and the dead, whose spirit is placed in a *govi* or clay pot and placed on the family altar, need this ritual of communication.

In a rhetorical move reversing Britain's universalization of its approach to settling accounts with the past, Lamming characterizes the affinity the English have for their radios as the sign of their "tribal habit" to listen to voices from beyond the grave. He proceeds to explain how engineers for the British Broadcasting Corporation summon these voices "to inhabit the little magic box of sound . . . bribing the sea to release its Dead for an interview with the living" ([1960] 1992, 14). By using the same language to describe sacred and secular practices separated by the vast expanse of the Atlantic Ocean, Lamming brings Haitian peasants who serve the *lwa* into a shared temporality they have historically been denied. His presentation of a BBC broadcast through the lens of a Vodou ritual can be understood as trivializing an English relationship to the past or ennobling a Haitian one. Lamming himself presents the opposition slightly differently by asserting the relationship between the lived reality of Caribbean people and a perspective designated as erroneous. Writing from London in the late fifties, he declares that, while the parallels he establishes might be condemned for their inaccuracies, his "mistake, lived and deeply felt by millions . . . proves the positive value of error" ([1960] 1992, 13). It is a value, he contends, that Europe, now on the verge of losing its colonies, must learn. Lamming's assertion of the necessity for Europe to learn from a perspective that it regards to be wrong is prescient of the intellectual project Dipesh Chakrabarty (2000) calls "provincializing Europe" and Sylvia Wynter (2013 calls "localizing" secular humanism. The next chapter turns to a work of fiction that, like Duval-Carrié's *The Indigo Room,* introduces Caribbean culture into the heart of American modernity. Erna Brodber's novel *Louisiana* defamiliarizes American culture while reconfiguring its historicist time to account for a sacred African diaspora temporality that anthropology relegated to the past. Since the novel's timeframe is the early twentieth century, it retroactively provincializes Europe through a black female anthropologist who, despite her university training, finds herself conversing with the dead.

CHAPTER 3

Word Holes

Spirit Voices in the Recording Machine

After we had learnt that the reel was full, not of silences but
of words, not of . . . Mammy reeling out her life story as
a parting gift to a well-favoured me, but of conversations
between two women, one of them Mammy, with interjections
from me in words I didn't know, we immediately forwarded
the spool and listened . . . right through to the end. We fell
right off the end of that reel right through those word holes.

—Erna Brodber, *Louisiana* (1994)

Erna Brodber's third novel, *Louisiana,* tells the story of a Jamaican
American anthropologist named Ella Townsend, who is charged with
collecting oral histories for the Federal Writers' Project on "the history
of the Negro of South West Louisiana" ([1994] 1997, 32). She travels
from New York to rural Louisiana in 1936 to interview Sue Ann Grant-
King, or Mammy King, known for her storytelling abilities. Equipped
with an early prototype of the recording machine, she is unprepared
for an informant who refuses to speak. But all of that changes after Sue
Ann dies two weeks into the oral history project. Her spirit enters the
anthropologist's body, causing her to hear snippets of stories and conversations that she had been unable to obtain from the elderly woman
when she was alive. Brodber does not use the term "spirit possession"
for the supernatural occurrence but the more colloquial expression of
a person serving as a horse for a spirit to mount or ride. The spirit of
Sue Ann's deceased friend Louise Ann points to Ella and says: "This is
the horse. Will you ride?" (17). Sue Ann responds with the short phrase,
"Let's see if she will." Accepting the dying woman's soul, Ella becomes
"a vessel, a horse" (46).[1] Dayan considers the usage of the term "possession" a barrier to understanding the idea of a spirit entering a hu-

man body due to the word forcing the experience of being ridden into a Western frame of reference. She explains that the Haitian Vodou concept of *monte chwal,* which is Kreyòl for "the *lwa* mounts the horse," does not suggest a spiritual being taking control of a person's body. Rather, it constitutes a "two-way process, postures or masks of servitude [that] act as the medium for renaming and redefinition" (Dayan 1995, 68). The bidirectionality of the process transforms a state of subjugation, particularly the kind that existed during slavery, into the far more contradictory state of a submission that allows a person to feel the power of a spirit inside her. In Brodber's novel, the three women—Ella, Suzie Anna, and Louise Anna (which are their familial names for each other)—are bound in a relationship described as a "marriage," after which Ella becomes a psychic called Louisiana. Like the *Marasa Trois* of the divine twins of Vodou, the two women are joined by a third, whose healing powers exceeds their own. Although orthographically different, the three names of Suzie Anna, Louise Anna, and Louisiana sound the same. The union of the three women is thus established through a phonological rather than orthographic relationship. As Brodber's sister, poet and fiction writer Velma Pollard, explains, "something one HEARS is key to this novel in which connections are made between this world and the other" (2009, 37). Since we can "see" the connection only if we have tuned our ears to listen for it, the novel shifts archival meaning from the visibility of writing to the audibility of orality. Brodber uses these and other shared names across the dispersed locations of the African diaspora as signposts for inaudible and often unacknowledged connections that can be seen and heard through an attentiveness to Jamaican oral culture.

Despite the explicit themes of pan-Africanism and hidden diasporic connections in *Louisiana,* my chapter foregrounds the localized Jamaican perspective that it introduces into early twentieth-century North American modernity. Unlike so many Caribbean writers of her generation who emigrated to Britain, Canada, or the United States, Brodber still resides in her village birthplace of Woodside in the rural parish of Saint Mary, Jamaica. Her home is known as BlackSpace, a place for overseas black artists and scholars to visit and for local community members to remember and reenact their own histories. In addition to writing fiction, Brodber is trained in psychiatric anthropology and history and has written the histories of her local community, *The People of My Jamaican Village, 1817–1948* (1999) and *Woodside Pear Tree Grove P.O.* (2004). While conducting research for these histories, she learned that a quarter of the slaves on a nearby plantation had been born in the United States (2012, 113–14).² Woodside does itself occupy the site of a former coffee plantation called Louisiana, which shares a name with the eighteenth state of the American Union but not for the same reasons since the plantation owner named it after his wife. Brodber's excavation of a hemispheric plantation history beneath the surface of her village prompts Alison Donnell to call Woodside "a very localized and yet profoundly diasporised place" and to offer Brodber's local rural perspective as a corrective to a "global village" one that collapses geographical distance and cultural differences across diasporas (2006, 483).

Although its action unfolds within the United States, *Louisiana,* like Brodber's other novels, displays a distinctively Jamaican sociocultural frame of reference through references to Rastafarianism and Jamaican orature by way of songs, hymns, folk tales, proverbs, and colloquialisms.³ My identification of Jamaican cultural and religious elements in a novel about diasporic connections is informed by Stuart Hall's (1990) insistence that we be attentive to not only intersecting and shared black histories but also their diasporic differences.⁴ Even as Brodber recovers the history of an early twentieth-century West Indian presence in the United States, she also obliges the reader to view its centered, mainland space through the rural environment of Woodside, Jamaica, which is a readerly experience she describes with self-irony as "dragging people through bush and weeds" (2012, 123). The purpose of this chapter, then, is not to measure the reality of the novel's world against a historical past, as have other critics who see it recovering a hidden history of Caribbean American and African American collaborations despite antagonistic relations (C. James 2001; Page 2005), or as a "lost diasporic history" of African religions that were driven underground during slavery (Roberts 2002, 76). Rather, I am interested in the novel's collapse of the division between science and superstition, the natural and supernatural through a transformation of the anthropologist's tool of the voice recorder into a conduit for spirits to enter a human world. As in Lamming's characterization of the BBC radio programming, the tape recorder transmits the words of people who are deceased. However, in *Louisiana* Ella is also confronted with the inexplicable evidence that the machine is capable of recording words that were uttered even prior to its invention. The scenario addresses both historiography, which reanimates a dead past, and anthropology, which preserves a dying present. By making a newly invented machine into a device for transmitting voices of the dead, the novel fuses Afro-Caribbean sacred worlds with the technologies of early twentieth-century modernity, which can be accomplished in fiction more so than historiography.

Due to the multiple fronts on which Brodber works, her approach to fiction writing is characterized as "interdisciplinary" (Roberts 2006, 37–46; O'Callaghan 2012, 66). In the paper she delivered at the First International Conference on Women Writers of the English-Speaking Caribbean at Wellesley College in 1988, she explains how her turn to fiction writing was an outcome of her experience with collecting oral histories, which forced her to rethink her social scientist training. She describes how she became frustrated with the demands for an objectivity that ignored "the affective interaction between the researcher and the researched" and how she also noticed that social scientists were accountable not to the people they were researching but to their fellow academics (Brodber 1990, 165–66). Both revisions to social science methodologies are presented in *Louisiana* through the ethnography that Ella finds herself practicing once she begins to hear the spirit voices. Arguably, Brodber is instructing us to listen carefully for an agency that exists in the silent spaces of history, and this is how the novel has been read. June Roberts characterizes *Louisiana* as introducing "new oral records acquired by Ella Townsend from sources beyond this world" (Roberts 2002, 82). Yet, I hesitate to consider Brodber's fiction only as an extension of her history-writing project, due to the experimental nature of its narrative form. The plot of *Louisiana* does not proceed linearly and, in places, is so disjunctive and fragmented that it is causes the reader to pause and even stumble. When Ella tries to organize the snippets of information she receives from the dead into fully fleshed-out stories, she discovers that she is unable to piece them together. Her failure points to the novel's interrogation of the efficacy of narrative itself, in both its written and oral form. My reading goes somewhat against the grain of the novel, since it *does* assert the value of recording oral histories and restoring subjectivity to forgotten agents of history, particularly black women. But I also want to suggest that we read the idea of speaking from beyond the grave literally in order to consider the effect an out-of-body experience has on our understanding of the materiality of the archives, whether they be textual, visual, or even aural.

Brodber's novels not only provide lessons on how to conduct responsible fieldwork but also are written in narrative forms that challenge the grounds of social realism. While the Rastafari proverb of "the half that's never been told," spoken by the spirit healer Ole African throughout her second novel *Myal* (1988), addresses the repressed and misrepresented life stories of black Jamaicans, Brodber does not simply recount the stories missing from colonial history books and archives.[5] Rather, as Shalini Puri notes, *Myal* introduces a different kind of realism than social mimesis through a literary form involving halvings and doubling, fragments, and nonlinearity that expose the contradictions of Science and Reason (2004, 139–70). This alternative reality, which she identifies as a marvelous realism preserving a tension between "the marvelous" and "the real," is presented through a Jamaican vernacular culture in which spirit thievery, exorcism, and repossession are very much part of the social reality of everyday life.[6] Due to its destabilizing of the documentary realism of anthropology and historiography, *Louisiana* also has elements of historiographic metafiction, which is a genre proposed by Linda Hutcheon for novels challenging a "separation of the literary and the historical" (1988, 105). Angeletta K. M. Gourdine (2004) uses the term "carnival-conjure" for describing the narrative form of *Louisiana,* where social history is accessed through the intervention of spirits. The unique characteristics of Brodber's fiction leads Patricia Saunders to distinguish her approach from other Caribbean women writers to addressing historical silences: "Where Nourbese-Philip and other writers like Dionne Brand and Merle Collins posit language and memory as the sites of engagement for wresting history away from the written word, Erna Brodber reaches beyond these paradigms to assert that the construction of knowing and being need to be reconsidered in a social-historical context" (2001, 141). Curdella Forbes (2007) considers *Myal* and *Louisiana* as going further than any other Anglophone Caribbean novel in depicting spiritualism as a historical phenomenon, arguing that to read the spirits only as metaphors for human actors displays faith in a secular vision of humanism. She explains the narrative style of *Louisiana*, "with its dissolution of event boundaries, its crossings to and fro between mental and geographical spaces, its refiguration of the journey as a spiritual rather than primarily cultural odyssey, its employment of multiple voice-narrators, and its removal of attributive hooks so that conversation floats in the air and floats into consciousness," reenacts the conjoining of a human and spirit world in Afro-Creole religions (2007, 14). The union of these two worlds also exists in the neologism of "word holes" uttered by Ella as she attempts to come to terms with an out-of-body experience that resembles the unexpectedness of the world Lewis Carroll's Alice encounters after plunging down a rabbit hole into Wonderland. Whereas Forbes's interest in reading the spirits as a phenomenological reality lies in tracing the place of Divine Power in human agency, my own approach is to explore the consequences of spirit possession being integrated into an anthropological methodology and not just as its object of study.

Louisiana brings together two seemingly incompatible bodies of knowledge: anthropology as a social science and spiritualism, for which Ella seeks to find an equivalent term. She asks whether she should call her practice "the anthropology of the dead" or a "Celestial ethnography," to which she responds, "Crazy" (Brodber [1994] 1997, 61) to show the impossibility of designating spiritualism as a social science. Due to the incompatibility of the two forms of knowledge, the idea of spirits speaking through a social scientist can only be presented as fictional rather than empirical evidence. "There has never been a scholar who really," writes Derrida, "and as scholar, deals with ghosts" (1994, 12). If a social scientist claimed her sources to be the spirits of people who were dead, she would probably be regarded as Ella is when she returns to the Social Research office of Columbia University, which is to say, "mad" (133). As Sylvia Wynter reminds us, African-derived religions occupied the same place in twentieth-century disciplinary forms of knowledge as madness during the Age of Reason (2013, 503n7).[7] The objective of a literary engagement with the past is thus different than a historical one, although the two projects have points of intersection. For this reason, my literal reading of spirit talk is in the interest of examining how Brodber's fiction creates an *imaginary past* in which mainstream American modernity is refracted through Jamaica's Afro-Creole epistemologies. Reading the spirit voices literally, instead of as metaphors for lost oral histories, allows one to find value, as does Ella, in the silence of her informant. More important, by demonstrating the heterologies of a universal vision of modernity that defines itself against its various Others (Certeau 1986; Trouillot 2002), the novel reframes an early twentieth-century anthropological perspective in which Jamaica, Haiti, and New Orleans exist as places of strange and exotic cultures.

ANTHROPOLOGIST AS CONJURE-WOMAN

Ella Townsend is a Zora Neale Hurston–inspired character, whose life story alludes to the African American anthropologist's autoethnographic works on Louisiana, Jamaica, and Haiti in *Mules and Men* (1935) and *Tell My Horse* (1938).[8] As a black female anthropologist,

Hurston has a unique style of writing ethnographies in her blending of the creative function of fiction with the social science one of anthropology through a black performative writing style that Houston A. Baker calls "spirit work" (1993, 69–101). Brodber goes even further than Hurston in fictionalizing anthropology though the real and not just metaphoric spirit work practiced by her anthropologist protagonist. Like Hurston, Ella is instructed by her teachers at Columbia University to collect black oral histories of the South for the Federal Writers' Project. And like Hurston, who had access to a cumbersome sound recorder for collecting folk songs, Ella has an early prototype of the recording machine she calls a "black box" (Brodber [1994] 1997, 12).[9] Unlike Hurston, Ella does not take the machine, along with its recordings, back to New York. Instead, it is reported that she ran away to become a "conjure-woman" (Brodber [1994] 1997, 4), which is derogatory name for a *manbo*. Ella prefers to call herself a female prophet (106) when, after Mammy dies, she moves to New Orleans to take over the business of psychic Madam Marie, whose name is reminiscent of the famous New Orleans "hoodoo doctor" known as Marie Leveau. In her first book of African American folklore, *Mules and Men,* Hurston tells the story of Leveau as recounted to her by her nephew, Luke Turner. She describes how she studied hoodoo under Turner for five months after which time he asked her to take over his business, an offer that with "great sorrow" ([1935] 1990, 205) she says she declined. The authority of a black female anthropologist's work depends on her not abandoning her scholarly objective by becoming a believer of the African-derived religion she is studying. As other critics note, Brodber is careful to distinguish Ella's practice from hoodoo and conjuring through the novel's biblical references (Toland-Dix 2007, 204) and "an ethics of surrender" to a Higher Power (Forbes 2007, 9). The spiritist tradition depicted in *Louisiana* is closer to Jamaica's Revival Zion, which is "biblically focused" but Afro-Creole in its emphasis on the spirit work of "divination, visions, prophecy, and healing" (Stewart 2005, 111, 108). As was common at the time she was writing, Hurston plays up the salacious and curious features of hoodoo and voodoo, the details of which were unquestioningly accepted as facts. In *Louisiana,* Ella defends the stories the spirits tell her as "facts" even though she "can't prove them to be so" (102) because they do not exist as material evidence. Her designation of ephemeral information as "facts" not only questions the factuality of ethnographic evidence but also invites the reader to imagine a different kind of archive, one where uncovering new evidence is not the sole objective of scholarly work.

The narrative form of *Louisiana* mimics the archive of a Harlem Renaissance writer like Hurston inasmuch as its story is presented as a manuscript consisting of a black female anthropologist's journal and diary written between 1936 and 1954, the transcript of interviews with her informant, a cover letter by the sender presumed to be her husband, and a note from the editor of a small black women's press as recipient of the manuscript in 1974. The editor's receipt of an unmarked manuscript during the seventies alludes to Alice Walker's visit to Hurston's unmarked grave in 1973 and the subsequent restoration of the anthropologist, folklorist, and fiction writer to her rightful place in an African American literary canon. Despite an attention to dates within the diary and at the moment of its discovery, time does not unfold chronologically in the novel. Its story is offered episodically through shifting voices and repetitious time sequences in which the same evidence is presented in multiple and diverse forms. In a statement that implicitly points to the creative anachronism of the novel's presentation of anthropological work, the editor of the Black World Press acknowledges that Ella's ethnographic study was ahead of its time. "Today," she notes, "the intellectual world understands that there are more ways of knowing than are accessible to the five senses" (Brodber [1994] 1997, 4).[10] The extra sense to which she alludes is one that exceeds the usual senses for working with archival materials, because it involves communication with the dead. The editor nonetheless attempts to understand the manuscript's significance in terms of traditional historiography by placing each chapter title as a sequence of cause and effect:

> The text came to us divided into six parts—1) I heard the voice from heaven say 2) First the goat must be killed 3) Out of Eden 4) I got over 5) Louisiana and 6) Ah who sey Sammy dead. Is there a message in these titles, we asked—I heard the voice from Heaven say, "first the goat must be killed (and you get) out of Eden and get over (to be) Louisiana." Den a who sey Sammy dead, (if this can happen). A hypothesis. (5)

She fills in the semantic gaps of each of the six parts with words to form grammatical sentences. Although there is a logic to the sentences constructed from the chapter headings, it does not deliver the full meaning of a story that is delivered in fragments, which interrogates the grammar of the master's language and casts suspicion on institutionalized methods of inquiry.

As a doctoral student in anthropology, Ella is trained in social scientist methods for collecting oral histories, but inasmuch as she is given a prototype for the recording machine, she is able to work with sound through a new medium that has not yet been systematized. Since the recording machine does not filter out noises that are extraneous to words, it captures emotional expressions that would be excluded from a written transcript. As a *black female* anthropologist, Ella ascribes value to the emotive quality of the words and sounds that might otherwise be treated as superfluous to the interview. Her refusal to reduce the interview to a process of information retrieval can be read as a lesson in how to collect and interpret oral histories. "These silences," writes Saunders, "include, but are not limited to, 'unsaid' and 'untold' stories; laughs and gestures which express ideas and emotions; voids, which at first appearance seem to be empty spaces" (2001, 156). The voids are not empty spaces because they are filled with spirit voices, which exist on a different register than the live recording of nonverbal emotive sounds.

Mammy's telepathic communication suggests an archive that exceeds even the emotive sounds of laughter and sighs. Ella captures the spirit voices on tape due to her habit of turning on the recording machine before each interview session in order to record not only voices but also nonverbal sounds. That is the explanation she gives to her husband, Reuben, when he inquires, "How come so much of the spool is used if there was so little conversation?" (Brodber [1994] 1997, 43). In response to her explanation, he tells her that he had heard "verbal activity" beyond the nonverbal sounds of her interview. On playing back the recording, she discovers voices in the silent parts and realizes that they are the same voices she heard inside her head during the times when Mammy King was silent. Ella records the conversation in her journal "as true and exact a transcription" (31) of the voices on the recording tape. To the reader, who has not yet learned the full story, the transcript of these voices appears as a series of disconnected snippets of songs and fragments of conversations, all of which add up to an incomprehensible babble. As a Canadian reviewer of *Louisiana* observes, the style of the first part is "very authentic in anthropological terms, but has the effect of blocking the reader at the very beginning of the narrative" (McNeil 1995). To an uninitiated reader the first section entitled "I heard the voice from heaven say" looks like, to quote a late nineteenth-century British colonialist's characterization of Ananse stories, "pointless, disjointed, mutilated fragments" (Rampini 1873, 117). The similarity between the transcript as authentic unframed ethnography and an outsider's perspective on Ananse stories licenses an interpretation of the first section as pure, unmediated orality.

However, if we read the opening scene literally and not only metaphorically, the transcript is also the raw text of beyond-the-grave conversations, against which the anthropologist's questions appear as background noise because she inhabits a different space. Having been introduced to the transcript before the description of the event in Ella's diary, the reader is privy to the knowledge that Mammy's silences, recorded by Ella as "full thick and deep" (Brodber [1994] 1997, 14), are filled with her conversations with Lowly. Ella notes that she "need[s] braille to access those thoughts" (14), which suggests the inadequacy of the usual senses for doing fieldwork, since braille involves the use of touch in the place of sight. In the context of the alternative reality belonging to a spirit world, the braille reference might also allude to the stroking of hands through which a soul is transferred from one body to another. Ella calls the process "passing the life-line" (121) and learns from Lowly that it happened when she placed the palms of her hands on Mammy's own palms in an effort to resuscitate her when she lost consciousness. After Ella receives Mammy's life-line, the trigger for opening up a sixth and psychic sense in her are the words—"*Ah who sey Sammy dead*"—which is the response to the refrain "Sammy dead, Sammy dead, Sammy dead oh" of a Jamaican call-and-response song. The mento song (mento being one of the root musics of reggae) tells the story of how a "grudgeful" neighbor, envious of Sammy's successful crop of corn, uses obeah to cast a spell that kills him. Brodber couples the response to a song about a violent and vengeful death with a hymn about a peaceful one—"It is the voice I hear / the gentle voice I hear / that calls me home" (9)—thereby changing the mento song's message of envy and discord into one of community. The hymn, which speaks of death not as an end but a journey to an afterlife, was sung at the funeral of Ella's grandmother, who died in St. Mary, Jamaica, when Ella was nine months old and of whom she has no conscious memory. It was also sung at Lowly's and Mammy's funerals, and both songs serve as pathways for their spirits to communicate with Ella via the recording machine.

The idea of a machine that can record the voices of the living and the dead suggests more than the division between written and oral archives; it also suggests a split within the archive itself between what is remembered and what is forgotten, a history that is preserved for posterity and the one that gets left behind and, as a result, is irretrievable. While hinting at these forgotten histories, the novel does not recover them despite Ella's access to voices from beyond the grave. One of the stories that Ella uncovers through her listening to the spirit voices is that Mammy was a United Negro Improvement Association (UNIA) organizer in Chicago for Marcus Garvey, who, like Lowly and Ella, was born in Jamaica. Since Garveyism was a black self-improvement movement that connected people of African descent in the United States, Central America, and the Caribbean, the novel returns to a past moment in time when the utopian vision of pan-Africanism was still in its infancy and Garvey's dream was alive.[11] Robert A. Hill's multivolume collection of the Marcus Garvey and United Negro Improvement Association Papers provides an expansive archive of UNIA activities across the African diaspora. Of the 250 of its West Indian and African American members from between 1917 and 1920 whom he is able to identify by name, 64 were women (2011, 794–95). In his introduction to the eleventh volume, the first of three on the Caribbean, Hill explains how influential West Indians were in the early formative years of the UNIA in the United States and how widespread its membership was in the Caribbean due to Garvey's attempts to mend the divisions, not always to success, between African Americans and West Indians (lxii–lxvii). The documents of everyday UNIA business offer glimpses into the identities of women leaders but less so of those belonging to the rank and file. While *Louisiana* reveals, as does Hill's massive archive, that UNIA organizers were both West Indian and African American whose numbers included women, it also presents the records of a prior generation of black women as inaccessible.

Instead of the spirit voices providing all of the missing pieces of lost stories, they speak only to confirm that these stories cannot be told. One of the stories that Ella attempts to reconstruct belongs to Mammy's mother, who led a cane workers' strike on the Teche plantation in Louisiana within a year after Mammy was born.[12] She disappeared shortly afterward, but there is no record of her death. Although Ella learns from Mammy King that her mother was one of the forgotten leaders of the strike, the mystery of her death remains unsolved. Ten years after she first heard the story, Ella researches the Teche strike in the library to the sound of Mammy's spirit laughing at the thought that her mother's life story would exist in so mighty a place as a library. All Ella is able to determine from her research is the year of the reported

"Disturbance in the canefield" (Brodber [1994] 1997, 139), 1878, and that both men and women participated in the work stoppage. Alluding to Mammy's mother, Ella reports that "it is the general assumption that she was disposed of by the planters because of her political activities" (151). However, she is unable to discover how. Was she the female cane worker spotted hanging from a tree? Or the one found drowned in the river, presumed to be death by suicide? Mammy does not know because the body was never recovered, and she was a young child at the time. But it is not simply a question of not having the information because even in her spirit form Mammy refuses to speak about incidents that are painful for her to recall. Her runaway slave grandfather, her father, and her stepfather were all lynched, but Mammy's spirit does not speak about these occurrences other than to tell Lowly's spirit to go talk to the ghost of her father, Ramrod Grant, who is still waiting by the cotton tree. Inasmuch as the dead speak, they do so to signal the stories they will not or cannot tell. In this way, the novel is as much about the impossibility of creating seamless stories out of fragments as it is about filling in archival gaps with oral sources. "Did the new data help to flesh out these themes?" Ella asks herself after recording the information she gets from Mammy's spirit. "They did not," she concludes (108). *Louisiana* points to broken spirit stories, the morsels of which do not fit together like so many pieces in a jigsaw puzzle.

Since the spirit voices do not provide the incomplete or missing data, Ella is obliged to consider the reasons for the reticence of her informants in recalling the past. While combing the tape for information, she places all of the pieces of data within an "analytical frame" in the interest of a "historical reconstruction of the life of Mrs Sue Ann Grant-King" (Brodber [1994] 1997, 64), which is the project with which the university entrusted her and also the history she seeks to write. Once she begins to really listen to the spirit voices, Ella arrives at a different kind of understanding than the one provided by dates, locations, and individual stories. She writes in her diary: "I think that for the very first time I have found my way into the depths of Mammy's sadness" (140). Her diary entry shifts the focus of oral histories away from collecting information in order to fill in the missing portions, which is the objective of history writing as recovery. Saunders observes that the novel makes an epistemological break with the Works Progress Administration (WPA) project by shifting the authority of history from "scientific procedures" to "ex-slaves as witnesses and participants" (2001, 157). But Ella's diary entry indicates that the value of Mammy's stories lies both in new participant evidence and also something information alone cannot convey—namely, the feelings accompanying silence. "What your granny felt," Ella tells Mammy, "what your mother felt, what you felt cannot be told any better than you have told it" (139). She concludes that "feeling is knowing," words alluding to a Rastafarian proverb, "he who feels it knows it," which was spoken by Madam Marie at a time when Ella did not understand its meaning (148).[13] She later understands that even her informants cannot consciously access a past that is too painful to remember and are obliged to "'feel' their way to it" (149). Ella thus identifies the silence of her informants as being more relevant to her project than a reconstruction of data derived from oral histories with which to fill the gaps of the written records.

The spirit voices that fill Ella's head, then, do not belong to a world of information but one of vision and affect. However, as Trouillot explains, North Atlantic universals of modernity also "do not describe the world; they offer visions of the world" (2002, 220). The vision of the world provided by Brodber's novel addresses a response of diasporic Africans to the social death of plantation slavery. The rules of reason cannot account for the understanding Ells obtains, for she is able to access a knowledge that exceeds her own individual mind. She likens the precise moment of being ridden to the feeling of a silver spear piercing through one side her head to the other. She goes on to explain that the spear leaves a trail of silver dust and "these particles of dust are absorbed into the brain and your whole mind becomes suffused with understanding" (Brodber [1994] 1997, 106). The relationship of the jab of the silver spear" to archival materials, both written and oral, can be likened to the natural light Ella observes shining through a stained-glass window at her mother's church. "The picture," she notes, "was a mosaic, like a jigsaw puzzle" (57). The colorful lead-soldered glass pieces form a dull and broken image until the sun streams through them during the long summer days. As a source of energy that is not part of the picture yet necessary for it to be seen, sunlight makes the depicted scene suddenly appear. "The whole picture was there," Ella declares, "and for a considerable time" (57). A picture of the past is acquired not only from the pieces of information assembled like a jigsaw puzzle. It also requires the trail of silver dust that infuses the brain, allowing one to see, hear, and feel things one did not before. The novel's integration of spirit possession into the social scientist's approach to collecting data offers a glimpse into the debris that a historicist temporality of modernity leaves behind.

A refusal of the binary logic through which modernity defines itself against its Others—the rural, the primitive, the supernatural—already exists in Jamaican vernacular culture. In response to Ella telling her that her parents emigrated from Jamaica, Mammy remarks that "they have high science there" (Brodber [1994] 1997, 20). She is using a Jamaican expression that she most likely learned from Lowly; namely, calling the ability to command and communicate with ancestors, and to draw on their power for healing the sick and determining the outcome of events, *science*. For Vodouisants, the same spiritual knowledge is called *konesans*, derived from the French *connaissance,* but the Kreyòl has stronger implications of experience and wisdom passed down from teachers to their disciples than the French (Michel 1996, 37–41). The Jamaican and Haitian use of the European words for disciplinary forms of knowledge constitute appropriations that repurpose their meaning. In *Louisiana,* Ella is Mammy's and Lowly's disciple, but the black vernacular appropriation of the word "science" is channeled through a new technology since she is unable to hear the voices that are communicating with her telepathically until they materialize on the tape. Ella's psychic abilities interject supernatural signification into the word "medium," which, according to *The Oxford English Dictionary*, refers to "any physical material (as tape, disk, paper, etc.) used for recording or reproducing data, images, or sound," but also "a person believed to be in contact with the spirits of the dead and to communicate between the living and the dead." *Louisiana* joins these two seemingly incompatible meanings. In like manner, Ella's personification of the tape recorder suggests a fusion of technological and spirit work. She writes that she does not want "the people's recording machine to hurt its head" (32) in allusion to the headache she feels whenever she hears voices. And, on one occasion when Mammy's voice is particularly loud and fierce because she is "vexed" (109), Ella is forced to turn down the volume on the machine, which suggests a fusion of the spirit with the recorder. By enlisting the aid of a sound recorder for expressing the idea of communication with the dead, the novel's presentation of spirit talk undermines the science/superstition dichotomy of industrial modernity.

What are the implications of the double meaning of the term "medium," recording tape as a physical material that can play back voices in the absence of their speakers and a person who has the special power to transmit the voices of the dead? Communication is implied in both, except that the former is scientific and technological, and the latter, spiritual and supernatural. Yet, the two discourses were historically intertwined in the emergence of industrialized modernity. British and American spiritualism reached its height in an era of an increasingly mechanized and industrialized society during the late nineteenth and early twentieth centuries. According to *The Oxford English Dictionary*, "medium" was first used for spiritualism during the 1850s. As Steven Connor (1999) explains, rather than denoting a retreat from machines into an ethereal realm of the supernatural, modern spiritualism drew on scientific inventions for explaining the phenomenon of ghosts. The invention of the telephone in 1876, the phonograph a year later, and the gramophone in 1887 enabled psychics to offer materialist explanations for their transmission of voices over great distance. Connor concludes that the effect of their analogies was "to 'materialize' spiritualism itself and to highlight the ghostliness of a new technological power to separate the voice from its source, either in space, as with the telephone, or in time, as with the gramophone" (212). His description also suggests that through the magic of new inventions, voices were freed from their physical bodies and able to exist outside of human time. The analogy made between spirituralism and new sound technology also worked the other way. Jonathan Sterne explains in *The Audible Past* that sound recordings were heralded as having the ability to preserve the voices of the dead forever, even though early sound archival materials were less than permanent. "Despite the ephemerality of the recordings themselves," he writes, "death and the invocations of 'the voices of the dead' were everywhere in writings about sound recording in the late nineteenth and early twentieth centuries" (2003, 289). By understanding the incipient technology of voice recordings through the conceptual apparatus of spiritualism, Victorians extended its immaterial and ephemeral qualities to a new archival material for preserving sound.

Brodber's novel makes evident a relationship that once existed but was left behind as the language of technology became increasingly codified through a separation of science, as forward and future-looking, from superstition, as a residual of the past. Early anthropological use of sound recorders was in the interest of saving a vanishing past that included folk songs and oral storytelling. "The time has come," reports a spokesperson for the Library of Congress about its folk music project, "when the preservation of this valuable old material is threatened by the spread of the popular music of the hour" (qtd. in Sterne 2003, 330n108, 409). The effect of this preservation act, however, was to place the vanishing past in a temporality outside of the present. Where popular music is timely, existing in the "hour" of the immediate present, folk music expresses a past way of life that is under threat of disappearance. Could the folk music have made its way into popular music, ever-present but transformed? The recordings do not say. As pure sound, they authenticate a dead past whose "pastness" is made evident by the quaintness of accents and ghostly presence of voices from beyond the grave. The idea of a recording as evidence of an authentic and unmediated voice adheres to the temporality of a historicism that makes a clean break between past and present. To see the recordings of Mammy's and Lowly's conversations as coming from the past, when the two women were still alive, is to adhere to the temporal logic of anthropology. As the novel reveals, the spirits exist in a different space but not a different time. In *The Writing of History,* Michel de Certeau characterizes the division between past and present, as a uniquely Western form for organizing time. "Modern Western history," he explains, "essentially begins with differentiation between the *present* and the *past*" (1988, 2), which is a differentiation that is not universal.[14] While the Derridean idea of hauntology inhabits Western historicist time in order to deconstruct it from the inside, the sacred worlds of Afro-Creole religions, as well as their accompanying imaginaries, do not disrupt the separation of past and present in the same way.

GHOSTS, SPECTERS, HAUNTING

The haunting of *Louisiana* is derived from Caribbean creolized religions, in which the spirits of the dead do not always return as ghostly doubles of the people who once lived, as they do in the ghost lore informing European literature. Derrida's philosophical meditation on the spectral logic of hauntology is based on a scene from Shakespeare's *Hamlet* (1609), where the deceased king of Denmark is seen nocturnally walking the ramparts of Elsinore castle (1994, 1–25). The apparition does not identify himself to the soldiers who see him; he is recognized as the former king only by the armor he wore when he was alive. To rephrase Pollard's assessment that what is *heard* is key to understanding the connection between the human and spirit worlds in Brodber's novel, what is *seen* is key to understanding the haunting of Shakespeare's play. The ghost of the murdered king leaves to return at a later time, and on seeing his son, Hamlet, silently beckons him to follow. Only when they are alone does he describe how he met his death and demands from Hamlet revenge for his murder. Since the specter has a physical form in the likeness of the king, Derrida describes it as an incarnation of spirit and in possession of a body that is neither living nor dead (4–5). The ghostly remains of a past that is declared to be dead continues to haunt like the specter of Hamlet's father. Derrida references Shakespeare's stage directions—"enter the ghost, exit the ghost, re-enter the ghost" (xix)—for figuring the untimeliness of a past that is not dead because it returns again and again.[15] In *Louisiana*, the spirit is not a ghost of the same order as the king because it has no spectral form of its own but speaks through a living human vessel. Unlike the king of Denmark, Mammy King, the daughter of a cane worker whose mother was a slave, passes her lifeline onto Ella when her spirit enters her body. The union of flesh and spirit suggests a different temporality than the one belonging to Derrida's hauntology as referencing the return of a past that appears to be dead but is not.

While hauntology is a useful concept for explaining how slavery has not ended because it returns in new forms of bondage, I also want to heed Wendy Brown's warning against deriving a "general historiography" (2001, 152) from Derrida's writings. As she proceeds to explain, his idea of haunting as being touched by a ghost that cannot be fully comprehended was intended to address a specific historical moment when the past was being recalled in a way that was "simultaneously an achievement of memory and a failure of memory" (153). Derrida was writing against the proliferation of pronouncements, for which Francis Fukuyama's book *The End of History and the Last Man* served as a prime example, declaring the "'end of history,' of the 'end of Marxism,' of the 'end of philosophy,' of the 'ends of man'" (1994, 16). As Derrida argues, the social exploitation that led Marx to identify class struggle as the motor of history did not end with the triumph of capitalism and liberal democracy after the fall of the Berlin Wall. In the context of race and slavery, the idea of a Derridean hauntology demonstrates that a declaration of the "end of slavery" or "the end of racism" is premature, as their reconstituted forms live on in the prison industrial complex, racial profiling, and police violence. While useful as a concept for explaining how the racist structures of slavery persist into the present, Derrida's hauntology is less useful for describing how black people combatted racism in the past.

Brown's advice against deriving a general historiography from hauntology can be equally applied to Morrison's *Beloved*, which serves as a literary device for scholars to describe the enduring trauma of slavery. The spiteful spirit haunting 124 Bluestone Road belongs to a baby girl who was killed by her fugitive slave mother, Sethe, to prevent her from being returned to slavery. Sethe's neighbor Ella (who shares a name with Brodber's protagonist) leads a group of thirty women to rid the community of the ghost, because she believes that by returning as an adult human, it had gone too far: "She didn't mind a little communication between the two worlds, but this was an invasion" ([1987] 2004, 302). When Ella says of the dead baby's return "that people who die bad don't stay in the ground" (221), she is alluding to African American lore about the spirits of those who died an unnatural death or did not receive proper burial rites remaining on earth to haunt a community. This belief, as Barbara Christian observes, also exists in the Caribbean, where she grew up hearing stories of the deceased who "have not resolved some major conflict, especially the manner of their death" returning to haunt the living in the shape of a newborn baby (1997, 43). Another indication of the hidden connection between African American and Caribbean cultures is that the ghost child emerges fully grown and in human form from a nearby stream (Morrison [1987] 2004, 60), which alludes to water's surface as the crossroad for a passage between the two worlds. The metaphoric implications of the haunting denote a deep and lasting loss that cannot be spoken, and the weight of that loss on subsequent generations.

Beginning in the 1990s, ghosts, specters, and haunting became more frequently used as metaphors for the residual effects of slavery that continued to be experienced and felt. Brodber describes how, on her return from England to Jamaica in the 1970s, the color prejudice she observed in the newly independent nation made it seem that "the enemy was a ghost that talked through black faces" (1990, 165). In *Silencing the Past,* Trouillot calls the invisible yet active form of slavery structuring contemporary racism a ghost (1995, 147). Avery Gordon's *Ghostly Matters* derives from the figure of the ghost a sociological methodology that attends to a past that is unspeakable, unrepresented, and disremembered (2008, 150). My own *Ghosts of Slavery* invokes Caribbean lore about wandering spirits as a metaphor for the necessity to narrate the untold stories about the everyday lives of slave women (J. Sharpe 2003). And Baucom's *Specters of the Atlantic* (2005), whose title echoes Derrida's *Specters of Marx* (1994), makes a case for the *Zong* massacre as a haunting presence in finance capital and human rights discourse. Yet, the spirits populating Afro-Creole religions are more diverse than the ones that have come to represent slavery. Some of them, like those summoned through the Haitian ritual of *wete mò nan dlo* return to settle disputes so that the living can proceed with their lives. While others, like the *lwa*, give the disenfranchised and disempowered access to a life force greater than their own. What would spectrality as a metaphor for an unacknowledged history look like from the perspective of one of these other spirit forms?

Brodber's *Louisiana* invokes haunting to figure the racial violence of slavery that continues to be repeated in the postslavery era, but it also references how a terror-inducing racial violence was resignified by free Jamaicans. At the outset of the novel, the reader hears about Mammy King's father, whose shadow spirit remains close to the cotton tree from which he was lynched. He belongs to those restless spirits who "die bad" and, in this regard, indicates the shared African American and African Caribbean lore that Christian describes. However, in those parts of West Africa and the Caribbean where the silk cotton, or ceiba, tree is native, the tree is considered sacred and its large roots a place where spirits reside. The legendary Kumina Queen, Imogene "Queenie" Kennedy, describes a silk cotton tree in this way: "because take for instant out at Morant Bay . . . when dey came here . . . you 'ave a cotton tree out dere . . . what dey buil' a gas station now . . . dat dey *use to heng men*" (Brathwaite 1978, 47). Miss Queenie is alluding to how the British used the wide expansive branches of the silk cotton tree for hanging black freemen involved in the 1865 Morant Bay rebellion. The brutality with which Governor Eyre responded to the demands of black freeman for a living wage is an indication of the failure of Emancipation to extend full rights to former slaves. Yet it is also the case that the potency of a tree at which the spirit of rebelliousness did not die is evident in Miss Queenie having received her powers to access the spirit world after spending twenty-one days inside the hollowed-out roots of a silk cotton tree.

The stronger retention of African spirituality in Jamaica has to do with the Africans who were transported as indentured workers, alongside those from India and China, between 1841 and 1865, which was a period shortly after the abolition of slavery and long after the end of the slave trade.[16] It is now recognized that Africans of the Kongo nation who arrived during the postslavery era brought with them Kumina rituals that revitalized the Myalism practiced by slaves (Stewart 2006, 136; Roberts 2006, 182).[17] Descriptions of possession as a spirit riding a person's head exist in both Kumina and Myal ceremonies (Warner-Lewis 2003, 147). We also now know that what the British called "obeah" or black magic was Myalism as a form of religious resistance that bridged the divisions of different African ethnic groups, uniting them for the first time (Schuler 1980, 33–37; Chevannes 1994, 17–18). If the colonial edict Philip incorporates into "Discourse on the Logic of Language" commanded that different linguistic groups of slaves be mixed to prevent them from plotting rebellions, in Myalism the severed tongue grew back in a different form. Beyond such moments of overt rebelliousness, these religions provided channels for community and survival because they were "life-affirming rather than death-dealing" (Stewart 2005, 223). The story of Miss Queenie receiving her healing powers from the same kind of tree used for lynchings indicates that not all spirits of a black supernatural world haunt in the same way as the ghost of 124 Bluestone Road. Drawing on this local Jamaican history, Brodber presents a different kind of apparition than either Hamlet's murdered father demanding revenge or a spirit child's hunger for maternal love that is so fierce it can kill. The two female spirits of *Louisiana* represent a history that does not materialize any more than Derrida's spectral one, but it is a history that disentangles enabling moments from potentially disabling ones.

In *Louisiana,* two conjoined black women pass their power to communicate with the dead on to a social scientist and, in doing so, change her relationship to her ethnographic work. At the precise moment of her death, Mammy's spirit leaves her physical body and enters Ella's living one, thereby passing on to her a psychic power as well as political commitment to combatting racism. It is only after her informant dies that the anthropologist learns that both she and her friend Lowly were clandestine UNIA organizers in Chicago. Sue Ann was also a psychic known as Mammy King, who merged her political and psychic work into "a combination which served to make her a legend" (Brodber [1994] 1997, 153). Mammy's character is loosely based on Audley (Queen Mother) Moore, a Garveyite and UNIA leader who was born in rural Louisiana in 1898. Mother Moore learned about Garvey and the UNIA from her Jamaican-born husband, who worked for a Jamaican-based shipping company and traveled between the United States, Latin America, and the Caribbean (Blain 2018, 87). Brodber recalls reading a newspaper story describing Mother Moore's visit to Jamaica to be with her dying friend and learning about how a soul leaves one body and enters another. "One person puts the palm of their hand on the other's upturned forearm," she explains, "and strokes down to the fingertips" (2003/2004, 31). Although African spiritual traditions were also integrated into African American churches, the particular form of the transference of Mammy's soul to Ella—stroking her arms with her fingertips—belongs to Jamaica's Myalistic and Revivalist religions. These religions, popularized in Jamaica during the early 1930s, which is the era of Ella's encounter with Mammy in Louisiana, played a healing role in the lives of socially marginalized people (Stewart 2017, 4–14). The 1930s were also when Rastafari emerged as a back-to-Africa moment and a religion that "synthesized Revival religion, religious Ethiopianism, Garveyism, and esotericism" (Paton 2015, 245). However, if Mammy and her Jamaican friend Lowly practice spirit work, it is not as Garveyites. The official position of the UNIA was to support an outlawing of African-derived religions like Revivalism and Pukumina (Paton 2015, 260). Despite Garvey being Jamaican, he disapproved of, to use his words, "religions that howl, religions that create saints, religions that dance to frantic emotion" (qtd. in Hill 2001, 24). Shirley Toland-Dix argues that the kind of spiritual leader Ella becomes resembles the black women healers of the Spiritual Church of New Orleans, which she offers as evidence of the diasporic connections Brodber seeks to illuminate (2007).

But what if instead of looking to the past for historical people, cultures, and events that can serve as sources for the novel's invented world, we examine the relationship between past and present within the novel itself? The first chapter, called "I heard the voice from Heaven say," contains the statement that "Anna sighed another sigh that leaked from our history" (Brodber [1994] 1997, 14). The reader has not yet been introduced to the person speaking these words and is obliged to circle back to the beginning after reading the entire chapter to figure out that the speaker is Sue Ann's best friend, Louise or Lowly, who is already deceased. There is also a temporality to the scene that has not yet been established because Mammy King's sigh is in response to something her friend said several years before Ella arrived with her recording machine. The conversation between Mammy and the spirit of her friend took place when Ella was interviewing Mammy, although she was unaware of Lowly's presence in the room when Mammy was not responding to her questions. The anthropologist conducting the interview is only able to hear the conversation between the two friends when she plays back the recording machine. From Ella's perspective, Anna's sigh in response to what Lowly is saying exists as an effect with no discernible origin or cause, which is why it is characterized as emerging from a different space. When Lowly describes Mammy's sigh as one that "leaked from our history" (14) and Ella records that her "other self entered their space" (33), they are each talking about the simultaneity of two temporalities characterized in the novel as "human time and other world time" (115). Ella wants to know how Lowly's request that Mammy attend her own funeral managed to be recorded by the machine if the words had been spoken before she, Ella, arrived in Louisiana. The word Ella uses for explaining the appearance of Lowly's voice on the tape is "recall," which suggests a different form of recollection than calling up events from the past:

> When and how did Lowly's speech get on the recording machine if she had spoken in the past when it was not there? Mammy must have recalled her. Mammy must have recalled her: "And I had heard you that time." Yes. Mammy on her way to the other world recalled that event and so powerfully that it was recorded on the machine. Or did the machine pull it from her, from her friend and from me? That meditation later. Mammy's recall was not the end of Lowly. She was there continually after and in the present. So was I. (60–61)

To recall, in this sense, is to hear the spirit voices that exist in a perpetual present. In other words, Lowly does not come to Ella from the past; her spirit already exists in the present but can only be heard after she has been called by Mammy's spirit as it transitions into Ella's body. Since the two spirits are not African ancestors but the recently deceased, they suggest an immediacy that does not conform to the idea of history as archeology. "This supports the suggestion," explains Forbes, "that the spiritual legacy is right here at our fingertips within reach—it does not have to be excavated from a distant past—it is even now in the making" (2007, 14). Unlike the most powerful *lwa* of Haitian Vodou and biblical prophets and saints of Revival Zion, the spirits of Pukumina, which Mammy mentions in addition to Jamaica's high science, are the recently deceased known as "ground spirits," who are seen as closer and thus more likely to come to the assistance of the living (L. James 2009, 325).

THE SHAPE-SHIFTING OF REGRAMMARING

The idea of a spiritual legacy that is not past because it is being made and remade encompasses a temporal logic in which historicism's clean break between past and present is muddied or "confounded," to use a word uttered by Ella in the context of trying to understand the voices she has heard. This temporality belongs to Afro-Creole religions. Ella explains that words she encountered in her mother's Episcopalian church—words like "dread," "aweful," and "confounded"—"control large spaces" and "sit over large holes" she likens to corroded metal plates on the pathway of her life (Brodber [1994] 1997, 43). She characterizes the experience of hearing speech in the silent portion of the tape as stepping on the "corroded words" (44), causing her to fall down a hole. "Do I need a psychiatrist?" she asks Reuben, who responds with the words, "actuality does not always accord with the literature" and "there are different yet logical systems of knowledge" (46). In travelling from the Belgian Congo to Europe and then to the United States, Reuben undertakes a reverse journey of Garvey's back-to-Africa movement in the sense of an African going west in pursuit of the teachings of W. E. B. Du Bois. But it is only while living among southern blacks in New Orleans's Congo Square, which is a diasporic doubling of his African home, that he understands the meaning of his race.[18] Reuben, the half-European, half-Congolese talented tenth who, due to his German university training, Ella considers a more "authentic" (34) anthropologist than herself, serves as her interlocutor for understanding the conversations on the reel. It is he who first draws her attention to the extra tape on the recorder's spool. When he says "actuality does not always accord with the literature," he is questioning the presumed superiority of his university training.

Ella and Reuben begin to unravel the limitations of analytical sciences like psychiatry and anthropology for understanding the black psyche, and of the grammar of European languages for accessing black vernacular cultures. According to grammatical rules, words do not sit on top of spaces, but the spaces between letters create words, and the spaces between words create meaning. The existence of "word holes" is at odds with a grammatical system in which holes are the antithesis of words. Ella's description of "word holes" and empty spaces as channels or pathways to a spirit world that coexists with the human one forces a rethinking of historicist time and even language itself. It is not only the recording machine but also the words from a mento song—"*Ah who sey Sammy dead*"—that provide a passageway for spirits to wrinkle the smoothness of human time. In this regard, sound machines are mere tools for hearing spirit voices rather than essential to them, as is evident in a second "black box" (Brodber [1994] 1997, 13), which is a Victrola or early phonograph with an internal horn that was called a "talking machine." The first time Lowly listens to the music coming from a Victrola was in the Chicago boardinghouse where she worked in the kitchen alongside Mammy. She is furious at the sound of the hateful words of a coon song "spewing" (145) from the device. However, Silas, a resident in the house and Mammy's future husband, instructs her to claim the power of the derogatory name for herself. "When next you hear that song," he instructs Lowly, "say to yourself, 'the coon can'" (145). "Coon" refers to a minstrel buffoon, and "coon can" is a popular card game that Ella plays with Mammy while interviewing her. The phrase "coon can" becomes a rallying cry for collective black agency, and even the Black World Press editor participates in "the community of the production" (5) of Ella's manuscript by adding the title of "Coon can" to its appended note.

The linguistic strategy of repurposing a racist expression by changing its grammar is conveyed by Mammy in the story of her Grandpappy Moses, who is described as "a thinking man" (Brodber [1994] 1997, 80) and whose benevolent master was fond of reminding him of the good life he had. In response to his master's claim that his black servant does not want for anything, Moses says: "Only difference Massa Sutton, you sleeps on the featherbed and I's on the moss" (81). In that one piece of folk wisdom Moses names the relationship that his master, having grown up alongside him as a child, is unable to acknowledge, which is that Moses is not his servant but his slave. As a means of asserting ownership once their true relationship is identified, Sutton responds to his slave's attempt to escape by lynching him from a branch of the same wide oak tree under whose canopy Moses once lay. Mammy characterizes her grandfather's speech act as a rearrangement of Sutton's words in order to bring into representation the relationship that existed in the silence between them. This is how Mammy tells the story her grandmother told her:

> Massa look at them strange and under his eye and he be so silent with Moses, but not a word yet called "slave." Things done get to my Grandpappy, my Granny say. This silence twixt him and the master when first it was Massa want his head clear he open up that head to Moses, Moses he put this word to the front, that to the back, this one twixt this and that and set the master's words in the right and proper fashion. Massa cast out that word, Moses take it, examine it, be it no good, he throw it out; can it be fixed, he fix it and put it in a right spot and so. (81–82)

Moses does not speak the unspeakable word of "slave" that Sutton cannot bring himself around to say. Instead, he "regrammars" the sentence just as Lowly teaches Ella to reconfigure words of derision by placing a comma between "coon" and "can," as Silas taught her. Their actions indicate that black agency might be hiding in plain sight—detectable only when regrammared—rather than in the silent spaces of history.

The shape-shifting form of Moses's "regrammaring" might explain why the novel provides the reader with more than one conceptual metaphor for understanding the kind of social science methodology it is proposing. The first is from a Jamaican Ananse (spelled Anancy in the novel) story about a trickster spider, a shape-shifter that is also a man who speaks in the lisping speech of black peasants (Tanna 1983). Ella derives a lesson about her fieldwork from a story Madam Marie recounts about the spider Anancy's possession of a pot that would cook him a meal whenever he said, "Cook mek mi see" (Brodber [1994] 1997, 78). Mrs. Anancy, wondering why her husband looked so well-fed when she and her eleven children were starving, spies on him and discovers the magic pot. She gets the pot to cook enough food to feed her children but, "in her tidiness" (79), cleans and rinses its magic away. On hearing the story, Ella realizes she has spent so much time "scouring and rinsing that tape" (79) to the degree of it losing its magic. If instead she allows herself to "suspend [her] own sense of right behavior" (80), she explains to herself, the recording machine, like Anancy's magic pot, will provide what she needs. The likely lesson to be derived from the folktale is that the social scientist should transmit oral histories without attempting to interpret them by scouring them for meaning. But Ella's understanding of the recording machine as a magic pot is based on her social scientist faith in the recorder as an instrument for collecting oral histories and the tape as material evidence. Moreover, the story is male-gendered, since the pot loses its magic only when a woman, out of domestic habit, scrubs it clean. The analogy between the magic pot and the tape recorder is an imperfect one, because the magic of the tape recording machine does not only issue from its technology but also the sensation of a spirit passing from one body to another. Five years after Mammy's death, Ella abandons the recorder in favor of a solid pendant pierced with a hole for communicating with the spirit world. The pendant can be seen as an allusion to Hurston's reference to the ethnographic demand for objectivity as "the spy-glass of Anthropology," which is a requirement that the participant-observer maintain a critical distance. Hurston writes that the "spy-glass of Anthropology" allowed her to see her own culture, which she couldn't previously see because "it was fitting [her] like a tight chemise" ([1935] 1990, 1).

Whereas the metaphor of a spy-glass privileges sight and distance, the pendant supplements the sense of sight with that of sound and replaces distance with intimacy. Unlike a recording machine or even a cooking pot, a pendant has no apparent utility. Yet, it is a superior tool since looking through its hole allows Ella to both hear and see things differently. Since Reuben purchased it for her in commemoration of their fifth wedding anniversary, the pendant also represents the joint agency of black men and women.[19] In Brodber's *Louisiana*, the new instrument triangulates the relationship between Ella and the spirit world through Reuben, who transcribes the voices speaking through her. As transcriber, he adheres to an anthropological demand for objectivity but soon records that he too is unable to "remain emotionally detached" (Brodber [1994] 1997, 143). The final entries of Ella's journal, written in his hand after her death, state his intent to return to his birthplace to join the Congolese struggle for independence. His own life story has become intertwined with the black people's stories they are collecting and recording, which itself becomes woven into a larger narrative of pan-Africanism. When Ella embraces a pan-African consciousness, she too undergoes a change. The language of magic shifts from the "thingness" of recorder or cooking pot to the presumed "nothingness" of a hole in the pendant, which she asks her reader to reimagine in this way: "Now put the tips of your index fingers and the tips of your thumbs together. Your extremities now form a diamond. Imagine the diamond to be solid, three dimensional. Now pierce a hole through the center of this. That hole, that passage is me. I am the link between the shores washed by the Caribbean sea, a hole, yet I am what joins your left hand to your right. I join the world of the living and the world of the spirits. I join the past with the present" (124). Like the word holes Ella has already mentioned, the void of a hole is transmuted into something: a pathway or passage to diaspora, ancestors, and history. The hole—a space between the touching finger tips of two hands and the water separating land masses—joins the Caribbean islands to North America and the living to the dead. It brings to mind the Ezili of Duval-Carrié's *The Indigo Room* and the Haitian expression of *lòt bò dlo* for the place of spirits of loved ones and the destination of those who cross the Caribbean Sea to the American mainland. As the novel develops, it invites the reader through the idea of an extra-ordinary sense, to think beyond an association of archival gaps and silences with absence, loss, and negation.

The recording machine, while instrumental to creating an oral record, necessitates filling an epistemological absence—emptiness and silence—with something, a voice recording that can be heard, seen, and measured on the tape. Ella can identify the length of an interview based on the length of the tape that has moved from one spool to the other and first realizes there are voices that do not belong to the interview by the amount of tape on the spool. The tape recorder represents Ella's desire for a complete narrative she can send to Columbia as proof that she did not stray too far from the task with which her teachers entrusted her and to avoid being accused of stealing the machine she was given. "Mammy is the key," she thinks to herself. "Would she be so kind as to give me a narrative plain and straight of her life and doings in South West Louisiana that I could send in this way to them?" she says after accessing her spirit voice (Brodber [1994] 1997, 109). The tape is a material embodiment of the linearity of chronological time, since each segment corresponds to the length of time it takes to unwind. The hole that joins two worlds exists, like word holes, as a passage that is spatial, temporal, and much more. When Ella Townsend, the daughter of Jamaican immigrants, crosses over from the rational and logical discourse of the social sciences to the presumed irrational and illogical language of spirit talk, she becomes Louisiana, which is a name that not only designates her new American domicile but also connects her to her birthplace, a small town in the Jamaican parish of St. Mary called Louisiana. Lowly is also from Louisiana, St. Mary, Jamaica, whereas Mammy was born in the village of St. Mary in the state of Louisiana. The novel addresses the interlocking struggles of African American and African Caribbean people by playing with the reverse mirror names of two places that actually exist: Louisiana in St. Mary, Jamaica, and St. Mary in Louisiana, U.S.A. The two place-names appear to be worlds apart not only because one is in Jamaica and the other, the United States, but also because the former is the place of African-derived spirituality and the other—well, it is too, although it is relayed more strongly through Christianity than some Afro-Caribbean religions. The proximity of the living to the dead is evident in New Orleans, where funeral marches and other mortuary rituals are joyful: "The dead seem to remain more closely present to the living in New Orleans than they do elsewhere" (Roach 1996, 15). Ella's African American informant, Mammy King, has the power to converse with the dead, which is a spiritual knowledge she passes on to Ella when she dies, leaving her soul with her. "I am Louisiana," records Ella; "I give people their history" (Brodber 1994 [1997], 125). West Indians, mostly Jamaicans, who arrive on the United Fruit Company's "banana boats" (78) seek her out for insights into traumatic pasts that continue to cause them pain. Roberts characterizes Ella as a "reverse clairvoyant" because "instead of reading the future she reads the past and makes the fragments of trauma legible as a life worth saving" (2002, 81). Yet, it is possible to make the case, as Barbara Christian does about Morrison's *Beloved,* that clairvoyance as history reflects African cosmologies in which "the future, in the Western sense, is absent, because the present is always an unfolding of the past" (1997, 45). To signal the absence of a future in the Western sense is not the same as saying that knowledge of the future is inconsequential. Jamaican Revival healers are described as having four eyes: two eyes like everyone else and two additional eyes that can see both the past and the future (Chevannes 1994, 32). And then there is the Warner, often a robed woman with a turban-wrapped head, who warns of an impending catastrophe. A member of the August Town Revival movement describes her childhood memory of a robed man who went from one Kingston street to the next warning of an impending disaster a few hours before the 1907 earthquake struck. With the decline of Revivalist religions, the role of the Warner passed to Rastafarians (Chevannes 1994, 81–83). A double vision—forward and backward looking—exists in Brathwaite's philosophy of history that combines Afrofuturism with the temporality of Rastafari warnings. It is to the poetic expressions and philosophic notes and musings of the visionary Bajan poet, historian, and cultural critic that my book now turns.

CHAPTER 4

DreamStories

The Virtuality of Archival Recovery

But Sycorax comes to me in a dream and she dreams me a
Macintosh computer with its winking *io* hiding in its margins
which, as you know, are not really margins, but electronic
accesses to Random Memory and the Cosmos and the *lwa*.

—Kamau Brathwaite, "Interview with Kwame Dawes" (2001)

Kamau Brathwaite famously proclaimed that a Caribbean history of catastrophe—beginning with early tectonic movement causing its islands
to rise from the sea to a more recent past of genocide, slavery, and neo-
colonialism—"requires a *literature of catastrophe* to hold a broken mirror up to broken nature" (1985, 457). The metaphor of literature as a
broken mirror is modernist in its implication of breaking and refracting
the mimesis of literary realism without attempting to restore wholeness
to its fragments. Yet, Brathwaite proceeds to explain that Caribbean
writers should not follow European modernists by remaining "trapped
and imprisoned within the detonations of our own fragmented worlds"
but instead find a way to write themselves out of their broken histories
(459). As he reminds us in *Contradictory Omens* (1974), the fragments
of Caribbean islands resulting from the violent upheaval of tectonic
activity are nonetheless linked underwater: the unity is submarine. The
year after declaring the requirement for a Caribbean literature of catastrophe, he suffered the first of three personal catastrophes that would
lead to a loss of his poetic voice. The first occurred in 1986, when his
Guyanese wife, Doris, whom he calls Zea Mexican in allusion to her
mixed-race Warao ancestry, passed away. They had met in Barbados in
1960, and in addition to being his lifelong companion, she also managed his work on a personal computer that he was unable to access after
her death. As his friend and literary critic Gordon Rohlehr explains,

"This increased his panic that aspects of his written life could perish" (2007, 420). Brathwaite's second catastrophe was the destruction of his thirty-year archive on September 12, 1988, when Hurricane Gilbert devastated his home in the Irish Town suburb of Kingston, Jamaica. The hillside behind the house became so waterlogged that it slid down onto the structure, ripping off its roof and burying its contents in mud and debris. Brathwaite characterizes the damage to his library as a loss of his personal memory because it constituted his own distinctive assemblage of a Caribbean cultural history (1994a, 306). The third catastrophic event was what he referred to as his murder by two gunmen in 1990, when thieves broke into the Kingston apartment to which he had moved following the collapse of his Irish Town house. One of the intruders put a gun to the back of his head and fired. Although no bullet penetrated his skull, Brathwaite felt its heat pass through his brain. In his recapitulation of the event, he reports a "ghost bullet" entering his imagination rendering him metaphorically dead and unable to write (Brathwaite 1999, 162). The period he calls his Time of Salt, in allusion to the wasteland left in the wake of a drought, was one of deep loss—the death of his lifelong companion and archivist of his work, the destruction of his library crushed and crumpled under a mountainside, and a gaping wound in the depths of his imagination.[1] From this devastation would emerge a new poetic style, one reverberating with the sounds and images of a destructive nature, expressing the pain and suffering of broken lives, and replete with the remains of his destroyed archives. His Time of Salt would end with the poet replacing the familial name of "Edward" with "Kamau," a Gikuyu name chosen for him by Ngũgĩ wa Thiong'o's mother, thereby signaling his rebirth as a new man.[2]

The new poetry books were written in a form that defied the conventions of prose and poetry writing through their use of pictograms, ideograms, text boxes, different fonts and font sizes, and varying degrees of margins. In some instances, just one or two words appear in large letters on the page. In others, the poems are accompanied by *vèvè*-like geometric signs and pixel drawings resembling crabs, spiders, birds, frogs, as well as the profile of a woman's face. The innovative writing style could only be accomplished on an Apple Macintosh computer and its Imagewriter printer, which was the earliest home computer to place an array of fonts and graphics for creative expression into a typist's hands. Brathwaite was obliged to start his own press for typesetting *SHAR: Hurricane Poem* (1990) and subsequent books, which were technologically difficult and expensive for standard presses to publish.[3] He christened the new poetics his "Sycorax Video Style" (SVS) after the powerful conjure-woman in Shakespeare's *Tempest* (1611), claiming that she resided within his Apple computer. How she revealed herself is the subject of "Dream Chad," the second story in *DreamStories* (1994b), a prose-poetic series weaving memories, allegories, and meditations into the time-space of dreams laid out in SVS. As Brathwaite explains in the passage serving as this chapter's epigraph, Sycorax appeared to the poet in a dream and dreamed for him a Macintosh computer. His presentation of the streams of computer code (*io*) as pathways to the *lwa* suggests an interface between computer memory and black diasporic memory, along with the shared immateriality of their forms. Brathwaite's analogy refers to random-access memory (RAM) rather than cyberspace because there was no internet at the time. Prior to the transference of a World Wide Web technology to the public domain in 1993, personal computers were relatively autonomous machines. For this reason, SVS is not a cybertext but a creative use of computer-generated fonts and layouts. Brathwaite's inventive style that uses the computer as a writing machine may reflect an analog rather than digital technology, but it nonetheless embodies the virtuality Brian Massumi characterizes as a realm of potential where opposites mingle and conjoin: "In potential is where futurity combines, unmediated, with pastness, where outsides are infolded and sadness is happy (happy because the press to action and expression is life). The virtual is a lived paradox where what are normally opposites coexist, coalesce, and connect; where what cannot be experienced cannot but be felt—albeit reduced and contained" (2002, 30). The potential of virtuality lies in its its propensity to dispense with binary systems, including the binary of the analog and digital, which is why Massumi argues for the superiority of the analog for accessing virtuality (2002, 133–43). He also makes a case that the imagination is especially suitable for expressing the virtual because it is a space of "thinking feeling" that can "diagram without stilling" (2002, 134). While Massumi's description of "the virtual" is in the interest of unleashing the limitless potential of affects, I find the term equally appropriate to Brathwaite's description of the computer as a machine that infolds writing into orality for his diagraming of African diaspora memory. Like electronic files hidden deep within the computer hard drive to be retrieved at a future point in time, the African gods and spirits were driven underground to a land of linguistic silence, awaiting their unspoken, dare I even say "felt," summoning on the other side.

Throughout the long span of his poetic career, Brathwaite has always been attentive to the gods and spirits that inhabit the Caribbean world, not in their original form but as they emerged from the wreckage of the Atlantic crossing. "But the nam/nommo capsule is not merely a machine," he declares about the ancestral spirits who accompanied enslaved Africans in the ship's hold; "(if that were so, our African New World gods would have arrived awesome, not crippled; cold and dead)" (Brathwaite 1982, 4). Brathwaite's characterization of ancestral spirits as cold and dead does not mean that they were forgotten. As NourbeSe Philip explains about embodied memory forms, it is not a question of forgetting as the antithesis of remembering because "when the African came to the New World, she brought with her nothing but her body and all the memory and history which that body could contain" (1996, 22). In his description of the Middle Passage gods belonging to Jamaican Ananse, Cuban Orishas, and Haitian *lwa*, Brathwaite writes against what he calls the "Greek symmetry" of balanced thought (1982, 7). "The gods," he declares, "do not 'survive,' they wait they listen they remain, as ancient and as modern as the morning star." The Middle Passage gods are both ancient and modern because they are the same as their African origins but also transformed. He proceeds to explain how his own work is "bitten bidden ridden by these gods," expressing "the feeling for the word, the song, the cadent vocable" and "the sense of contradiction: 'fragments/whole'" (8). To think of Brathwaite's description of fragments and wholeness as working against Greek symmetry is to see the potential for wholeness in the fragment that cannot be made whole again. As Colin Dayan tellingly observes, "No other poet has recognized so fully the power in fragments, the pull of detritus on the life of the spirit" (1994, 726). The power of fragments is evident in the poet's computer-generated style, which stitches together scraps and pieces of earlier poems, letters, and document in a manner that leaves their seams exposed. Brathwaite was filled with the sense of contradiction between word fragments and their cadence in song when he began experimenting on Doris's computer after her death. As his fingers moved across the letters on the keyboard of what was previously a cold and dead machine, he felt a silent and unseen spirit move him.

Brathwaite characterizes his computer-generated poetics as "writing in light," a phrase that alludes not only to the light of the computer screen but also to the vision the new form of writing provides since it enables him to bring visibility to the spoken word. "When I discover that the computer cd write in light," he explains, "I discovered a whole new way of SEEING things I was SAYING" (1994a, 378). Critics have followed suit by describing his poems as "visual noise caused by the graphics" (Torres-Saillant 1994, 701); a "performance on the page, an alternative to a taped reading" (Walmsley 1994, 749); "jazz texts" (S. Brown 1995, 134); a "secondary orality" (Rodriguez 1998, 126); and "voice made visible" (Reed 2014, 62). When asked whether he perceived a contradiction to accessing black vernacular culture through modern technology, Brathwaite responded by explaining that, unlike the typewriter, the computer is an extension of orature:[4] "The computer has moved us away from scripture into some other dimension which is 'writing in light.' It is really nearer to the oral tradition than the typewriter is. The typewriter is an extension of the pen. The computer is getting as close as you can to the spoken word—in fact it will eventually I think be activated by voice and it will be possible to sit in front of the computer and say your poem and have it seen" (Brathwaite 1989b, 87). Whereas Brathwaite's earlier formulation of orality turned its back on technology as a product of the European industrial machine he calls Prospero's Plantation, he now began to embrace the computer as a tool for delivering the same effect as speech. He even predicted the ability of a computer to convert speech into written text.

Brathwaite's description of the computer as connecting preliteracy to postliteracy bends what he calls the "missile logic" of a progress-driven modernity back upon itself to resemble the curved space and nonlinear temporalities of African cosmologies he likens to round objects such as pebbles and capsules. The missile stands for a Western modernity identified equally with its soaring buildings of gothic spires and skyscrapers as its projectile weapons of missiles and spears (Brathwaite 1985, 472–76). The circle represents not only the target on the backs of subjugated peoples but also the hole through which they "crashed into history" (476). The Haitian Revolution, as the first successful slave revolt that would inspire countless others across the Americas, constitutes one such disruption of the smooth passage of historicist time. Alluding to the hurtling of the Haitian Revolution into Western history, Brathwaite presents "space capsule" logic as the kernel of hope that widens like ripples formed by dropping a pebble in water: "From capsule core (*religion/nam*) the circles widen outwards/back: explode: : at times of crisis: : in response to dream or hope or vision" (1983, 39). The widening ripples allude to a related concept of tidalectics as tidal flows that go back and forth without synthesis, which Brathwaite offers as an alternative to the progress-driven narrative of a Hegelian dialectics. Silvio Torres-Saillant explains tidalectics as "a centripetal approach to the philosophy of history of the Caribbean" that addresses both hope

and catastrophe (2006, 241). Elizabeth DeLoughrey develops the endless motion of water between the African and Caribbean shores into "a
geopoetic model of history" for her study of "a dynamic and shifting
relationship between land and sea" (2007, 2–3). And Toni Pressley-Sanon uses Brathwaite's tidal metaphor as a frame for her study of Haitian
sacred memory by relating it to the "transition, transformation, and the
creative potential of chaos" of Legba, the Vodou *lwa* of the crossroads
(2017, 10).

My reason for focusing on the astrophysical metaphor of the rocket
ship and space capsule rather than the oceanic one of tidal flows has to
do with Brathwaite's description of capsule logic as a response to not
only hope but also *dreams and vision*, the immaterial forms of which
open the imagination to affects, temporal incongruities, and the limitless potential of virtuality. The space capsule contains the "atomic core"
of *nam*, which is etymologically an African word but also a spelling of
"man" backward, thereby representing for Brathwaite the human core
of slaves that Western humanism masks (1983, 36–39, 53). According
to his missile-and-capsule model, a rocket ship launched from West African shores and landed in the Americas, but it was not the end of the
journey because diasporic Africans traveled imaginatively "back across
the Atlantic in the other direction" (1994a, 50). Due to it expressing the
temporality of diasporic modernity, the curvature of capsule logic is not
simply a return to a precolonial African past. Brathwaite's merging of
science, technology, magical realism, and African cosmologies embraces
the sensibility of Afrofuturism, particularly through an allusion to the
Middle Passage as a futuristic alien abduction suggested by his comparison of slaves in the ship's hold to "the capsule powered by that rocket
of the slave trade" (1983, epigraph on title page).[5] The Afrofuturism of
his computer-generated poetics performs what he calls an "alter/native"
move by abducting a modern machine and transforming it into a gate-
way to Ginen, home of ancestral spirits but also the recently deceased.[6]

This chapter argues that behind the looming presence of Sycorax exists the shadowy figure of Doris, Brathwaite's recently deceased wife. It
is only when flesh turns to spirit that she ceases to exist as his muse, as
she did in life, and assumes the shape of a powerful woman who haunts
his imagination. Just as Brodber introduces black women's agency into
written and oral archives through the idea of Mammy's and Lowly's
voices appearing on a recording machine, I want to entertain the possibility of a once living woman as the spirit inhabiting Brathwaite's
writing machine. And, like Brodber's presentation of archive creation as

emerging from the joint effort of Ella and her husband, Reuben, I will argue that Doris provided a similar partnership that becomes legible to Brathwaite only after he suffers the loss of her life. My intention is to bring visibility to a woman's labor in the male poet's creative process, even though the poet himself understands this contribution in terms of the more traditional female role of muse. Brathwaite's alignment of the typewriter with writing and the computer with the spoken word erases the female-gendered space of his computer-generated poetics. This space, like the black female agency NourbeSe Philip characterizes as "dis place" (1997, 85), is one of silence and invisibility. Critical readings of Brathwaite's SVS only as a visualization of the voice overlook the female labor embedded in his new poetics. This is why, rather than treating his new style as an extension of orality, I maintain a separation of the two forms of poetic expression—the spoken word and a creative use of fonts. While Brathwaite appears to be in full control of his new computer writing style, the process by which he arrived at it was more labored, tentative, and even painful. I trace the development of his video style over the several works emerging from his Time of Salt—*X/ Self* (1987), *SHAR: Hurricane Poem* (1990), *The Zea Mexican Diary* (1993a), *Barabajan Poems* (1994a), and *DreamStories* (1994b)—in order to foreground the slow process of recovering his poetic voice. In the last of these works, *DreamStories*, Doris appears as a powerful female spirit who saves his archives from future destruction. This haunting points to a different kind of archive fever than the one Derrida identifies in Freud—less a desire to return to a moment of complete knowledge about the past than a movement toward a future of archival destruction and its re-creation in a different form.

My chapter reads along the jagged edges of Brathwaite's dreamstorie "Dream Chad" for a puncturing of, or, to use his words, crashing into, the dream sequence of Wilhelm Jensen's novel *Gradiva: A Pompeian Fantasy* (1902), which Freud turned into a modern parable and which Jacques Derrida deconstructs in *Archive Fever* ([1996] 1998). Each dream describes a monumental catastrophe: the volcanic eruption that destroyed the city of Pompeii in A.D. 79 and the hurricane that devastated Kingston in 1988. The archaeologist of *Gradiva* travels via a dream to ancient Pompeii to witness the creation of the stone record of a person who once lived—the footprint of a Roman virgin in volcanic ashes at the precise moment she and all of Pompeii are destroyed by the molten rock flow of Mount Vesuvius. Brathwaite's dream, on the other hand, is not a return to the past but the vision of an impending disaster. I derive from his dreamstorie a parable for the impermanence and precarious status of Caribbean archives, for which there is no return to the origin as there is in a story about an enduring archive of Western civilization: ancient Pompeii and its artifacts preserved in stone. I also establish an analogy between Brathwaite's and Derrida's incorporation of their scenes of writing into the story each recounts. Each wrote his account on an Apple computer within a year of each other and presents his writing process as a preamble to the narrative. Brathwaite completed his dreamstorie in Kingston in August 1993, while Derrida finished his meditation near Pompeii in June 1994. The two scenes of writing—a modern Jamaican city and ancient Roman one—point to a divergence in underlying assumptions about the archive at each site. Whereas the archival impulse in the metropolis is to discover the first and most original document, in the periphery it assumes the form of converting originals into their virtual forms. I characterize Brathwaite's new style of computer writing as a salvage poetics that figures the salvaging of Caribbean archives through digitization. If this final chapter is more focused on the life of the artist than the previous ones, it is only because Brathwaite weaves his vision of Caribbean history and culture into personal anecdotes, private memories, and the unconventional archive he calls his Library of Alexandria.

CONJURE-WOMAN AS ARCHIVIST

In naming his new poetic style after a character from *The Tempest*, Brathwaite draws on a Shakespearean imaginary of the supernatural as does Derrida in *Specters of Marx* (1994). However, in Caribbean literature, the North African witch, who was banished to a remote enchanted island, and her son Caliban, who was born there, are no longer the same characters because they have undergone the metamorphosis of creolization.[7] As Simon Gikandi explains in his study of the relationship of Caribbean literature to European modernism, creolization diverts European literary culture through African orality to create "a unique kind of Caribbean modernism" (1992, 16). We are by now familiar with Caribbean appropriations of *The Tempest* that occurred between the late fifties and early seventies when European colonialism was coming to an end. Rob Nixon concludes his study of these appropriations with the assessment that the value of *The Tempest* for African and Caribbean intellectuals declined with national independence, especially since there was no female counterpart to the rebellious male slave (1987, 576–77). Sycorax does not appear as a character in Shakespeare's *Tempest* or even in Aimé Césaire's rewriting of the play as *Une tempête* (1969), where she is identified with the native land. Caliban nonetheless continued to serve as a seditious and recalcitrant figure for Brathwaite, who embraces the beautifully poetic passages Shakespeare gave his savage slave while rejecting the mimicry of their imperfect iambic pentameter. In his manifesto on creolized speech as a language for poetic expression, he locates a uniquely Caribbean linguistic style in its lilt and rhythm through his famous statement that "the hurricane does not roar in pentameters" (1984, 10). As Brathwaite shifted from writing in Standard English to Nation Language, Caliban was transformed into "an anti-colonial/Third World symbol of cultural and linguistic revolt" (1987, 116n). In this way, he moved the slave off Prospero's Plantation and into a rebellious and runaway maroon culture, despite the character's origination in English literature. By naming his new poetic style after an African conjure-woman, Brathwaite sees himself accessing a language that even Prospero's rebellious slave does not have. Since Sycorax is Caliban's deceased African mother, she represents for him a buried mother tongue submerged within Afro-Caribbean spirituality. She appears in *Mother Poem* as a female-embodied knowledge of spell-making that "crumples words / into curses" (1977a, 41–51). When asked about Lamming's ([1960] 1992) claim that Caliban is trapped within the prison of Prospero's language, Brathwaite responded that "instead of Caliban revolting even against the language of Prospero he is really trying to hack his way back to the language of the forgotten, submerged mother, Sycorax" (Brathwaite 1991, 45). By naming the spirit inhabiting his computer Sycorax, Brathwaite is indicating that the machine has connected him to his lost mother tongue.

This critical move is nonetheless limited by the colonial exchange of *The Tempest*, provoking Sylvia Wynter to characterize the absent black woman as the "demonic ground" of Shakespeare's play due to her existing outside the frame of its narrative plot (1990, 361). Saunders similarly identifies postcolonial rewritings of Shakespeare's play as being locked into its dynamics even when attempting to escape them (Saunders 2001, 139). Within the wider context of Brathwaite's metaphor of linguistic creativity, Bev E. L. Brown (1985) is critical of what she calls a Brathwaitian manscape in which women figure the birthing of the male poet. Rhonda Cobham-Sander, by contrast, considers the female names Brathwaite assigns to language and his computers as expressions of "kinship and solidarity" with black women. She defends him against Brown's criticism by describing his depiction of man as creator and alienated subject and woman as mother and land as a "productive opposition" (2004, 205, 212n6). The feminist impulse of my chapter follows a different path of inquiry than these diverse positions by bringing greater visibility to Doris as Brathwaite's creative partner in life, the place of her death in the loss of his poetic voice, and the fragile and broken masculinity of his slow recovery to regaining it. Unlike the mythic presentation of Sycorax as a powerful woman representing a lost African heritage, the life of the real woman embedded in his poetics, like the small fishing sloop alongside the mythic proportions of the slave ship, tells a different kind of story.

Despite the linguistic mythopoesis that Brathwaite provides, his identification of a female spirit inside his computing machine has everything to do with Doris's strong attachment to her Kapro, a first-generation home computer that preceded the Apple Macintosh. She was responsible for typing his work into the machine and generating printouts for his review. Until Apple introduced its mouse technology as a navigation tool for clicking on icons to create documents and to access files, a writer had to know specific codes to activate the blinking cursor on the blank screen. Brathwaite, not knowing the codes, was unable to open his files. This private history reminds us of how a technology generally associated with men was more likely to be used by women in its early stages, particularly since word processing and data entry emerged from all-female typing pools (Abbate 2012; Machung 1988). Although Brathwaite has called Doris his muse, a woman who inspires but lacks creativity of her own, others speak highly of her literary and artistic talents, her presence as a center of energy at literary gatherings, and her partnership in his creative, publishing, and archiving enterprises (Walmsley 1992, 40). As Velma Pollard explains, "She was aware that he was special and had unique gifts that the Caribbean needed and was willing to support them at the expense of her own creativity which included a gift with art" (Velma Pollard, email interview by author, March 10, 2015). Brathwaite himself provides a glimpse of Doris Monica Brathwaite as the woman behind the muse in *The Zea Mexican Diary,* which includes extracts from the diary he kept during the months leading up to her death along with letters he wrote to his sister, Mary Morgan. The highly personal work is a raw expression of mixed emotions—grief, guilt, fear, shame, pain, remorse, and anger. Cobham-Sander describes the readerly experience of seeing the poet without the mask of his poetic personae as one of severe discomfort. "This mask is ripped off," she explains, "taking with it the first layer of skin on the public orator's face" (2004, 199). The grieving husband is remorseful for taking his wife for granted and guilt-ridden for his relationships with women he calls his "other muses" (1993a, 78). He writes to free himself of the belief that her cancer was sent as punishment for his neglect and infidelity.

Upon publishing his private journal after Doris's death, Brathwaite publicly recognized her contributions to his literary and archiving projects. *The Zea Mexican Diary* acknowledges the wider role she played in his professional life: typing his thesis, proofreading his poetry, arguing with him over its meaning, publishing *Savacou*, and "break[ing] into computers long before the current craze" (1993a, 191). In poetic memories of shared moments like "long crazy drives back from Accra on Nkrumah's new lonely highways when possessed by the red firefly eyes of *sasabonsam*" (73), he conveys her participation in the experiences that nourished his artistic vision. Brathwaite presents the portrait of a woman possessing her own creative energy: playing piano, painting, and helping him with the Caribbean Artists Movement (CAM), which was a London community of artists, writers, intellectuals, filmmakers, and musicians that existed between 1966 and 1972.[8] The artists' movement that would become instrumental in defining a Caribbean cultural identity began with informal meetings in their Bloomsbury basement flat. Being a meticulous archivist, Brathwaite insisted on tape-recording, transcribing, and publishing the proceedings of every meeting in bimonthly newsletters. Doris was responsible for transporting the large Akai reel-to-reel tape recorder on her motorcycle and operating the machine during the sessions. Together, they transcribed the tapes for publishing in the CAM newsletters. When the couple returned to Jamaica in 1968, she similarly assisted him in publishing the literary journal *Savacou* (Walmsley 1992, 89, 307–8).

Doris became a librarian out of a desire to catalogue Brathwaite's expansive literary and cultural archive but found the "vast and undisciplined" collection too unmanageable for one person to organize (Walmsley 1992, iii). Instead, she embarked on the smaller project of compiling a bibliography of his published prose and poetry. She continued to labor on this task until September 7, 1986, her sixtieth birthday, when her life was cut short but a few months after being diagnosed with an advanced stage of cancer. As she lay dying, Brathwaite took over the task of finishing the bibliography in the hope that it would prolong her life. For the first time, he experienced a role reversal in typing up her work, but he also noticed that it was still his work because the manuscript was about his literary life: "it was her work & therefore her life that I was dealing with esp since it was her life dealing with my life" (Brathwaite 1993a, 89). He records that he had just "dotted the last i of it that night—when she died—w/ the computer room in darkness" (90), which is a phrasing that suggests Doris and her computer lost their life forces at the same time.

Brathwaite first presents himself as writing his poems on a computer in *X/Self*, a collection published in 1987 and which he records as having "revisited" during the days immediately following Doris's death (1993a, 129). In the poem "X/Self's Xth Letters from the Thirteen Provinces," he announces he is writing "pun a computer" as if he "jine the mercantilists!" (1987, 80). He qualifies this declaration by proceeding to describe his theft of the master's tools as an act that reverses the "tief/ in" of slaves from Africa. And, he proceeds to describe the difference between a typewriter, which requires feeding paper between rollers and painting on liquid paper for corrections, and "this obeah blox," which "get a whole para / graph write up & / quick" (81). The poet's voice is one of awe and admiration for a technology to which he is being newly introduced. "Since when I kin / type?" he asks in the inquiring voice of one who is surprised at his newfound skill (82). By the end of the poem, he sees himself as Caliban "learnin prospero linguage & / ting" (84). His Sycorax Video Style is accompanied by what he calls Calibanisms—a breaking of language through erratic punctuation, idiosyncratic spelling, mixed fonts, wordplay, neologisms, and puns. Echoing the words Caliban famously hurls at Prospero, "You taught me language; and my profit on't/Is, I know how to curse" (Shakespeare 1611, 1.2.366–67), Brathwaite proclaims that "prospero get / curse / wid im own / curser" (1987, 85). The wordplay on cursing not only refers to Caliban's revolt against the English language but also the computer's cursor, which Brathwaite characterizes as a "tongue" enabling him to speak out against Prospero's plantation culture (127). He identifies the new voice as issuing from a "muse / in computer" that the reader presumes to be Sycorax since the letter is addressed to Caliban's mother (84). However, none of the poems in this collection are published in the layout of creative fonts and pictograms of his video style.

It was in "X/Self's Xth Letters from the Thirteen Provinces" that Brathwaite first used the phrase "writing in light" to describe the experience of seeing his words magically appear on a computer screen (1987, 87). The same poem reappears in *Middle Passages* (1992) and *Ances-*

tors (2001) in video style as "Letter Sycorax," which makes the original version of the poem prophetic of the style he would later attribute to Caliban's mother as the spirit inside his computer. Now laid out in dark, bold script, including large graphic *X*'s as the poet's signature scoring its pages, the new versions overwrite the earlier awe and smallness of the poet's voice with a visually dramatic speech form. Also missing from the new version are the last two lines of "X/Self's Xth Letters from the Thirteen Provinces," which ends on a questioning note of the inexplicable nature of the marvelous writing machine:

> *why is*
> *dat*
> *what it*
> *mean?* (1987, 87)

The lines from "The Dust," which first appeared in *Rights of Passage* (1968), echo the mystified voice of a peasant woman responding to the withering of her crops "without rhyme, without reason." A version of the same lines appears in the dedication of *X/Self* to Zea Mexican as an expression of bewilderment over the suddenness and swiftness of her death. As the first book of poems written after Doris's passing, *X/Self* introduces a more vulnerable Calibanesque voice, one that is in awe of a new technology and attempting to come to terms with loss. This fragile and inquiring male voice, which echoes a female voice from an earlier poem, recedes into the background as Brathwaite increasingly gains mastery over the computer.

The first poetic venture exhibiting Brathwaite's initial experimentation with SVS is *SHAR: Hurricane Poem* (1990), which he read at Harvard University just ten days after Hurricane Gilbert destroyed his Irish Town home. The poet's voice echoes the hurricane's roar through large bold-faced fonts that jump out at the reader. The word "sing," in particular, is repeated throughout, becoming larger and larger as if to suggest a crescendo, until the only words on a single page are the large bold-faced lowercase letters of "the song." As many critics have remarked, the poem transforms the storm's destructive energy into song (Torres-Saillant 1994, 700; Dayan 2001, 335–39; Reed 2014, 80–82; Deckard 2016, 29). *SHAR* is also an elegy since its title alludes to Brathwaite's niece, Sharon Marie Morgan Lake, who loved to sing. Since Sharon died in 1990, the first version of the poem, which he read at Harvard on September 22, 1988, could not have possibly been an elegy to her, although Doris also liked to sing. This earlier version consisted of only the first part, with an appendage of lines from "Vèvè," the penultimate poem of *The Arrivants*, describing Legba as the crippled *lwa* of the crossroads with his satchel of dreams (1989a). Brathwaite's sister reports that he revised the hurricane poem after the death of her daughter (M. Morgan 2001, 328), and the revision is confirmed in his dedication of *SHAR* "version September 1990" to his niece. The version he read at Harvard University does not exhibit his new video style, instead conveying the storm's fury through repetition, onomatopoeia, and the rhyme of language. In the third stanza, where a creative use of font is minimalized even in the 1990 published version, the roar of the hurricane is mimicked in the poem's stuttering rhythm and creative use of punctuation rather than fonts. This effect is achieved through a repetition of the words "what" and "winds" in order to re-create the whooshing sound of the 175-mile-per-hour winds. The poem shifts to the harsh tone of "stop" as the storm gathers strength, before ending in a swirling scream. The lines express the poet's bewilderment at the enormity of the destructive energy of the storm:

> **A**nd what. what . what . what more. what more can I tell you
> on this afternoon of electric bronze
> but that the winds. winds. winds. winds came straight on
> & that there was no step . no stop . there was no stopp.
> ing them & they began to reel . in circles . scream. ing like Ezekiel's wheel
> (Brathwaite 1990, I)

In this stanza, Brathwaite uses a bold font only for the first letter of the first line. By contrast, the poetic style of II is quite different as it illustrates his more extensive use of fonts for experimenting with a visualization of voice and sound. Written exclusively in video style, it poetically transforms the wind-whipped rain of the storm into rainbow and song. The poet had not yet arrived at this style when he read his poem in September 1988, because it was during his stay at Harvard that Sycorax revealed herself through an Apple Macintosh, to which he was being newly introduced.

SHIPWRECKED IN DREAMSPACE

"*DREAM CHAD* a 🍎 *story*" (1994b), takes the reader on a journey into the days preceding the hurricane, which is also a voyage into the future through an apocalyptic warning. Although the short piece is based on events that happened in Brathwaite's life, I read them through the experimental form of the dreamstorie, which weaves together myth, allegory, memories, and dreams in computer-generated typography. While citing from the dreamstorie, I make every effort to approximate its fonts as a way of conveying the textured textual meaning of its poetic style. The preamble addressed to the reader, which is as much a part of the story as the dreams, describes the bizarre occurrences affecting his composition of the dreamstorie at Harvard University in the summer of 1988.[9] It was such an unseasonably hot August day, Brathwaite reports, that the university was forced to close due to a heat wave for the first time in its history. He explains from the perspective of writing the preamble at a future location and time—Kingston, July 1993—that earlier drafts of his dream disappeared until the story taking over was the one "of Chad materializing out of that HEAT from tropical Jamaica into the summer of Harvard" (1994b, 48). Chad or Dream Chad, named after the Saharan oasis he identifies as "the soul / of the world" (1973, 105), is Beverley Reid, a Jamaican who is the new woman and muse in his life.[10] In the preamble, Brathwaite explains how he rented a Macintosh computer from student services at Harvard Yard to make a permanent record of his dream. It was his first experience with an Apple, as he had left his Eagle, an early personal computer like the Kapro, with Chad at his Irish Town home as an "emotional anchor or icon" (1994b, 48). He reports how, after finishing his dreamstorie on the Macintosh, each time he tried to save his work the writing would disappear, forcing him to reconstruct his words from memory. While the most logical explanation was that the machine had "malfunctioned" or was infected with a "virex or bug," it also seemed to the poet as if a "**spirit in the machine**" was preventing him from recording the dream. Calling the "loss of <txt" a "strange **decon-struction**," Brathwaite notices that whenever he attempts to reconstruct his words after they are erased, the new words he writes are not quite the same. "w/ each re/byte, as it were," he reports, "I must have been making subtle perhaps changes" (1994b, 48). He metaphorically extends the language of computer memory to his own memory for suggesting that both rememoration forms—electronic and human—constitute an impermanent and changing record.

Brathwaite interprets the actions of the spirit in the machine to mean that it wants him to write a "less ?dangerous—even perhaps less ?truthful version of event(s) that had in fact **not yet taken place(!)**" (1994b, 49). His suspicion is confirmed when a message flashes on the screen informing him that he could not continue writing the dream because "**SOME-BODY ELSE WAS USING IT**" (49). Brathwaite wonders whether his Eagle computer was "jealous because [he] was into a Ma(c)" (49). The "c" in parentheses indicates a feminization of the Apple machine as "Ma," which alludes to Sycorax as submerged mother. Brathwaite's attribution of emotions to the computer he calls an "obeah blox" indicates his development of an affective relationship with a machine that is connected to his memories of Doris. Although her physical body has been destroyed by the metastasis of cancer cells, the machine embodying her lifelong labor comes to life through its anthropomorphization in a language resembling the description of Ella's black box in Brodber's *Louisiana*. His recording of the story is deferred until he is able to obtain a second computer on which he is finally able to save the dream. A few days after Brathwaite's failed efforts to record his dreamstorie on the initial Apple computer, Hurricane Gilbert destroyed his Irish Town home. However, as he explains in the preamble, his old Eagle computer, with all of its stored files, was in a room that did not get crushed by the landslide. Seeing "the looting & fire of his dream be / coming instead the wind & water of the hurricane" (1994b, 49), he interprets its meaning as both a warning of the impending destruction of his library as well as its preservation. The spirit's refusal to archive the dreamstorie every time he pressed "save" prevented the total catastrophe he witnessed in his dream from becoming a reality. Brathwaite takes the warning to heart by reminding himself that even if his library was not completely destroyed, he could lose everything unless he finds a more permanent home for his archives:

> if I dont take care and get the archives out of there—as Yale (1991) had < so generously invited me to do (nobody in the Caribbean being, as far < as I can see, remotely interested or concerned)—that the story of this < Dream cd very well eventually come true (50)

Despite Brathwaite attributing the saving of his archives to Chad, the last "word" on the page, which appears after these lines, is a pixel drawing of a woman's profile (1994b, 50) (figure 4.1). It is the pictogram for Doris as Zea Mexican, alluding to her Amerindian heritage.[11]

New York Feb 93. the Stark version

Figure 4.1. From *The Zea
Mexican Diary* (1993a)

And so, the preamble ends with the sign of Zea, as the dreamstorie itself begins.

In the second beginning, Brathwaite describes himself walking across Harvard Yard with the blond-haired American Randy Birkenhead, who through dream condensation is also a homeless Bajan beggar called Horsehead Birken. Brathwaite compares Birken to "**BarbajanSpiders**" (1994b, 51), thereby alerting the reader to the presence of "Ananse, West African/Caribbean spider/god of tricks, stratagems, transformations, disputations, Nommo/The Word, and of 'fallen' creativity" (1987, 114). Like Ananse, a shape-shifter who is both spider and man, the time of the dreamstorie shifts between the temporalities of memory, dreaming, and writing. Its space is equally fluid, traveling between North America and the Caribbean, which at times become superimposed upon one other. The hot summer day in Cambridge appears in the dreamstorie as Jamaica's tropical heat drifting across the water to envelop the northern Atlantic city. Walking across Harvard Yard with its multitude of people, Brathwaite spies Chad in the distance. He tries to catch up with her, but she always stays a few paces ahead. Initially, he is able to single her out from the crowd by her white island cotton dress and her graceful posture and athletic stride, which he compares to "fierce AfricanAmerican panthers like Ashford or Slo-Joe or Florence Joyner-Kersee" (1994b, 54–55). A quick-paced step replaces her usual languid gait because she was "in this diff erent time in this stranger place where she nev er was out of place though as usual she was" (55). Brathwaite draws attention to the stone, statues, and "monarchic emblems" of Harvard's historic buildings that have never experienced a "destructive hurricane" as have buildings in the Caribbean (53). And he imagines a more modern building shaped like a ship with round windows resembling portholes as among those "ancient stone galleons on which she [Chad] might have arrived in this part of the dream" (59–60). The dream language invoking metaphoric implications of the Middle Passage reveals how that originary crossing haunts Brathwaite's poetic imagination. Even the beggar with his "slooped-over shoulder" who scoops up cans to crush with his foot appears "like e shipwreck" (61). At this stage of the dreamstorie, Brathwaite shifts to addressing himself in the third person as if to suggest that he too is shipwrecked and lost in dreamspace. Unable to see around the corner of his dream, he loses sight of Chad, who disappears into the time lag between his recollection/vision and its writing. When he is able to locate her once again, "she wasn't lookin at him anymore but at like a fly on fire alight/in a darken room" (1994b, 61). The small point of light in a darkened room resembles "the computer room in darkness" (1993a, 90) at the moment the light of Doris's life, like the computer's life light, was extinguished. The reference to the darkened room is followed by a picture of a door in the place of the letter "w" belonging to the short phrase "which is how it began in my dream" (61) (figure 4.2).

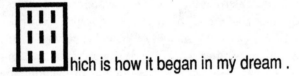

Figure 4.2. From "Dream Chad" (1994b)

The phrase denotes yet another beginning in the disjuncture between the time of the dream and its telling, and the weaving of different dreams into a single dreamstorie.

The door introducing the dream into the dreamtime memory is depicted as a stark black-and-white drawing of a rectangle containing nine short thick lines, which also represents the "dark front door" to Brathwaite's mind (1994b, 63). The line drawing invokes Vodou *vèvès*, which serve as the doors through which the *lwa* enter the human world, thereby suggesting the presence of a spirit inside him. In fact, Rohlehr invokes a Caribbean language of spirit possession for explaining Doris's presence in Brathwaite's dreamstorie, saying that, although "physically dead," she is "spiritually very much alive in Brathwaite's *ridden head*" (2007, 421; emphasis added). While walking alongside Birkenhead, Brathwaite feels a shooting pain emitting from the top of his skull, causing his eyes to appear "red & flickering & the pain how li-ke it curled up thru my hair" (62). His headache resembles "the silver spear that goes slowly from one side of the head and through to the other" (Brodber [1994] 1997, 105–6) that Ella experiences whenever a spirit rides her, allowing her to access past lives of which she has no memory or prior knowledge. The headache also brings to mind the "pain pressing down like a cap that fits to your skull and the back of your eyes" that Carolyn Steedman detects in the anxiety-ridden historian entrusted with deriving from the smallest morsel of archival information the lives of the forgotten and the dead (2002, 19). In Brathwaite's case, the anxiety concerns the loss of his personal archives that are also intimately bound up with the diasporic history informing his creative life.

The historian-poet's archive fever is both a malaise and its cure because in the third and final section, Zea Mexican appears as a powerful spirit woman who saves his library. Watching himself in the dream as if in a video, Brathwaite visualizes the shooting pain in his head as a "great leap of flame" (1994b, 62) emitting from the right side of his skull. Birkenhead, whose names shifts between Bajan/Birkenbridge and Bajan/Birkett, cannot see the flame because he is walking on Brathwaite's left side. Chad, seeing Brathwaite's flushed face, realizes that he is in distress. Inside his head, he and Chad are back at Bougainvillea, their Irish Town home with its bamboo railing. When Bajan/Birkett does notice his friend's suffering, the pace of the dream quickens "like he pressin the key on a VCRs **fast far. ward mode**" (63). Brathwaite's punning of the word "forward" as "far ward" transforms its linear temporality into a spatial movement that also alludes to the vast distance between Cambridge and Kingston being contracted. Birkenhead rushes toward him and, pushing open the door of his head, sees the fire and "flash of pain" within and people "like magnified ants" (64) running around ransacking the poet's brain, picking up things, grabbing them, and tossing them around.

Another time/space shift occurs as Chad calls out to Brathwaite in a loud voice, although he cannot hear her because this part of the dream unfolds in complete silence. He writes that "this dream wasn't makin no so und though she was callin out loud w/ that voice like a banjo or banshee or" (1994b, 64–65), breaking apart the word "sound" in the middle of an unfinished sentence. When her words do appear, they are visualized in the large bold-faced cursive script of SVS and express concern for the potential destruction of his computer along with its contents: "suppose the Eagle damage or gone or knock ova or bush & she cdnt get it re-pair" (figure 4.3). Here, the video style of the warning represents not the orality of the voice, as it does for the word "sing" when it reaches a crescendo in *SHAR*. Rather, it stages the power of silence due to there being no sound in this part of the dream. Chad appears to be channeling Zea Mexican since it is Doris who cherished her computer and who feared for its loss. Brathwaite recalls a letter Chad wrote to say how the Eagle had become his "constant comfort companion," words expressing her suspicion of his continued attachment to Doris because, he writes, she expected him to deny the relationship (68). Rohlehr describes Chad at this stage of the dreamstorie as being transformed into "a medium possessed by the urgent prophetic spirit of Zea Mexican" (2007, 421). Although the critic follows the poet in identifying Zea as his muse, despite her appearance as a powerful spirit, he nonetheless credits her with preventing the computer's destruction.

If in life Doris performed invisible labor for Brathwaite while serving as a source of inspiration for his poetry writing, in the dream she still remains hidden because she is unnamed, silent, and unseen. But her power has grown, allowing her to take over Chad's body to warn him of an impending disaster. A dream logic of association connects this scene to the final dream scene of

Figure 4.3. From "Dream Chad" (1994b)

Wide Sargasso Sea (1966).[12] In Jean Rhys's retelling of the story of the mad Creole woman of Charlotte Brontë's *Jane Eyre* (1847), Antoinette (Bertha Mason's name in Rhys's novel) jumps off the roof of Thornfield Hall toward her former slave and childhood friend Tia, as the Great House goes up in flames. She is attempting to escape from England, where her husband keeps her locked in the attic, by returning to her Jamaican home in Coulibri. The flame leaping from Brathwaite's head resembles Bertha Mason's streaming hair surrounded by flames, while Chad/Zea's shout becomes Antoinette's calling out for Tia (called Tina in the dreamstorie). Like Brathwaite's one-room house, Coulibri is on fire except that it is a Great House set aflame by newly emancipated slaves. In jumping toward Tia, Antoinette desires to return to a time before emancipation when they were still friends, but there is no return because her idyllic memory of plantation life belongs to, as Brathwaite explains in an earlier essay about Rhys's novel, "the carefully detailed exotic fantasy of the West Indies" (1974, 36).

In *Wide Sargasso Sea*, Antoinette Cosway/Bertha Mason awakens from her dream, knowing what she must do because her future has already been prophesied in *Jane Eyre*. In his dream, Brathwaite sees Chad/Zea jumping from Harvard Yard trying to reach "Bougainvillea/Coulibri" (1994b, 71), but Harvard Yard and Bougainvillea are now the same place, denoting his refusal to envision his home through the lens of colonial nostalgia. The Barbadian poet and Jamaican/Guyanese woman are shipwrecked and out of place in Harvard Yard with its stones, statues, and monarchic emblems, but so are they at their Irish Town home. The dreamstorie ends with Brathwaite ("this ole Bajan Man") standing alongside Chad/Zea, surrounded by mist and ashes, as she tries to prevent herself from voicing the destruction of their home:

> ...*& trying not*
> *to make her mouth shape shout*
> *out in the dream*
> *that this wasnt no dream*
> *where she was standing alone w/*
> *this ole Bajan Man in the mist &*
> *midst of the ash of the one*
> *one-room oneliest house she had*
> *never had in the Harvard Yaad >*
> *or anywhere else for that matt-*
> *er*
> (71–72)

The repetition of "one / one-room oneliest" for a house that did not exist in Harvard Yard or anywhere else indicates Brathwaite's sense of homelessness that follows him from place to place. It is no accident that Horsehead Birken is a homeless and itinerant man as he is a figure for Caribbean dispossession and even the poet himself. While Brathwaite tries to reassure Chad that what they are seeing is only a dream, she wants to tell him that the dream is real. However, the energy of her voice is directed into preventing her mouth from forming the words. Silence here does not represent a woman's voicelessness but her power to prevent an impending catastrophe because to utter those words, as Rohlehr (2007, 420–421) explains, would make it a reality, thereby transforming the warning into prophecy. Brathwaite's dream of his pursuit of an elusive woman that ends with the two of them surrounded by ashes resembles the dream that Freud analyzes in "Delusion and Dream in Jensen's *Gradiva*" (1907) and that Derrida deconstructs in *Archive Fever* ([1996] 1998). Despite these resemblances, the two dreams cannot be reconciled due to the asymmetrical histories of imperial centers and their colonies. Like my discussion of Derrida's *Specters of Marx* in the previous chapter, I foreground here the local rather than universal attributes of European literary works and their accompanying imaginaries that the French philosopher weaves into his theories of archival knowledge. In this chapter, I present Brathwaite's "Dream Chad" as a literary work from the periphery, one that provides an imaginary for the precarious status of Caribbean archives.

CONTENDING PARABLES OF THE ARKHĒ

Derrida's characterization of archive fever as a compulsion to find the commencement or beginning of things is based on the parallels he establishes between Freudian psychoanalysis and archaeology. He explains that Freud turned Wilhelm Jensen's novel *Gradiva: A Pompeian Fantasy* (1902) into an archaeological parable for how the psychiatrist can arrive at the past event responsible for a patient's psychological condition. The novel is also a parable for the historian's search for a document having the greatest proximity to the lives it records. *Gradiva* tells the story of an archaeologist, Norbert Hanold, who becomes obsessed with the woman depicted in an ancient bas-relief he sees in a Roman museum. Fascinated by the grace and agility of her gait, which gives the appearance of being captured midstride, he names her Gradiva, meaning "the woman who walks." The carving is the archaeological remains of what was once living flesh, and the movement suggested by the forward motion of her lifted foot, with only her toes making contact with the ground, indicates the living origins of inanimate stone. A feverish dream transports Hanold to ancient Pompeii at the exact moment of its destruction by the eruption of Mount Vesuvius, an event Derrida refers to as "the catastrophe of 79" ([1996] 1998, 85). The dead are brought back to life when Hanold spies the woman of the bas-relief walking ahead of him. He recognizes her by the languid swiftness of her gait but also loses sight of her amid the fiery grit and ashes raining down from the sky. He finds her again only to see her body become completely encased in hot ashes. The lasting impression of the dream makes Hanold feel as though he actually witnessed the destruction of Pompeii, and now he can only see the bas-relief as Gradiva's tomb. Since Freud had a plaster cast of the bas-relief alongside replicas of Florentine statues in his Vienna office, their shared passion for antiquities leads Derrida to call Freud a "lover of stone figurines" and a "brother to Hanold" (92, 83).

Derrida sees the psychiatrist as always trying to outdo the archaeologist in his ability to derive from a memory trace the imprint it has left on the psychic substrata of the unconscious. He understands Freud's fascination with archival stratification, as expressed in a letter to Wilhelm Fleiss, to prefigure his presentation of the mystic pad as a writing device for explaining memory work ([1996] 1998, 83n17).[13] While the tablet allows writing to be erased by separating the top layer from the one beneath it, the underlying wax slab contains the permanent marks of its impressions. This depth model allows Freud to explain the permanent archiving of a repressed memory on the unconscious even if at the surface level of consciousness it has been forgotten. Derrida explains Freud's desire to establish the permanent archiving of a repressed memory as being fueled by the death drive of its disappearance through forgetting (12). This is why he considers archive preservation to be in tension with archive destruction, memory with forgetting, which is a tension that permits him to derive a different kind of parable from Jensen's *Gradiva* than Freud's.

Derrida's *Archive Fever* is as layered a text as Brathwaite's "Dream Chad," consisting of the core section called "Theses" embedded within an "Exergue," preamble, foreword, and postscript, which is a narrative structure designed to imitate archaeological stratification. In the "Exergue," Derrida calls his book a "retrospective science fiction" in which he imagines the archiving machine to be a modern "machine tool" rather than a newly invented "child's toy" ([1996] 1998, 14–16). Like the preamble to "Dream Chad," where Brathwaite describes the process of writing his dreamstorie on an Apple computer, Derrida's preamble and postscript introduce the reader to his writing machine. The preamble presents us with an image of the philosopher "tinkling away" on his "little portable Macintosh . . . on a beautiful morning in California" (25), while the postscript shows him transported a few weeks later to the "rim of Vesuvius, right near Pompeii" (97), where he finished writing his lecture.[14] Derrida ponders whether Freud would have been able to derive the permanence of an ephemeral trace if computers, printers, faxes, and other late twentieth-century inventions had been available to him. Since the virtual writing that appears on a computer screen leaves no permanent impression, surface is indistinguishable from substrata. How then, Derrida inquires, does one determine the exact moment when computer writing is transformed into the permanency of an archive?

> Was it not at this very instant that, having written something or other on the screen, the letters remaining as if suspended and floating yet at the surface of a liquid element, I pushed a certain key to "save" a text undamaged, in a hard and lasting way, to protect marks from being erased, so as to ensure in this way salvation and *indemnity,* to stock, to accumulate, and, in what is at once the same thing and something else, to make the sentence available in this way for printing and for reprinting, for reproduction? (25–26)

The moment the virtual words and letters are saved onto the computer's hard drive, they achieve the permanency of an archival record. However, since this permanency allows endless reproduction through the ability to print and reprint what was typed, there is no material original; only copies.

Just as the mystic pad provides Freud with an archaeological model for moving from the surface trace to the substrata of repressed memories, the computer serves as a model for Derrida's description of the nonoriginary nature of the *arkhē*, the Greek root of archive meaning "beginning," "source," or "origin." The German archaeologist of *Gradiva* visits Pompeii to see if he can find the Roman virgin's footprint in the solidified volcanic ash, what Derrida calls "the uniqueness of the printer-printed" ([1996] 1998, 99). Yet, his ability to recognize the distinctive footprint resulting from her unique gait is based on having seen her walking in his dream. In other words, Hanold's access to the historical event and living woman is only through the immaterial form of a dream. Derrida characterizes the archive as holding within it the memory of *arkhē,* which refers to the beginning of things, the original, or first. But the archive is also not the *arkhē* because it is a record or, using Derrida's computer analogy, a copy or reprint of an event rather than the event itself. This is why, for the archive to be considered the same as the event, its secondary relationship to the *arkhē* has to be forgotten (2). Derrida's explanation of the nonoriginary status of historical events fueled the archival turn of historians, anthropologists, and literary critics who foregrounded the mediation of the past through the records in which they appear.

Social historian Carolyn Steedman expresses displeasure with theoretical abstractions and metaphoric treatments of the archive like Derrida's *Archive Fever* because they do not attend to physical archives or the labor of historians who use them (2002, 1–15).[15] And she is impatient with readers she calls "sad fetishists" (2), who presume the French philosopher is talking about archives when his lecture, written for the opening of new Freud archives in London, is about psychoanalysis. Steedman counters Derrida's abstract philosophy with what she playfully calls a Philosophy of Dust derived from physical archives, where nothing perishes or becomes waste because those records that disintegrate into shreds and end up in rubbish heaps are gathered by rag pickers to be made into new paper for subsequent documents (157–70). For her, "the impossibility of things disappearing" (163) is a metaphor for how the smallest speck of dust can lead to a larger story. For Derrida, the speck of dust belongs to the vanishing point of a past that is irretrievable, producing a condition of being "in need of archives" (*en mal d'archive,* which is closer to the book's French title) through the pursuit of an event or life at the moment of its disappearance ([1996] 1998, 91). Derrida's *Archive Fever* addresses the imaginary status of the archive, just as Steedman's response in *Dust* returns it to the material world of books, documents, and stately buildings.

As a story about Brathwaite's personal library that is also a parable for the constant threat to archives within the Caribbean region, "Dream Chad" traverses the boundaries of the archive's imaginary and material status. Whereas Hanold's dream transports him to the past to witness

the creation of an archive, Brathwaite's takes him to the future, where he
sees its impending destruction. The temporality of his dreamstorie does
not belong to the retrospection of history but to the futurity of warning
and prophecy, the objective of which is to incite action. And, instead
of existing only as an object of desire and figure for the elusiveness of
the *arkhē*, as does Gradiva, the woman in Brathwaite's dreamstorie has
the power to warn him in large graphic typography. Inasmuch as the
dreamstorie is prophetic, it approximates the messianic temporality of
Derrida's suggestion that the archive speaks to the future more than the
past through a "perhaps" in which its meaning will be known "in times
to come, later on or perhaps never" ([1996] 1998, 36). However, as
an expression of the prophetic time belonging to Afro-Creole religions,
the futurity of the promise in "Dream Chad" is presented in the more
radical move of a spirit preventing the liquid letters floating on the computer screen from being saved. For Brathwaite, the electronic streams
of what he calls "random-memory" do not lead to the computer's hard
drive but to Ginen, where the *lwa* and spirits of the recently deceased
reside. Instead of the spirit woman enabling his words to be transferred
to the computer's hard drive, she causes them to vanish through what
he calls "a strange deconstruction," which, unlike Derrida's use of the
term for undoing a metaphysics of presence, refers to the undoing of
writing in a "loss of < txt." But that does not mean that it is irretriev-
ably lost. As NourbeSe Philip explains about the sudden disappearance
of words that have been entered into a computer, "*When a text goes
missing in the computer, it is not completely lost—another language is
needed to translate the language of the 'missing' text so that it becomes
readable once again*" (1997, 83). For her, the missing computer text
is analogous to the silenced spaces in which black women have left
their marks. Unlike Jensen's story of Gradiva, where an event and its
imprint or record are perfectly matched, there exists a space between
the archive and event that necessitate "translation," which is the same
term Mammy King uses in *Louisiana* for her transformation from flesh
into spirit (Brodber ([1994] 1997, 42). The agency of black women in
"finding" a language for translating the missing text is undeniable. Her
agency exists in Brathwaite's dreamstorie, if only in virtual form. The
black female spirit's erasure of his writing does not mean that it is per-
manently lost, even if the exact words cannot be recovered. Since they
have not been saved, they change with each rewrite, or "re / byte" to
use his poetic pun, which transforms a space of loss into one of creation
(1994b, 48–49). Brathwaite sees the spirit as wanting him to write not a

more but *less* truthful version of an event that had not yet taken place, words that suggest a demand for his record not to approximate the original that was lost. Her invisible presence that causes a dematerialization of his words paradoxically preserves his material archives: the impending destruction of the archive cannot itself be archived because the spirit in the machine refuses to record the future. Brathwaite's library is a private collection that is not yet part of a public domain, and by virtue of that exclusion, its archival status exists in a future that may or may not arrive.

When Brathwaite watched Hurricane Gilbert make landfall in Jamaica on his television screen in his New York apartment, the video unfolded in silence as in his dream because the sound to the livestream had been muted. He describes how, as he saw the hurricane gather speed and build the force of its destructive energy, he became filled with a sense of helplessness:

> As soon as I saw that storm come up out of the sea just south of Puerto Rico, I knew this was it this was the dream this was the horror and there was nothing nothing nothing **nothing** I could do about it. [. . .] All I could do was watch that approaching terror without its sound on television and not reach anybody . . . And as far as I could see, nothing was being done to help that house that heart that home . . . Who cares about Irish Town? what after all is "Irish Town". . .?
>
> **'Irish Town' is one of the largest & most important archives of Cari bbean literature & culture in the Caribbean . . . It contains a record—since I keep almost everything— of many of our writers' progress (drafts unpublished manuscripts letters diaries artefacts books books books books thousands of miles of tapes LPs)—possibly one of the largest collections of Caribbean poetry in the world** (Brathwaite 1990, in Carolivia Herron, "Saving the Word," para 2–3)[16]

The question "Who cares about Irish Town?" expresses Brathwaite's frustration with the recognition that others may not share the same value he ascribes to his library. However, his answer to the open-ended question "What after all is 'Irish Town'. . .?" reveals the "impulse to collect" that David Scott identifies in other black memory historians, which is an impulse to create a counterarchive of Caribbean history and culture, to transform absence into "a domain of positivity, of pure materiality" (2008, v–vii). The creation of a domain of pure materiality is necessary for the enterprise of archive building, of gathering in one place the scattered pieces, and finding the resources to ensure they do not turn to dust. Brathwaite's is a Sisyphean effort to prevent a particular black memory archive from vanishing into oblivion due to an absence of institutional funding and government support.

By calling the collection his Library of Alexandria, Brathwaite alludes to not only the fabled grandeur of the ancient Egyptian archive but also the equally legendary enormity of its destruction. On later reflection, he describes the Irish Town library in more modest terms as one of those "personal, even somewhat idiosyncratic collections, which, unlike official collections, have the value & virtue of this very personal element" (1999, 299). As a private collection, the holdings have not undergone the critical eye of an archivist who painstakingly goes through materials, classifying and cataloguing its contents, in order to decide which portion to preserve and which to place in storage or even discard. Brathwaite's library was too unmanageable even for Doris to catalogue, as it contained thousands of notebooks, books, magazines, clippings, pamphlets, letters, manuscripts, photos, records, spools of films and sound recordings, art, and musical instruments. It consists of the heterogeneous materials of raw archives as they exist outside of libraries, repositories, and special collections, although I have sifted through boxes of unsorted and uncatalogued materials at a few National Libraries in the Caribbean. Following a large SVS banner of the word "HELP," place/date-stamped as "Mona 20 June 1989," Brathwaite's *ConVERSations* provides a brief inventory of the sound recordings dating back to 1960 of poetry readings, live music, sacred rituals, radio broadcasts, conversations, and all of the CAM meetings (1999, 298–301). It is possible to argue that the collection is important to Brathwaite only because it represents one man's poetic and cultural journey, including his personalized relationship to African and Caribbean cultures. But one can equally turn that statement around and say that one man's journey is important to African diasporic memory due to his central role in the formation of a Caribbean cultural identity. I have already mentioned Brathwaite's cofounding of CAM and his manifestos on Caribbean poetics, including sound poetry. Doris's bibliography of his books of poems, literary criticism, writings on history and aesthetics, and recordings between 1950 and 1982 is 140 pages long, while Gikandi reminds us that he "has written more on creolization than any other Caribbean historian" (1992, 17).[17]

Brathwaite's approach to creolization has come under criticism for its treatment of the cultures of Asians and Amerindians as raw materials for Afro-Caribbean writers and artists rather than creolized creative expressions in their own right. His dualist perspective of creolization as primarily a mixing of European and African elements overlooks the greater heterogeneity of Caribbean peoples, particularly indentured workers who were transported from India and China (Nair 2000, 237–42; Puri 2004, 62–66). As early as 1967, Kenneth Ramchand expressed in a letter that Brathwaite read aloud at a CAM meeting his disappointment in the movement's attention to "the African presence" but not his own Indian ancestry, an ignoring that he described as "deliberate and reasoned" (Walmsley 1992, 53–54). A dualistic and unidirectional model of cultural creolization is also present in Brathwaite's incorporation of pre-Columbian glyphs and stone carvings into his SVS. Linda Lizut Helstern (2000) identifies the resemblances between SVS symbols and Mesoamerican glyphs, while Brathwaite himself acknowledges that he is accessing Egyptian, Mayan, and Aztec hieroglyphs as well as the Warao *timehri* of Guyana (1999, 167). Critics like Jodi Byrd (2011, 92) and Shona Jackson (2012, 48–51) see in such assertions of "primordial" connections between Africans and Amerindians an ignoring of historical and cultural differences, thereby allowing Afro-Caribbeans to claim indigeneity for themselves. Rather than positing Brathwaite's private collection as an archive of *all* Caribbean culture, then, I understand its value as residing in its recording of African diaspora culture and cosmologies that he has so painstakingly documented.

The current condition of Brathwaite's library is difficult to determine. He has written about his failed effort to access the funds that had been raised in the United States for retrieving and recovering what was left from his destroyed Irish Town home or to have the library moved to the University of the West Indies at Mona (1999, 147–51). He further reports that his collection was not the only one damaged by Hurricane Gilbert. Poets Lorna Goodison and Louise Bennett Coverley lost portions of their manuscript collections, as did the novelist John Hearne, whose papers included letters from Ernest Hemingway (Brathwaite 1999, 306–7). A Jamaican government archivist explains that the hurricane was not only the worst the island had ever experienced but also a forerunner to future megahurricanes resulting from climate change. Moreover, the common salvage procedures available in some other parts of the world, of freezing waterlogged materials and vacuum drying them, could not be undertaken to save even official Jamaican archives due to extended power outages after the storm (Aarons 2005). In 2005, Brathwaite reported that thousands of photos and reels of 16mm film he took in Ghana were lost to "fungus, work and water" as they languished unrestored. What was left of his collection was placed in boxes, which in the absence of climate-controlled storage facilities, were invaded by termites (Brathwaite 2005d).

SALVAGING CARIBBEAN ARCHIVES

Barabajan Poems: 1492–1992, which appeared the same year as *DreamStories,* can be read as Brathwaite's effort to salvage the fragments of his destroyed self and ruined archives by converting them into digital form. The large volume is a disjointed and perplexing work that begins as a 1987 lecture he gave at the invitation of the governor of the Central Bank of Barbados. The book's title references the Columbus Quincentenary, which makes it a sort of history book— or perhaps the inverse of a history book through its references to the dismal archiving practices of the Barbadian government. Brathwaite poetically laments the decrepit condition of the National Archives that were "allow(ed) the pox & pot & rat & warm & damp & rat & rot & sworms of our **neglect neglect neglect** to ravage & destroy these things because(se) we didn know the value of them" (1994a, 161). Since he was obliged to self-publish the volume, its 8½-x-11-inch letter-size paper permitted him to display his computer-generated layout to fullest visual effect with bold type, small type, italics, and pictures, right-justified margins, text boxes, and margins drawn on the left or right or left and right sides of the page. Some of the pages, with their apparently unrelated snippets of texts of different font sizes and styles and accompanying graphic images, invite the reader to see them as picture puzzles. However, Cobham-Sander considers the book more as a metaphor for archive building, calling the large volume "a plastic artifact that enacts the process of creating an archive through its innovative form" (2004, 300). This experimental archival form is not exclusive to *Barabajan Poems.* Due to Brathwaite's inclusion of small pieces of different cultural artifacts, including "newspaper clippings and letters, anecdotes, essays" in a subsequent book of poems, *Born to Slow Horses* (2005), Joyelle McSweeney observes that "the archive itself is almost becoming a poetic form" (Brathwaite 2005c, 7). To rephrase her words, I would say that Brathwaite has made the digital *salvaging* of archival materials into a poetic form through his incorporation of scraps and archival remains into his video style.

Brathwaite's predicament is symptomatic of the vulnerability of Caribbean archives even beyond his personal collection, as libraries and archives are at risk of damage due not only to natural disasters like hurricanes and earthquakes but also to the manmade ones of understaffing, underfunding, and neglect. The discrepancy between salvage procedures available in Jamaica and metropolitan centers is captured by Brathwaite's punning of the "savage" implicit in Caliban's name (an anagram for "cannibal") as "salvage" (1994a, 188), which is a term he uses for referring to the precariousness of Caribbean lives, livelihoods, and land.[18] As Guyanese media artist Roshini Kempadoo observes, "Researching material *in* the Caribbean recognises the distinction between material retained and conserved in Britain and other imperial metropolitan centres and the *residual* material left in the postcolony" (2016, 4). Her characterization of Caribbean archives as "residual material" points to a splitting of "the archive" itself. Caribbean National Archives are not always housed in the stately buildings Mbembe characterizes as belonging to the archive's architectural design. After Hurricane Ivan struck Grenada in 2004, the building for its national archives was rendered unusable. Its roof was so severely damaged that water flooded inside, causing its manuscript collections to become waterlogged. Ten years later, it was reported online that a new building had not been found and the archives were deteriorating: "We have no building and the ancient documents we do have left are suffering heavily from rot, mould and other damage from poor treatment" (Bdosparks 2014). In what amounts to an online plea resembling Brathwaite's video style banner of "HELP," this commentator provides a list of other national archives—Barbados, the British Virgin Islands, Guadeloupe, Haiti, Jamaica, Saint Vincent and the Grenadines, Saint Kitts, Saint Lucia, and Trinidad—that are also in need of assistance. And the neglect, in many instances, has been for a much longer period than the recent past. Documents pertaining to the early settlement of the colonies have been particularly vulnerable. The high humidity of the Caribbean and improper storage facilities have left them exposed to the attack of fungus, worms, termites, and rodents. The Turks and Caicos National Museum reports that its archives have suffered from the islands' lack of a central government dating back to the time of its early colonial days. When museum staff inventoried its holdings in 1983, they discovered that most of the early records had been damaged beyond recovery. However, the museum has been able to save more than fifty thousand of the documents and is in the process of digitizing them through the British Library's program to save endangered libraries, which was started in 2004.

One of the few hopes for rescuing Caribbean archives is digitization, and several initiatives funded by the British Library's Endangered Archive Programme (EAP) have already been undertaken. Yet, the objective of the grant-oriented program is to save archival materials from the premodern period, which not only shows a preference for antiquities but also necessarily excludes a black cultural archive like Brathwaite's. Even in the instance of records pertaining to the early colonial period of the islands, the EAP favors archival access and preservation over conservation. As the cofounders of the funding agency explain, "We chose digitisation because it preserves the content of the archives, even if the physical materials may disappear in the future" (Rausing and Baldwin 2015, xxxvii). Should the manuscripts continue to undergo rot, ruin, and decomposition or, to use Brathwaite's words, "fungus, work and water" (2005d), they can at least survive in virtual form. Digitized copies serve as a means of saving the archives if not the documents themselves, which with imminent deterioration could crumble beyond recognition. Although lacking the tactile quality of the originals, the high-resolution reproductions perhaps constitute an even more perfect and democratic form. A researcher can zoom in, print, or save digitized documents to a hard drive, while a searchable online catalogue makes them globally available. The archive is no longer the sacred destination of a chosen few who have the funds to travel great distances to access them. One can argue conversely that a loss of materiality is accompanied by a loss of aura in the sense that virtual records lack the tangible quality of documents that were created in past times and touched by the hands of people long dead. Historian Natalie Zemon Davis describes the loss a researcher experiences in using digitized copies of archival records as "the loss of the object itself, of the marginal notations missed by the camera, the signatures cut off, the paper not available to the touch, the bindings unseen" (2013, xvi). The desire for personal encounters with physical archives is understandable because it represents the lure of the *arkhē* of which Derrida speaks ([1996] 1998, 2). But it is equally important to recognize that this lure is not always fulfilled in the Caribbean, where images can—and do—serve in the place of physical archives. While heroic in its own way, the salvaging of endangered archives through digitization involves the conversion of material archives into an immaterial form.

The restoration of Caribbean archives takes documents farther away from the *arkhē*, unlike the archival impulse in metropolitan centers, where the future holds the promise of bringing documents closer to their origins. As chapter 1 demonstrates, what we know about the

Zong massacre relies heavily on the testimony of the ship's first mate, James Kelsall. However, until Martin Dockray found the original transcript of Kelsall's sworn statement in the Court of Exchequer, the primary document was the authentic copy Granville Sharp acquired and classified as Voucher No. 1. Dockray's discovery revealed that the first mate's sworn statement was prepared for separate proceedings in the Court of Exchequer. The existence of the new document makes evident that Kelsall did not testify at the more famous trial, even though historical accounts make it appear as if he did due to the statement being presented as evidence (Oldham 2007, 316–17). The impulse for seeking out originals is not limited to historians. Literary scholar Michelle Faubert (2017) reports that her recent discovery of Sharp's letter to the Lords Commissioners of the Admiralty at the British Museum makes the document at the National Maritime Museum an "extant copy." What role do discoveries of this kind play in our perception of material archives, especially when considered alongside archives in those parts of the world where preservation is equated with transforming originals into digital copies?

The recent unearthing of the official printed version of Haiti's Declaration of Independence in the most unexpected of places demonstrates the necessity for a transatlantic perspective on the power and status of the archive. Haiti does not possess the official printed document of its 1804 Declaration of Independence but only hand-transcribed or newspaper print versions. Until 2010, historians who have searched for the original presumed all to have been destroyed, but that turned out not to have been the case. While conducting research for her dissertation, Julia Gaffield (2014) decided to take an Atlantic World approach by visiting the archives of seven countries instead of immersing herself in a single linguistic or national archive. She explains how a letter in a box of documents at the National Library of Jamaica in Kingston took her to the National Archives of the United Kingdom (TNA) in London, where she found a packet of Haitian documents that Governor Nugent had sent to his home government. Among them was an official printed version of the very piece of paper that was believed not to exist. Her trans-island and transcontinental approach, one that did not adhere to the linguistic boundaries of colonial cartographies, led her to the eight-page Declaration of Independence that had been printed by the newly formed Republic of Haiti. Since her discovery was made but a few weeks after the 2010 earthquake that severely damaged the Archives Nationales d'Haiti and its heritage libraries, the news was received as all the more fortuitous. A year later she found a second copy of the Declaration that was stored in the most unlikely of places due to it being catalogued as a map. Not only was the broadside print, made for public posting, stored with maps and plans in TNA, but also there was no mention of it originating in Haiti. Gaffield describes the circuitous paths to finding both documents as a sign of "the complex and integrated place that Haiti occupied in the Atlantic World in the nineteenth century" (2014). Her discoveries demonstrate that the archive as object and not only as source can equally be a commentary on lost pasts. Since both documents were lost inside a European archive, archival loss indicates not only an absence of records but also their invisible presence.

The invisibility of documents within the archive speaks to the subject of this book for which the term "immaterial archives" refers to the narratives and codes informing our perception and reception of archival materials. The classification of documents resulting in the belief that they had been irrevocably lost is an outcome of Haiti's marginalization in cataloguing practices inherited from colonialism. Gaffield's find perhaps proves Steedman's point that nothing is lost in the archives (2002, 157–70). That might have been the case had Steedman not opened her book with a small footnote mentioning how the Spanish conquistadores burned an entire Aztec archive with the exception of three Maya manuscripts and fifteen Aztec texts (xi n1). Consigned to the margins as an aside, the note points to the uneven distribution of archival loss across the globe and a heterogeneity to the forms that loss takes. A digitized image of the Haitian Declaration of Independence is now available online, while the original at TNA has been removed from circulation in order to preserve it. Unlike Americans who can view their Declaration of Independence on display at the National Archives in Washington, D.C., Haitians will be able to see their original Declaration only in its digital form, even if they have the means to make the long journey across the Atlantic to London.

The compulsiveness with which Brathwaite has worked and reworked his earlier poems in SVS is fueled by a desire to bring permanence to his poetic legacy in the face of its destruction. This is the Caribbean historian-poet's archive fever. Just as archiving is an ongoing process, so is archival destruction in countries where national governments do not have the resources or inclination to protect them. Brathwaite alludes to the government of Barbados ignoring its literary heritage through a declaration in uppercase, dancing Calibanesque letters that "we is also the only maj-or literature-producing Caribbean territory with out a national anthology of any sort to its nature" (1994a, 120). The adversarial role of the government to its national literature was played out in his efforts to bring the "shattered" Irish Town library together with the "scatta archives" of his New York apartment to a new location on his home ground (Brathwaite 2005b, 3). In 1996, Brathwaite purchased a parcel of rural land on the outskirts of Bridgetown, which he named CowPastor in reference to its pastoral terrain but also the Pastor who helped him locate it. A few miles south of the Newton Plantation, which is known for having the only surviving slave cemetery in Barbados, CowPastor is believed by Brathwaite to have once belonged to "that complex of early southern Bajan plantations" (2004b, 161). He hoped to realize his dream of finding a permanent home for his archives in addition to building a cultural center with a conference room, performance spaces, and living quarters for writers and artists, only to come up against a series of obstacles. He was initially informed that he could not build on the land due it being in the flight path of airplanes. He was subsequently notified that the land was being claimed as the site of a new road for the airport's expansion with the objective of increasing tourism. When he and his neighbors organized against their impending eviction, they were accused of squatting on the land (Brathwaite 2005a). Brathwaite responded with the declaration that tourism was unlawfully occupying his poetic imagination:

Hotels are Squatting on my Metaphors

All the places where I use(d) to write my poetry in Barbados from (see **BarabajanPoems** <1994> are gone. replace(d) by hotels & ocean-side apartments & enclave- (a) villas" (2004b, 151)

This paving over of poetic sites with tourist dwellings makes evident the struggle for memory between an industry that extends colonial nostalgia for plantation culture into the present and creative works that offer counterimaginaries.

In March 2005, tractors were brought to raze the bushes and trees on Brathwaite's property, including a bearded fig tree after which the island was named. When he describes the choking experience of inhaling the dust stirred up by the tractors, he is alluding to how he is being forced swallow the particles of his crushed dream (Brathwaite 2005b, 1–3). The sickness he suffers from the ruin of his land resembles the occupational hazard Steedman identifies as belonging to historians who inhaled the poisonous dust released by the leather, parchment, and vellum of old manuscripts (2002, 19–29). In Brathwaite's case, the dust he inhales belongs to the destruction of the physical space for his archives, which themselves are in a state of decay. While attempting to preserve a photographic memory of CowPastor before it was razed, Brathwaite was confronted with the inexplicable appearance of a black woman's face in the photograph Beverley took of a spider with her old Kodak camera, which, like the recording machine in *Louisiana,* resembles a black box or even the "obeah blox" of his Apple computer. And, like Ella's black box that records a conversation between two women who are deceased, a segment of the spool of film on the Kodak camera displayed an unexpected female face: "from this box we get this pic. ture. not of spiders spiderwebs. but this. the one shot out of a whole wide roll of blacks & blanks of flim. **this Nam-setoura**" (2004b, 168). Brathwaite identifies Namsetoura as a slave woman who informs him that they are standing on the sacred land of a slave burial ground, which is information he uses to request that the property be declared a national historical site. The furious spirit also tells him she has lingered at the spot for three hundred years due to the absence of having received appropriate burial rites and that she views even him as an intruder (Brathwaite 2005c, 3). In view of the "Nam" in her name, which alludes to an ancestral African spirit, Namsetoura appears to be an avatar of Sycorax. In explaining the Namsetoura period of Brathwaite's life, Anthony Carrigan describes how the slave woman's appearance "drives him to the archives, to historical resources, stories, and imaginative reconstructions in order to 'develop' a fuller understanding of CowPastor which he then self-reflexively refashions as aesthetic artefact" (2011, 85). In other words, the appearance of Namsetoura fuels a poetics in which "the imaginary" comingles with "the historical."

Brathwaite's ongoing battle over his archives continues to fuel his writing. In the poem called "**meʃon (2),**" belonging to his more recent collection *Strange Fruit,* he compares the undoing of the work he put into assembling his library to the theft of the labor of Africans who were brought over as slaves (2016, 39). The sense of violation, loss, and homelessness does not go away, despite the almost two hundred years since Britain ended slavery in its West Indian colonies. June Roberts describes Brathwaite as belonging to a group of male writers "who seem never to move beyond the quandary of physical and metaphysical catastrophe" (2006, 59). This may be the case in the poet-historian's constant return to the loss of his archives and artifacts, which is an activity that belongs to what David Eng and David Kazanjian (2003) would describe as the creative impulse of melancholia—but only if we make Brathwaite's action conform to a Freudian model. Instead, I would like to consider his poetic enterprise in terms of the philosophy of writing oneself out of catastrophe that he himself provides. "One thing about catastrophe, for me," explains Brathwaite, "is that it always seems to lead to a kind of magical realism. That moment of utter disaster, the very moment when it seems almost hopeless, too difficult to proceed, you begin to glimpse a kind of radiance on the other end of the maelstrom" (2005c, 2). The radiance of magical realism—whether the Sycorax of his Apple computer or the Namsetoura of Beverley's Kodak camera—belongs to the futurity of the Caribbean poet's "perhaps," which diverges from a Derridean vision of the "perhaps never." While the title of the poem, "**me/on (2),**" alludes to the bleakness that accompanies a catastrophe, Brathwaite's two volumes on magical realism, *MR,* open with an explanation of the transformation of meson into the new vision of mesong: "we begin by locating where the BLACK HOLES in the CLOSED (PROSPEREAN) SYSTEM are and GO THRU THERE . . . INTO ALL (NEW) KINDS OF ENVISIONING/REVISIONING" (2002, 1:39). Just as the poet is forced to rewrite his dreamstorie through "subtle perhaps changes" (1994b, 48) whenever the spirit in the machine causes his writing to disappear, archival loss necessitates the intensive labor of confronting black holes each time with a new vision or perspective.

The radiance of a book of poems that opens with two blurry photographs of racial violence—one close up—from the not too distant past (Brathwaite 2016, 17, 25) is almost as imperceptible as the sonic difference between "meson" and "mesong" is inaudible. The two pictures, the first in a series of visual archives included in *Strange Fruit,* show the inert bodies of Laura Nelson and her teenage son, Lawrence, hanging from a suspension bridge over a river—victims of a 1911 Oklahoma lynching. The curious white onlookers assembled on the bridge pose with the hanging bodies for the photographer, who, standing in the distance, is removed from the brutality of the event he is recording. Although Brathwaite opens the poetry book with a scene of violence that was turned into postcards to be passed from hand to hand as obscene souvenirs, he follows them with a different set of photographs—sparrows outside his CowPastor window (54, 56), young Bajan girls whose corn-rowed hair has been lovingly braided by their mothers (75), the Mandelas with their raised fists clenched high in the air (81), and the backs of two scantily clad Bajan women holding each other's waist in a casual embrace at the Kadooment Crop Over Parade (113). The accompanying text to the Crop Over Parade pictures describes the women's "joy & doan-care caring" in turning their exposed buttocks to the camera's "stare" (112). The jubilant dancing belonging to Caribbean masquerades, despite their recent tourist commodification, represents for Brathwaite not only a history of self-expression but also turning one's back on the camera's transformation of black bodies into spectacles for the white gaze.[19]

While Brathwaite's conversion of meson into mesong may be as indiscernible as the presence of Doris in "Dream Chad," it does not mean that, like the immaterial archives this book has been tracing, it is not there. His dreams for CowPastor still exist, even if the cultural center and library have not materialized. As Philip (2005) expresses in an open letter to him, "Cow Pastor appears to point to a daring to dream, a willingness to imagine other possibilities or ways of being where we can be in active contact with all that has contributed to our terroir and terror."[20] Her own conversion of the traumatic loss of *Zong* into *Song* sonically resonates with Brathwaite's transformation of *meson* into *mesong*. In the Caribbean art and literature of this study, the past does matter because the legacies of slavery remain. Yet the works not only allude to a past that did happen or might have happened but also introduce into material archives the astonishing potentialities of affects, dreams, and visions. They offer more contradictory and paradoxical relationships of the present to the past: a language in silence, the light and airy world of an island under the sea, word holes through which spirits communicate, the saving of physical archives through a dematerialization of words, and the imaginings of futures that may exist only as a "perhaps" but without which there would be no beyond to tomorrow's horizon.

AFTERLIFE

I felt a presence on that land, Kamau. It had a patient, serene, windswept quality to it. As if it was waiting for something. I saw the pond, or what is left it, the lone bearded fig-tree. It did feel magical. Was it my imagination . . . ? – (And) if it was my imagination – all the better. For that is what we will need to do – imagine worlds that defy the. . . nightmare that presently holds the world hostage

Brathwaite, "**Baptism Poem**" (2017)

Notes

INTRODUCTION

1. For an account of the archival, oral, and written stories about Nanny, see my *Ghosts of Slavery* (Sharpe 2003, 1–43).

2. While a complete list is too long to provide, the scholars whose work have informed my study include Foucault (1972), Certeau (1988), Derrida (1994, [1996] 1998), Dayan (1995), Trouillot (1995), Roach (1996), Chakrabarty (2000), W. Brown (2001), Mbembe (2002), Steedman (2002), Taylor (2003), Baucom (2005), Wynter (2013), Hartman (1997, 2007, 2008), Scott (2008), Arondekar (2009), V. Brown (2009), Stoler (2009), Helton et al. (2015), Lowe (2015), and Best (2018).

3. The book's chapter "On Failing to Make the Past Present" first appeared as an essay in *Modern Language Quarterly* in 2012. For responses to Best's argument, see Fleissner (2013), Goyal (2014), Helton et al. (2015), and Warren (2016). For a criticism of the melancholic historicism of queer studies, see Arondekar (2015). Also relevant to Best's argument is Wendy Brown's explanation of Benjamin's identification of a "left melancholia" as occurring when "attachment to the object of one's sorrowful loss supersedes the desire to recover from this loss, to live free of it in the present, to be unburdened by it" (2001, 169).

4. While Derrida's and Morrison's figurations of spectrality are not quite the same, they have become conjoined in recent years (Baucom 2005; Weber 2005; J. Miller 2007; A. Gordon 2008, 183–84).

5. Clark explains that she is building on the black vernacular models for literary theory initiated by Houston Baker and Henry Louis Gates Jr. (1991, 59n17).

6. Clark notices that Milo Rigaud's collecting of the sacred signs of the *Marasa Trois* has not received the scholarly attention it deserves due to "his eccentric approaches [being] devalued in the wider field of cultural criticism at the time" (1991, 59n24).

CHAPTER 1

1. The term "neo–slave narratives" was first used by Bernard Bell (1987) and formalized as a genre by Ashraf H. A. Rushdy, who describes the literary work as "both a site for historical recovery and a space for intervening in the cultural debates of the post–civil rights era" (1999, 180). Arlene Keizer (2004) explains that she prefers the term "contemporary narratives of slavery" so as to broaden the scope of the slave narrative's historical form. For an overview of scholarship on the neo–slave narrative, see Valerie Smith (2007).

2. John Weskett's *A Complete Digest of the Theory, Laws, and Practice of Insurance,* published two years before the *Zong* case, explains the determination of insurance liability in this way: "The insurer takes upon himself the risk of the loss, capture, and death of slaves, or any other unavoidable accident to them: but natural death is always understood to be excepted:—by natural death is meant, not only when it happens by disease or sickness, but also when the captive destroys himself through despair, which often happens: but when slaves are killed, or thrown into the sea in order to quell an insurrection on their part, then the insurers must answer" (qtd. in Oldham 2007, 303). Saidiya V. Hartman's explanation of this insurance law is that the death of slaves classified as commodities exists as "a variant of spoilage" like the loss incurred in "rotten fruit" (2007, 148).

3. Equiano would not publish his slave narrative, *The Interesting Narrative of the Life of Olaudah Equiano, or Gustavus Vassa, the African,* until six years later.

4. For a more detailed discussion of the specularity of antislavery sympathy, see my *Ghosts of Slavery* (2003, 79–81).

5. The only detailed description of a Middle Passage experience appears in Equiano's 1789 slave narrative. In his survey of the fifteen autobiographical accounts of the Middle Passage that he was able to find, Jerome S. Handler (2002) concludes that the lack of details has to do with whether white transcribers who were not abolitionists would have asked the right questions, which is an observation pointing to the highly mediated status of slave testimonies.

6. Gilroy describes Ruskin's sale of Turner's *Slave Ship* to an American buyer as emblematic of "the Atlantic as a system of cultural exchanges" that his *Black Atlantic* charts (1993, 14). The painting is currently in the permanent collection of the Boston Museum of Fine Arts, where I viewed it.

7. The ship was a traditional Baltic trader that had been converted to a tall ship for TV and film productions, including the biopic of the antislavery movement *Amazing Grace,* which was released the year of the Bicentenary.

8. While Philip's poem is not a countermonument of the sort Young describes, Paul Ricoeur reminds us that "archives were for a long time designated by the term 'monument'" (2006, 68).

9. "As long as language is considered as a system in equilibrium, the disjunctions are necessarily exclusive (we do not say 'passion,' 'ration,' 'nation' at the same time, but must choose between them), and the connections, progressive (we do not combine a word with its own elements, in a kind of stop-start or forward-backward jerk)" (Deleuze 1997, 110).

10. For a more complicated portrait of Mansfield as Dido's guardian, see Krikler (2007).

11. For a discussion of the images of black people in eighteenth-century British art, see Dabydeen 1997; Tobin 1999; and Wood 2000.

12. The 1779 portrait of Dido Elizabeth Belle and Lady Elizabeth Murray was formerly attributed to Johan Zoffany, but the artist is now considered unknown. The only textual description of Dido is a racist portrait in the diary of Thomas Hutchinson, an American loyalist in London.

CHAPTER 2

1. The earliest art form on the island belongs to the native Taíno/Arawak people, the cultural elements of which *oungans* and *manbos* incorporated into Vodou. After the revolution, the French colony of Saint-Domingue was renamed Haiti as a restoration of the Taíno name Ay-ti, meaning "land of mountains."

2. *Pwen* can be used in a variety of contexts, including verbally "throwing the point," but in all instances signals "a condensation point for symbolic meaning" (McCarthy Brown 1995, 32).

3. The *lwa* are also known as *zanj* (angels), *mistè* (mysteries), *sen* (saints), and even *djab* (devils), as Colin Dayan explains, due to Christian efforts at religious conversion that Voudouisants resignified (1995, 104).

4. Anthropologist Karen E. Richman explains that the frequency with which the Kreyòl word *dyaspora* or *jaspora* became used during the late eighties denotes a shift in the consciousness of Haitians living in the United States from a condition of exile to one of immigrant (2005, 28–29). Yet, as Edwidge Danticat explains, *dyaspora* is used by Haitian migrants not only to claim American nationality but also to feel connected to each other and to Haiti: "Haiti then had nine geographic departments and the tenth was the floating homeland, the ideological one, which joined all Haitians living outside of Haiti, in the *dyaspora*" (2010, 49).

5. One of the first of Zépherin's paintings Rediker purchased was *The Spirit of the Indian Facing Colonization,* which shows a Taíno woman with a Spanish ship behind her and a black face emerging from her chest as the subjugated race that will replace the exterminated native population. Rediker calls it "a stunning allegory of the origins of the New World" (2014).

6. The ship's name was misspelled as *Brookes* in the text of *Description of a Slave Ship*, the abolitionist broadside in which the diagram first appeared.

7. The Comte de Mirabeau commissioned the making of a three-foot wooden model, complete with wooden men and women painted black to represent the slaves, which he planned to use as a prop in his antislavery speeches (Finley 2018, 77–81).

8. The ubiquity of the *Brooks* diagram in black culture is evident in its appearance on the album sleeve of roots reggae artists Bob Marley & The Wailers' *Survival* (1979).

9. A color image of Zéphirin's *The Slave Ship Brooks* can be view at https://www.beaconbroadside.com/broadside/2014/08/the-art-of-frantz-zephirin.html

10. Trouillot's well-known assessment speaks more to the official French and American positions on Haiti. During the early nineteenth century, free African Americans and white abolitionists like William Wilberforce and Clarkson celebrated the new black republic (Sinha 2016, 62–64). The African American activist Prince Saunders collaborated with Clarkson on a plan to resettle American freemen in Haiti by having Henri Christophe offer them citizenship and land, which they hoped would be a step toward an official recognition of the new nation's sovereignty. Their plan was interrupted by the revolt that resulted in Christophe taking his own life, but in 1824–25, under President Jean Pierre Boyer, six thousand African Americans emigrated to Haiti (C. Miller 2013, 88–126).

11. As C. L. R. James explains about Clarkson's assistance to Vincent Ogé, the free mixed-race leader of a 1790 revolt against the French colonialists in Saint-Domingue, the abolitionist would not have aided and abetted a revolt in any of the British colonies ([1938] 1989, 73).

12. Cécile Fatiman was a light-skinned mulatto woman who was also a *manbo*. She is reported as being the daughter of an African woman sold into slavery and a Corsican prince (Dayan 1995, 47; Dubois 2004, 99–100).

13. When Clarkson showed the stowage plan of the *Brooks* to Mirabeau during a trip to Paris in 1789, the French statesman described it as a "living coffin" (Sinha 2016, 99). An 1827 American version of the diagram was accompanied by a description of the space allocated to each slave as approximating the amount of space in a coffin (Rediker 2007, 329; Wood 1997, 226).

14. The two sea *lwa* are among the most powerful ancestral spirits, but as Dayan reminds us, there are thousands of *lwa* that cannot be classified because "they are ever being born or reconstructed, dying or being forgotten" (2000, 21).

15. The racial significance of "black" and "white" is as complex as the gendering of the mermaid and the whale. Alfred Métraux explains that white is the symbolic color of water spirits, which is why Agwe appears as a mulatto ([1959] 1972, 102). Although Agwe and Lasirèn are generally depicted as light-skinned *lwa*, they are not always represented in that way. Moreover, the color of their skin alludes to their rule over the riches of the ocean and wealth being associated with a proximity to whiteness. I am indebted to Katherine Smith for explaining this aspect of whiteness in Vodou iconography.

16. Since Vodou signification resists the singularity and fixity of codified religions, "Ginen" is used in a variety of contexts beyond the sense of a "spiritual Africa" I am invoking here. For the wider usage of Ginen, see Rachel Beauvoir and Didier Dominique (2003, 70–72). I am grateful to Michel DeGraff for translating these pages from the Kreyòl for me.

17. Jean-Daniel Lafontant similarly described to me the sacred significance of reefs between the Haitian coastal town of Petit-Goâve and the Île de la Gonâve

in the gulf adjacent to Port-au-Prince (Jean-Daniel Lafontant, interview with the *oungan*, March 3, 2016). Métraux also mentions the reef known as Trois Islets as the site of sacrifices for Agwe (103).

18. Duval-Carrié explains that his family, belonging as they do to Haiti's elite social class, which is overwhelmingly Catholic, initially disapproved of his affinity for Vodou and the arts (1995, 76).

19. For a criticism of the category of the primitive underlying the naïve/modern classification of Haitian art, see Lerebours (1989, 1, 264–66); Alexis (2007; and Célius (2016).

20. The exhibition of Duval-Carrié's work at the Museum for African and Oceanic Art reflects the classification of art from the Global South as primitive, which is a classification that has since changed.

21. Danticat's short story "Children of the Sea" (1995), originally published as "From the Ocean Floor" in 1993, invokes a Middle Passage memory for telling the story of Haitian refugees fleeing the political instability of their country by boat. Its title refers to the underwater spirits that the male narrator has already seen in a dream and eventually joins when his boat springs a leak and sinks. For a discussion of a Vodou imaginary in Danticat's story and other *botpippel* fiction, see N'Zengou Tayo 1998. For a discussion of Haitian *botpippel* songs, see Averill 1997, 147–54.

22. For a discussion of Leys's work, see Philogene (2004).

23. The transition from life to death involving a passage through water exists in Dahomean and Kongo religions and is a sacred attribute that survived in Vodou (Desquiron 1990, 106).

24. Duval-Carrié acknowledges an explicit use of *pwen* as "a major, reiterated feature of his work" (Benson 2008, 156).

25. A color image of Duval-Carrié's *The Indigo Room* can be viewed at https://www.lotsafunmaps.com/viewm.php?id=8691

26. Duval-Carrié spotted a museum poster of his painting *Azaka, Agro Rex (Azaka, King of Agriculture)* in the Vodou community of Sucrée in Haiti (Duval-Carrié 1995, 75). In the painting, the *lwa* of farmers, who usually wears peasant clothes, is dressed in aristocratic finery and is also is blind in one eye as a critical commentary on the ecological devastation of the Haitian countryside. A Vodou appropriation of Duval-Carrié's unorthodox depiction of the *lwa* is an indication of the religion's capacity to incorporate objects that originate from outside the community.

27. The Ezili of *The Indigo Room* is a version of Duval-Carrié's (2004) painting of Ezili Dantò, in which she is holding a boat in each hand to represent the African and Haitian diasporas.

28. Danticat explains *lòt bò dlo* as signifying "the eternal afterlife as well as an émigré's eventual destination" (2010, 94).

CHAPTER 3

1. In Jamaica, Spiritism is more strongly articulated through a Christian idea of "the soul." Its tri-part conception of the soul nonetheless approximates Vodou's tri-part self, which consists of the *kò kadav* (cadaver), the *gwo bon*

anj (big guardian angel), and the *ti bon anj* (little guardian angel). Once the life force or *nam* has left the the *kò kadav*, the *ti bon anj* goes to heaven. The *gwo bon anj* has a life that is separate from the body as it can travel during sleep, visit others in dreams, and after death is sent to Ginen to join ancestral spirits (Desmangles 1992, 68–71; Dayan 1995, 67–68; McCarthy Brown 2006, 8–11). Barry Chevannes describes the idea of the soul belonging to Jamaican creolized religions in this way: "The multiple concept of the soul is still found in Jamaica: the soul, which goes to hell or heaven; the spirit, which can journey during sleep; and the shadow, or inner self, of which the visible shadow is but a reflection" (1998, 7). The shadow remains with a corpse after death but can wander if the deceased has not received a proper burial (Schuler 1980, 72–73).

2. American plantations are now included in hemispheric approaches to a plantation economy, which at the time of the British Emancipation Act of 1834 extended from Maryland and Delaware in the north, to Brazil in the south and the English, French, Spanish, and Dutch colonies on the Caribbean islands and along the South American coastal areas. "The configuration of the Plantation was the same everywhere," writes Glissant, "from northeastern Brazil to the Caribbean to the southern United States: *casa grande e senzala,* the big House and the slave hut, masters and slaves" (1999, 10).

3. Since 1976, Brodber has been a member of the Twelve Tribes of Israel, to which Bob Marley also belonged, and while not a strict follower of its teachings, Rastafarianism, along with black nationalism and black feminism, inform her work (Roberts 2006, 13–26).

4. For a more extensive discussion of Hall's diasporic model, see my "Thinking 'Diaspora' with Stuart Hall" (2018).

5. In Myal spirit possession, ancestral spirits are referred to as old Africans (Brathwaite 1978, 48; Warner-Lewis 2003, 147).

6. Carolyn Cooper (1992) examines spirit possession as a trope in an earlier body of Caribbean and African American women's writing, including Morrison's *Tar Baby* (1981) and Brodber's *Myal.* In the latter novel spirit possession appears as a healing process to "spirit thievery" or zombification.

7. We are reminded that in the not too distant past, Revival religions were called Pocomania, or "little madness," in allusion to the state of mind when a spirit mounts. Pocomania is believed to be a corrupt form of Pukumina, which means "small dance of ancestral possession" (L. James 2009, 322).

8. For comparison of Ella to Hurston, see Roberts (2006, 215–68); Toland-Dix (2007); and Pinto (2013, 106–41).

9. Roberts points out that whereas Ella receives royalties from the recordings she makes, Hurston did not receive any payments due to the recorder being given to the white male ethnomusicologist, Alan Lomax, who accompanied her (2006, 222).

10. The editor, known only as E. R. Anderson, is not gender-identified and could potentially be either male or female since pan-Africanism promoted a racial solidarity between men and women. However, since the Black World Press is identified in *Louisiana* as a small black women's press, I understand the editor to be female.

11. Brodber recounts how *Louisiana* was written, in part, as a response to a 1979 trip she took to Somalia and Egypt, where the interaction of African Caribbeans, African Americans, and Africans was informed by their internalization of racist stereotypes each group had about the other (2012, 125).

12. The Bayou Teche belonged to a Louisiana sugar plantation region, the stately homes of which have been preserved as historic sites.

13. "He Who Feels It Knows It" is the title of a 1966 song by the Jamaican ska band The Wailers, which was reformed in 1974 as the reggae band Bob Marley and the Wailers.

14. Certeau provides examples of different conceptions of time from non-Western cultures, ending with a West African one that, he claims, ethnography forced into a modern Western frame: "Among the Fô of Dahomey, history is *remuho*, 'the speech of these past times'—speech (*ho*), or presence, which comes from upriver and carries downstream. It has nothing in common with the conception (apparently close to it, but actually of ethnographical and museological origin) that, in *dissociating* current time from tradition, in thus imposing a break between a present and a past, and in actually upholding the Western relation whose terms it simply reverses, defines identity through a return to a past or marginalized 'negritude'" (1988, 4–5).

15. Translator Peggy Kamuf notes that Derrida uses the French word *revenant*, which literally means "that which comes back" (Derrida 1994, 224n1).

16. The first Asian indentured workers were transported to Jamaica in 1845, a few years after those from West Africa, but continued well into the early twentieth century. While those numbers from China remained small, East Indian indentured workers in Jamaica, behind Trinidad and Guyana, were the third-largest in the English-speaking Caribbean. Today, Indo-Jamaicans constitute less than 1 percent of the nation's population. For discussions of the history and culture of Indians in Jamaica, see Bryan (1991, 149–53); Shepherd (1993); and Mansingh and Mansingh (1999).

17. Brathwaite explains that Miss Queenie distinguishes Zion from Kumina, since the possession rituals of the former are articulated through a Christian language of the Holy Spirit and speaking in tongues as opposed to the Kikongo of Kumina (1978, 52).

18. Congo Square, the place where slaves and black freemen gathered to sing and dance to African-based musical instruments, is often identified as a birthplace of jazz.

19. For an overview of a depiction in Caribbean women's literature of black men as "helpers, healers" and "co-conspirators" of black women, see Valovirta (2013).

CHAPTER 4

1. Brathwaite provides the following definition of Salt: "Time or temne of . loss of waters . oases . leaving (only) a wilderness of bleak white mineral" (2002, vol. 2).

2. As Ngũgĩ wa Thiong'o recalls: "It was during the ceremony, with the women singing Gĩtiiro, a kind of dialogue in song and dance, that Edward

Brathwaite was given the name of Kamau, the name of a generation that long ago had struggled with the elements to tame the land and make us into what we now were. Edward, the name of the British king under whose brief reign in the 1920s some of the Tigoni lands had been appropriated by blue-blooded aristocrats who wanted to turn Kenya into a white man's country, had now been replaced by Kamau" (1994, 678).

3. Characterizing Brathwaite's dream as the typesetter's nightmare, Graeme Rigby (1994) describes the difficulty of preparing his Sycorax Video Style for print through laborious acts of translation that inevitably involved a loss of the original form. Since Brathwaite self-published his books as computer page printouts, Rhonda Cobham-Sander refers to the press as "a chronically under-funded one-man publishing enterprise" (2004, 198).

4. Ngũgĩ, who uses orature for aligning oral cultures with literature, reports having been "mesmerized by the voice of orature" (1994, 678) while listening to Brathwaite reading his work. My students have expressed a similar experience whenever I play recordings of Brathwaite performing his poems.

5. Cultural critic Mark Dery coined the term "Afrofuturism" in 1993 for de-scribing a black perspective on and inventive usage of technological culture. In addition to African American science fiction, he includes Jean-Michel Basquiat's paintings, Lizzie Borden's *Born in Flames,* Sun Ra's Omniverse Arkestra, Par-liament-Funkadelic's astrofunk, and black-written and black-drawn futuristic comics. "African Americans, in a very real sense," he explains in reference to a common futuristic story line, "are the descendants of alien abductees; they inhabit a sci-fi nightmare in which unseen but no less impassable force fields of intolerance frustrate their movements; official histories undo what has been done; and technology is too often brought to bear on black bodies (branding, forced sterilization, the Tuskegee experiment, and tasers come readily to mind)" (1994, 180). There is now an emerging scholarship on Afrofuturism in Carib-bean women's literature such as Brodber's *The Rainmaker's Mistake* (Josephs 2013) and Nalo Hopkinson's speculative fiction (Boyle 2009; Faucheux 2017; Moynagh 2018). Declaring Afrofuturists to "prize the histories encoded in the left over, the discarded, the scattered" (2017, 178), Somalian American poet and fiction writer Sofia Samatar (2017) makes a case for the planetary history of a genre more closely identified with African American and Caribbean science fiction and music.

6. Brathwaite explains that the Industrial Revolution "wasn't only one-way traffic. The slaves too used this Revolution" (1983, 33). In *X/Self,* he describes the fashioning of a new musical instrument from industrial waste as "discarded Trinidad oil industry drums converted into steel drum pans, regarded as one of the genuinely new (certainly ingenious) musical instrument creations of the twentieth century" (1987, 123).

7. The Sycorax of Shakespeare's *Tempest* is from Algiers in North Africa, which belongs to the Mediterranean world of its plot. Brathwaite, however, identifies Algiers as the name of the New Orleans neighborhood where "that first 'modern' Sycorax, Marie Leveau, lives" (1999, 189). The phonological as-sociation and diasporic doubling of names connects his writings, via Zora Neale Hurston's *Mules and Men,* to Brodber's *Louisiana.*

8. The Caribbean Artists Movement was founded by Brathwaite, John La Rose, and Andrew Salkey. For a description and history of the movement, see Brathwaite (1968) and Walmsley (1992).

9. The period to which Brathwaite refers would be the summer after his 1987–88 Fulbright Fellowship at Harvard University.

10. The freshwater Lake Chad that serves as an oasis metaphor for Brathwaite has itself become a wasteland due to drought and overuse. This historical reality points to the divergence of modern Africa from the imaginary Africa that Stuart Hall identifies as existing in African diaspora culture (1990, 231–32).

11. The pictogram that Brathwaite calls the Stark version appears after the title page of *The Zea Mexican Diary* (1993a) and is the one that is reproduced in "Dream Chad." He named the Apple computer he purchased for himself Stark, which is also his invented name for Caliban's sister and, as such, alludes to black women's writing. He includes in "STARK WRITING" Mary Prince, Mary Seacole, Paule Marshall, Alice Walker, Toni Morrison, Erna Brodber, Jamaica Kincaid, Maryse Condé, Carolivia Herron, and Cynthia James (1994a, 316).

12. Brathwaite describes the temporality of historical events and people in his poems as approximating that of dreams because they do not proceed chronologically but through metaphors and associations (1985, 465–67). Unlike Duval-Carrié's use of the Sargasso Sea as a metaphor for the Middle Passage and Caribbean creolization, for Rhys it represents the spatial distance between Europe and its West Indian colonies, between the English and the white Creole who were the Caribbean-born people of European descent.

13. The mystic writing pad, or magic slate, was invented two years before Freud wrote his "Notiz über den Wunderblock" in 1925.

14. *Archive Fever* is the published version of a lecture Derrida gave on June 5, 1994, at the Freud Archives in London. Since he joined the faculty of the University of California at Irvine's Critical Theory program in 1986, it is likely that the California location he mentions is Irvine.

15. Steedman (2002, 2) reminds us that Derrida's *Archive Fever* did not initiate "the archival turn" but followed the scrutiny of the archive that preceded it. Laura Ann Stoler also mentions the longer history of the treatment of the archive as subject, at least since Foucault's writings during the seventies (2009, 4).

16. "Saving the Word" is Carolivia Herron's introduction to Brathwaite's reading of *SHAR* at Harvard University, where in the place of her own "lost words" she reads a written note by Brathwaite. Cobham-Sander observes that the circulation of Herron's introduction some two years before *SHAR* appeared in print is a sign of "the kinds of inefficiencies around the distribution and preservation of the written word in the Caribbean that cause the frustration so evident in Brathwaite's words" (2004, 198).

17. The journal *Small Axe* initiated an online digital bibliographic project in December 2014 as a living library that builds on Doris's bibliographic work.

18. In the dreamstorie "Dream Haiti" (1994b, 94–111), "Salvages" is the name of the boat containing Haitian refugees attempting to escape a U.S. Coast Guard cutter. DeLoughrey (2010) explains the "savage/salvage" pun in the two dreamstories "Dream Haiti" and "Salvages" as figuring the wasted lives of Atlantic modernity. "Salvages" is also about a loss of land because the narrator

aboard the boat is washed up on Sandylane Beach, a place from Brathwaite's childhood that the government sold to private interests during the fifties (2004b, 150). The word "salvage" equally channels T. S. Eliot's poem "The Dry Salvages," the "Legba voice" of which Brathwaite reports hearing during his Time of Salt (2002, 2:571). His invocation of a Euro-American modernist like Eliot as Legba points to his idea of creolization as a diversion of Western culture through African orality. He explains how orality in Caribbean poetry is indebted to Eliot's introduction of "the speaking voice, the conversational tone" into modernist poetry (1993b, 286).

19. Brathwaite considers carnivals like the Crop Over Parade to be a public and secular practice that shares the same cosmology of private and sacred ones like Vodou (1996, 4). For an explanation of the *mampi*-sized (full-figured) black female body as a rejection of the white gaze and Western standards of beauty, see Cooper (2004, 138–40).

20. This, and other writings, appeared on the "Save CowPastor" website established by British poet Tom Raworth. As an indication of the nonpermanency of web pages, the site was deactivated with the passing of Raworth in 2017. Despite its death as a live web page, "Save CowPastor" can be accessed through the Wayback Machine, which as an archive of past digital content retrieves lost words from the depths of cyberspace: https://web.archive.org/web/20130629230449/http://tomraworth.com/wordpress/

Bibliography

Aarons, John A. 2005. "Hurricanes and Disaster Response: Lessons Learned in Jamaica from 'Gilbert.'" In *Preparing for the Worst, Planning for the Best: Protecting Our Cultural Heritage from Disaster,* edited by Johanna G. Wellheind and Nancy E. Gwinn, 117–25. Boston: De Gruyter.

Abbate, Janet. 2012. *Recoding Gender: Women's Changing Participation in Computing.* Cambridge: MIT Press.

Alexis, Gérald. 2007. "Devotion to Style and Color." *Américas* (May 1): 28–36.

Anglade, Pierre. 1998. *Inventaire étymologique des termes Creoles des Caraïbes d'origine Africaine.* Paris: Harmattan.

Anim-Addo, Joan. 2013. "Gendering Creolisation: Creolising Affect." *Feminist Review* 104, no. 1: 5–23.

Appadurai, Arjun. 1990. "Topographies of the Self: Praise an Emotion in Hindu India." In *Language and the Politics of Emotion,* edited by Catherine A. Lutz and Lila Abu-Lughod, 92–112. Cambridge: Cambridge University Press.

Apter, Andrew, and Lauren Derby. 2010. Introduction to *Activating the Past: History and Memory in the Black Atlantic World,* edited by Apter and Derby, xiii–xxxiii. Newcastle upon Tyne: Cambridge Scholars Publishing.

Arondekar, Anjali. 2009. *For the Record: On Sexuality and the Colonial Archive in India.* Durham, N.C.: Duke University Press.

———. 2015. "In the Absence of Reliable Ghosts: Sexuality, Historiography, South Asia." *Differences* 25, no. 5: 98–122.

Asquith, Wendy. 2012. "Beyond Immobilised Identities: Haitian Art and Internationalism in the Mid-Twentieth Century." In *Kafou: Haiti, Art and*

Vodou, edited by Alex Farquharson and Leah Gordon, 40–44. Nottingham: Nottingham Contemporary.

Austen, Veronica J. 2011. "*Zong!*'s 'Should We?': Questioning the Ethical Representation of Trauma." *English Studies in Canada* 37, no. 3–4: 61–81. doi: 10.1353/esc.2011.0038.

Averill, Grage. 1997. *A Day for the Hunter, a Day for the Prey: Popular Music and Power in Haiti.* Chicago: University of Chicago Press.

Baker, Houston A., Jr. 1993. *Workings of the Spirit: The Poetics of Afro-American Women's Writing.* Chicago: University of Chicago Press.

Barrows, Adam. 2010. "'The Shortcomings of Timetables': Greenwich, Modernism, and the Limits of Modernity." *Modern Fiction Studies* 56, no. 2: 262–89.

Baucom, Ian. 2005. *Specters of the Atlantic: Finance, Capital, Slavery, and the Philosophy of History.* Durham, N.C.: Duke University Press.

Bdosparks. 2014. Comment on webpage About the Library, Archival, Museum Services, National Archives of Grenada (July 27). https://grenadanationalarchives.wordpress.com/about/.

Beaubrun, Mimerose P. 2013. *Nan Dòmi: An Initiate's Journey into Haitian Vodou.* Translated by D. J. Walker. San Francisco: City Lights.

Beauvoir, Rachel, and Didier Dominique. 2003. *Savalou E.* Montreal: Éditions du CIDIHCA.

Bell, Bernard W. 1987. *The Afro-American Novel and Its Tradition.* Amherst: University of Massachusetts Press.

Benjamin, Walter. 1975. "Eduard Fuchs: Collector and Historian." Translated by Knut Tarnowski. *New German Critique,* no. 5 (Spring): 27–58.

Benson, LeGrace. 2006. "How *Houngans* Use the Light from Distant Stars." In Michel and Bellegarde-Smith, 155–79.

———. 2008. "On Reading *Continental Shifts* and Considering the Works of Edouard Duval-Carrié." *Small Axe* 12, no. 3 (2008): 151–64.

Bernier, Celeste-Marie. 2014. "'The Slave Ship Imprint': Representing the Body, Memory, and History in Contemporary African American and Black British Painting, Photography, and Installation Art." *Callaloo* 37, no. 4: 990–1022.

Best, Stephen. 2018. *None Like Us: Blackness, Belonging, Aesthetic Life.* Durham, N.C.: Duke University Press.

Blain, Keisha N. 2018. "'To Keep Alive the Teaching of Garvey and the Work of the UNIA': Audley Moore, Black Women's Activism, and Nationalist Politics during the Twentieth Century." *Palimpsest* 7, no. 2: 83–107.

Boime, Albert. 1990. "Turner's *Slave Ship*: The Victims of Empire." *Turner Studies* 10, no. 1: 34–43.

Bolster, W. Jeffrey. 1998. *Black Jacks: African American Seamen in the Age of Sail.* Cambridge: Harvard University Press.

Boyle, Elizabeth. 2009. "Vanishing Bodies: 'Race' and Technology in Nalo Hopkinson's *Midnight Robber* 7, no. 2: 177–91.

Brathwaite, Doris Monica. 1986. *EKB: His Published Prose & Poetry, 1948–1986: A Checklist.* Mona, Jamaica: Savacou Cooperative.

Brathwaite, Edward. 1968. "The Caribbean Artists Movement." *Caribbean Quarterly* 14, no. 1/2 (1968): 57–59.

———. 1973. *The Arrivants*. New York: Oxford University Press.

———. 1974. *Contradictory Omens: Cultural Diversity and Integration in the Caribbean*. Mona, Jamaica: Savacou.

———. 1975. "Caribbean Man in Space and Time." *Savacou* 111/112 (September): 1–11.

———. 1977a. "Hex." In *Mother Poem*. New York: Oxford University Press.

———. 1977b. *Nanny, Sam Sharpe, and the Struggle for People's Liberation*. Kingston, Jamaica: API for the National Heritage Week Committee.

———. 1978. "The Spirit of African Survival in Jamaica." *Jamaica Journal*, no. 42: 44–63.

Brathwaite, Edward Kamau. 1982. *Gods of the Middle Passage*. Mona, Jamaica: E. K. Brathwaite.

———. 1983. "Caribbean Culture: Two Paradigms." In *Missile and Capsule*, edited by Jürgen Martini, 9–54. Bremen, Germany: University of Bremen Press.

———. 1984. *History of the Voice: The Development of Nation Language in Anglophone Caribbean Poetry*. London: New Beacon.

———. 1985. "Metaphors of Underdevelopment: A Proem for Hernan Cortez." *New England Review and Bread Loaf Quarterly* 7, no. 4: 453–76.

———. 1987. *X/Self*. New York: Oxford University Press.

———. 1989a. *Atumpan*. Sound recording, cassette tape, 53 min., 30 sec. Recorded September 22, 1988. Washington, D.C.: Watershed Intermedia.

———. 1989b. "Interview with Stewart Brown." By Stewart Brown. *Kyk-over-al* 40: 84–93.

———. 1990. *SHAR: Hurricane Poem*. Mona, Jamaica: Savacou.

———. 1991. "An Interview with Nathaniel N. Mackay." By Nathaniel N. MacKay. *Hambone* 9 (Winter): 42–59.

Brathwaite, Kamau. 1993a. The Zea Mexican Diary: 7 Sept 1926–7 Sept 1986. Madison: University of Wisconsin Press.

———. 1993b. *Roots*. Ann Arbor: University of Michigan Press.

———. 1994a. *Barabajan Poems: 1492–1992*. New York: Savacou North.

———. 1994b. *DreamStories*. Harlow: Longman.

———. 1994c. *Trench Town Rock*. Providence: Lost Roads.

———. 1996. "Note(s) on Caribbean Cosmology." *River City* 16, no. 2 (Summer): 1-17.

———. 1999. *ConVERSations with Nathaniel Mackay*. Rhinebeck, N.Y.: We Press.

———. 2001. "Interview with Kwame Dawes." In *Talk Yuh Talk: Interviews with Anglophone Caribbean Poets,* by Kwame Dawes, 22–37. Charlottesville: University Press of Virginia.

———. 2002. *MR (Magical Realism)*. 2 vols. New York: Savacou North.

———. 2004a. "Interview with Emily Allen Williams." In *The Critical Response to Kamau Brathwaite*, edited by Emily Allen Williams, 294–314. Westport, Ct.: Praeger.

———. 2004b. "The Namsetoura Papers." *Hambone* 17 (Fall): 125–73.

———. 2005a. "Letter to Mervyn Morris." *Save Cow Pastor,* April 23. http://tomraworth.com/kambay.html.

———. 2005b. "My Emmerton 2005." *57 Productions*. http://www.57produc-
tions.com

———. 2005c. "Poetics, Revelations, and Catastrophes." Interview by Joyelle
McSweeney. *Rain Taxi* (Fall): 1–8.

———. 2005d. "The Rosie Doc." *Save Cow Pastor,* May. http://tomraworth.
com/25may05.html.

———. 2016. *Strange Fruit*. Leeds: Peepal Tree.

———. 2017. *the lazarus poems*. Middletown, Ct.: Wesleyan University Press.

Brennan, Teresa. 2004. *The Transmission of Affect*. Ithaca, N.Y.: Cornell University Press.

Brodber, Erna. 1984. "The Second Generation of Freemen in Jamaica, 1907–
1944." Ph.D. diss., University of the West Indies, Mona.

———. 1990. "Fiction in the Scientific Procedure." In *Caribbean Women Writers: Essays from the First International Conference,* edited by Selwyn Regi-
nald Cudjoe, 164–68. Wellesley: University of Massachusetts Press.

———. (1994) 1997. *Louisiana*. Jackson: University Press of Mississippi.

———. 2003/2004. "Erna Brodber." Interview by Keshia Abraham. *Bomb* 86
(Winter): 28–33.

———. 2012. "Me and My Head-Hurting Fiction." *Small Axe* 39: 119–25.

Brown, Bev E. L. 1985. "Mansong and Matrix: A Radical Experiment."
Kunapipi 7, no. 2: 68–79.

Brown, Stewart. 1995. "'Writin in Light': Orality-thru-typography, Kamau
Brathwaite's Sycorax Video Style." In *The Pressures of the Text: Orality,
Texts and the Telling of Tales,* edited by Brown, 125–36. Birmingham: Uni-
versity of Birmingham.

Brown, Vincent. 2008. *The Reaper's Garden: Death and Power in the World of
Atlantic Slavery*. Cambridge: Harvard University Press.

———. 2009. "Social Death and Political Life in the Study of Slavery." *American Historical Review* 114, no. 5: 1231–49.

Brown, Wendy. 2001. *Politics out of History*. Princeton, N.J.: Princeton University Press.

Bryan, Patrick. 1991. *The Jamaican People 1880–1902: Race, Class and Social
Control*. Kingston: University of the West Indies Press.

Byrd, Jodi A. 2011. *The Transit of Empire: Indigenous Critiques of Colonialism*. Minneapolis: University of Minnesota Press.

Carrigan, Anthony. 2011. *Postcolonial Tourism: Literature, Culture, and Environment*. London: Routledge.

Carson, Rachel L. 1989. *The Sea around Us*. New York: Oxford University
Press.

Célius, Carlo A. 2016. "'Hatian Art' and Primitivism: Effects, Uses and Beyond." In *The Haiti Exception,* edited by Alessandra Benedicty-Kokken,
Jhon Picard Byron, Kaiama L. Glober, and Mark Schuller, 120–34. Liverpool: Liverpool University Press.

Certeau, Michel de. 1986. *Heterologies: Discourse on the Other*. Translated by
Brian Massumi. Minneapolis: University of Minnesota Press.

———. 1988. *The Writing of History*. Translated by Tom Conley. New York:
Columbia University Press.

Césaire, Aimé. (1956) 2017. *Journal of a Homecoming / Cahier d'un retour au pays natal*. Translated by N. Gregson Davis. Durham, N.C.: Duke University Press.

———. 1969. *Une tempête*. Paris: Éditions du Seuil.

Chakrabarty, Dipesh. 2000. *Provincializing Europe: Postcolonial Thought and Historical Difference*. Princeton, N.J.: Princeton University Press.

Chevannes, Barry. 1994. *Rastafari: Roots and Ideology*. Syracuse, N.Y.: Syracuse University Press.

———. 1998. "Introducing the Native Religions of Jamaica." In *Rastafari and Other African-Caribbean Worldviews*, edited by Chevannes, 1–19. Brunswick, N.J.: Rutgers University Press.

Christian, Barbara. 1997. "Beloved, She's Ours." *Narrative* 5, no. 1: 36–49.

Clark, VèVè A. 1991. "Developing Diaspora Literacy and *Marasa* Consciousness." In *Comparative American Identities: Race, Sex, and Nationality in the Modern Text*, edited by Hortense J. Spillers, 40-61. New York: Routledge.

Clarkson, Thomas. 1788. *Essay on the Slavery and Commerce of the Human Species, Particularly the African*. London: J. Phillips.

———. 1792. *The True State of the Case, Respecting the Insurrection at St. Domingo*. Ipswich: J. Bush.

———. 1839. *History of the Rise, Progress, and Accomplishment of the Abolition of the African Slave-Trade by the British Parliament*. London: John W. Parker.

Clough, Patricia Ticineto. 2007. Introduction to *The Affective Turn: Theorizing the Social*, edited by Clough and Jean O'Malley Halley, 1–33. Durham, N.C.: Duke University Press.

Cobham-Sander, Rhonda C. 2004. "K/Ka/Kama/Kamau: Brathwaite's Project of Self-Naming in *Barabajan Poems*." In *The Critical Response to Kamau Brathwaite*, edited by Emily Allen Williams, 197–212. Westport, Ct.: Praeger.

Connolly, Brian, and Marisa Fuentes. 2016. Introduction to "From Archives of Slavery to Liberated Futures?" Special issue, *History of the Present* 6, no. 2: 105–16.

Connor, Steven. 1999. "The Machine in the Ghost: Spiritualism, Technology and the 'Direct Voice.'" In *Ghosts: Deconstruction, Psychoanalysis, and History*, edited by Peter Buse and Andrew Stott, 203–25. Basingstoke, United Kingdom: Macmillan.

Cooper, Carolyn. 1992. "'Something Ancestral Recaptured': Spirit Possession as Trope in Selected Feminist Fictions of the African Diaspora." In *Motherlands: Black Women's Writing from Africa, the Caribbean, and South Asia*, edited by Susheila Nastra, 64–87. New Brunswick, N.J.: Rutgers University Press.

———. 2004. *Sound Clash: Jamaican Dancehall Culture at Large*. New York: Palgrave Macmillan.

Copeland, Huey, and Krista Thompson. 2017. "Afrotropes: A User's Guide." *Art Journal* 76, no. 3–4, 7–9. doi: 10.1080/00043249.2017.1412741.

Cosentino, Donald J. 2004. *Divine Revolution: The Paintings of Edouard Du-val-Carrié*. Los Angeles: UCLA Fowler Museum of Cultural History.

———. 2016. "Frantz Zéphirin." In *Dictionary of Caribbean and Afro-Latin American Biography*, edited by Henry Louis Gates Jr. and Franklin W. Knight. Oxford: Oxford University Press. http://www.oxfordaasc.com.ezp-prod1.hul.harvard.edu/article/opr/t456/e2242.

Courlander, Harold. 1973. *The Drum and the Hoe: Life and Lore of the Haitian People*. Berkeley: University of California Press.

Cugoano, Ottobah. 1787. *Thoughts and Sentiments on the Evil of Slavery*. London.

Dabydeen, David. 1994. *Turner: New and Selected Poems*. London: Cape Poetry.

———. 1997. *Hogarth's Blacks: Images of Blacks in Eighteenth-Century Art*. Manchester: Manchester University Press.

D'Aguiar, Fred. 1999. *Feeding the Ghosts*. Hopewell, N.J.: Ecco.

Danticat, Edwidge. 1995. *Krik? Krak!* New York: Vintage.

———. 2010. *Create Dangerously: The Immigrant Artist at Work*. Princeton, N.J.: Princeton University Press.

Davis, Natalie Zemon. 2013. Foreword to *The Allure of the Archive*, by Arlette Farge. Translated by Thomas Scott-Railton, ix–xvi. New Haven, Ct.: Yale University Press.

Dayan, [Colin] Joan. 1994. "Who's Got History? Kamau Brathwaite's 'Gods of the Middle Passage.'" *World Literature Today* 68, no. 4: 726–32.

———. 1995. *Haiti, History, and the Gods*. Berkeley: University of California Press.

———. 2000. "Vodoun, or the Voice of the Gods." In *Sacred Possessions: Vodou, Santería, Obeah, and the Caribbean*, edited by Margarite Fernández Olmos and Lizabeth Paravisini-Gebert, 13–36. New Brunswick, N.J.: Rutgers University Press.

———. 2001. "A New World Lament." In *For the Geography of the Soul: Emerging Perspectives on Kamau Brathwaite*, edited by Timothy J. Reiss, 333–42. Trenton, N.J.: Africa World Press.

Deckard, Sharae. 2016. "The Political Ecology of Storms in Caribbean Literature." In *The Caribbean: Aesthetics, World-Ecology, Politics*, edited by Chris Campbell and Michael Niblett, 25–45. Liverpool: Liverpool University Press.

Deleuze, Gilles. 1997. "He Stuttered." In *Essays Critical and Clinical*, translated by Daniel W. Smith and Michael A. Greco, 107–14. Minneapolis: University of Minnesota Press.

DeLoughrey, Elizabeth M. 2007. *Routes and Roots: Navigating Caribbean and Pacific Island Literatures*. Honolulu: University of Hawai'i Press.

———. 2010. "Heavy Waters: Waste and Atlantic Modernity." *PMLA* 125, no. 3: 703–12.

Deren, Maya. 1953. *Divine Horsemen: The Living Gods of Haiti*. New York: Thames and Hudson.

Derrida, Jacques. 1976. *Of Grammatology*. Translated by Gayatri Chakravorty Spivak. Baltimore: Johns Hopkins University Press.

———. 1994. *Specters of Marx: The State of the Debt, the Work of Mourning and the New International.* Translated by Peggy Kamuf. New York: Routledge.

———. [1996] 1998. *Archive Fever: A Freudian Impression.* Translated by Eric Prenowitz. Chicago: University of Chicago Press.

Dery, Mark. 1994. "Black to the Future: Interviews with Samuel R. Delany, Greg Tate, and Tricia Rose." In *Flame Wars: The Discourse of Cyberculture,* edited by Mark Dery, 179–222. Durham, N.C.: Duke University Press.

Desmangles, Leslie G. 1992. *Faces of the Gods: Vodou and Roman Catholicism in Haiti.* Chapel Hill: University of North Carolina Press.

———. 2006. "African Interpretations of the Christian Cross in Vodou." In Michel and Bellegarde-Smith, 39–50.

Desquiron, Lilas. 1990. *Racines du Vodou.* Port-au-Prince: Editions Henri Deschamps.

Diouf, Sylviane A. 2013. *Servants of Allah: African Muslims Enslaved in the Americas.* 15th anniversary ed. New York: New York University Press.

Donnell, Alison. 2006. "What It Means to Stay: Reterritorialising the Black Atlantic in Erna Brodber's Writing of the Local." *Third World Quarterly* 26, no. 3: 479–86.

Dowling, Sarah. 2011. "Sounding Impossible Bodies in M. NourbeSe Philip's *Zong!*" *Canadian Literature* 210/211: 43–59.

Dubois, Laurent. 2004. *Avengers of the New World: The Story of the Haitian Revolution.* Cambridge: Harvard University Press.

Dunham, Katherine. (1969) 1994. *Island Possessed.* Chicago: University of Chicago Press.

Duval-Carrié, Edouard. 1995. "Interviews with Contemporary Haitian Artists: Edouard Duval-Carrié." In *Tracing the Spirit: Ethnographic Essays on Haitian Art,* edited by Karen McCarthy Brown, 75–77. Seattle: University of Washington Press.

———. 2004. *The Indigo Room or Is Memory Water Soluble?* Fort Lauderdale: NSU Art Museum.

———. 2007. "Plunder and Play: Édouard Duval-Carrié's Artistic Vision." Interview by Jenny Sharpe. *Callaloo* 30, no. 2: 561–69.

———. 2013. "My Spirit Is There." Interview by Kaiama L. Glover. *Transition* 111: 14–20.

———. 2016. "The Crossing/La Traversée: Art in Haiti and the U.S. (1915–1986)." Symposium address at Pomona College Museum of Art, March 3.

Eichhorn, Kate. 2010. "Multiple Registers of Silence in M. Nourbese Philip's *Zong!*" *XCP: Cross-Cultural Poetics* 23: 33–39.

Eng, David L., and David Kazanjian. 2003. "Introduction: Mourning Remains." *Loss: The Politics of Mourning,* edited by Eng and Kazanjian, 1–25. Berkeley: University of California Press.

Eskin, Blake. 2010. "Cover Story: The Resurrection of the Dead." *New Yorker,* January 15. http://www.newyorker.com/news/news-desk/cover-story-the-resurrection-of-the-dead/.

Farquharson, Alex, and Leah Gordon, eds. 2012. *Kafou: Haiti, Art and Vodou.* Nottingham: Nottingham Contemporary.

Faubert, Michelle. 2017. "Granville Sharp's Manuscript Letter to the Admiralty on the *Zong* Massacre: A New Discovery in the British Library." *Slavery & Abolition* 38, no. 1:178–95.

Faucheux, Amandine H. 2017 "Race and Sexuality in Nalo Hopkinson's Oeuvre; or, Queer Afrofuturism." *Science Fiction Studies* 44, no. 3: 563–80.

Fernández Olmos, Margarite, and Lizabeth Paravisini-Gebert. 2000. "Introduction: Religious Syncretism and Caribbean Culture." In *Sacred Possessions: Vodou, Santería, Obeah, and the Caribbean,* edited by Fernández Olmos and Paravisini-Gebert, 1–12. New Brunswick, N.J.: Rutgers University Press.

Finley, Cheryl. 2018. *Committed to Memory: The Art of the Slave Ship Icon.* Princeton, N.J.: Princeton University Press.

Fleissner, Jennifer. 2013. "Historicism Blues." *American Literary History* 25, no. 4: 699–717.

Forbes, Curdella. 2007. "Redeeming the Word: Religious Experience as Liberation in Erna Brodber's Fiction." *Postcolonial Text* 3, no. 1:1–19.

Foucault, Michel. 1972. *The Archeology of Knowledge.* Translated by A. M. Sheridan Smith. New York: Pantheon.

Francis, Jacqueline. 2009. "The Brooks Slave Ship Icon: A 'Universal Symbol'?" *Slavery and Abolition* 30, no. 2: 327–38.

Frost, Mark. 2010. "'The Guilty Ship': Ruskin, Turner and Dabydeen." *Journal of Commonwealth Literature* 45, no. 3: 371–88.

Gaffield, Julia. 2014. "Haiti's Declaration of Independence: Digging for Lost Documents in the Archives of the Atlantic World." *Appendix* 2, no. 1. http://theappendix.net/issues/2014/1/haitis-declaration-of-independence-digging-for-lost-documents-in-the-archives-of-the-atlantic-world.

Geggus, David Patrick. 1982. "British Opinion and the Emergence of Haiti, 1791–1805." In *Slavery and British Society, 1776–1846,* edited by James Walvin, 123–49. London: Macmillan.

———. 2014. *The Haitian Revolution: A Documentary History.* Indianapolis: Hackett.

Gikandi, Simon. 1992. *Writing in Limbo: Modernism and Caribbean Literature.* Ithaca, N.Y.: Cornell University Press.

———. 2006. "Picasso, Africa and the Schemata of Difference." In *African and Diaspora Aesthetics,* edited by Sarah Nuttall, 30–59. Durham, N.C.: Duke University Press.

Gilroy, Paul. 1990. "Art of Darkness: Black Art and the Problem of Belonging to England." *Third Text* 4, no. 10: 45–52.

———. 1993. *The Black Atlantic: Modernity and Double Consciousness.* Cambridge: Harvard University Press.

Glissant, Édouard. 1992. *Caribbean Discourse: Selected Essays.* Translated by J. Michael Dash. Charlottesville: University Press of Virginia.

———. 1999. *Faulkner, Mississippi.* Translated by Barbara Lewis and Thomas C. Spear. Chicago: University of Chicago Press.

Gold, Jennifer. 2007. "Slave Ship Comes to London to Mark 20th Anniversary of Abolition." *Christian Today,* March 10. www.christiantoday.com/article/

slave.ship.comes.to.london.to.mark.200th.anniversary.of.abolition/9865.
htm.

Gomez, Michael A. 2005. *Black Crescent: The Experience and Legacy of African Muslims in the Americas.* New York: Cambridge University Press.

Gordon, Avery F. 2008. *Ghostly Matters: Haunting and the Sociological Imagination.* 2nd ed. Minneapolis: University of Minnesota Press.

Gordon, Leah. 2018. "You Can't Always Curate Your Way Out! Reflections on the Ghetto Biennale." In *Situating Global Art: Topologies, Temporalities, Trajectories,* edited by Sarah Dornhof, Nanne Buurman, Birgit Hopfener, and Barbara Lutz, 129–54. Bielefeld, Germany: Transcript-Verlag.

Gourdine, Angeletta K. M. 2004. "Carnival-Conjure, *Louisiana,* History and the Power of Women's Ethnographic Narrative." *Ariel* 35, no. 3–4: 139–58.

Goyal, Yogita. 2014. "Africa and the Black Atlantic." *Research in African Literatures* 45, no. 3: v–xxv.

Gregson v. Gilbert. 1783. *Commonwealth Legal Information Institute, English Reports,* 629–30. http://www.commonlii.org/int/cases/EngR/1783/85.pdf.

Hall, Catherine, Nicholas Draper, Keith McClelland, Katie Donington, and Rachel Lang. 2014. *Legacies of British Slave-Ownership: Colonial Slavery and the Formation of Victorian Britain.* New York: Cambridge University Press.

Hall, Stuart. 1990. "Cultural Identity and Diaspora." In *Identity: Community, Culture, Difference,* edited by Jonathan Rutherford, 222–37. London: Lawrence and Wishart.

———. 1999. "A Conversation with Stuart Hall." *Journal of the International Institute* 7, no. 1 (Fall). Permalink: http://hdl.handle.net/2027/spo.4750978.0007.107.

Handler, J. S. 2002. "Survivors of the Middle Passage: Life Histories of Enslaved Africans in British America." *Slavery and Abolition* 23, no. 1: 25–56.

Hartman, Saidiya V. 1997. *Scenes of Subjection: Terror, Slavery, and Self-Making in Nineteenth-Century America.* Oxford: Oxford University Press.

———. 2007. *Lose Your Mother: A Journey along the Atlantic Slave Route.* New York: Farrar, Straus and Giroux.

———. 2008. "Venus in Two Acts." *Small Axe* 12, no. 2: 1–14.

Helstern, Linda Lizut. 2000. "Sycorax Video Style: Kamau Brathwaite's Middle Passages." In *African Images: Recent Studies and Text in Cinema,* edited by Maureen Eke, Kenneth W. Harrow, and Emmanuel Yewah, 139–52. Trenton, N.J.: Africa World Press.

Helton, Laura, Justin Leroy, Max A. Mishler, Samantha Seeley, and Shauna Sweeney. 2015. "The Question of Recovery: An Introduction." *Social Text* 33, no. 4: 1–18.

Hesse, Barnor. 2002. "Forgotten Like a Bad Dream: Atlantic Slavery and the Ethics of Postcolonial Memory." In *Relocating Postcolonialism,* edited by David Theo Goldberg and Ato Quayson, 143–73. Malden, Mass.: Blackwell.

Hill, Robert A. 2001. *Dread History: Leonard P. Howell and Millenarian Visions in the Early Rastafarian Religion.* Chicago: Miguel Lorne.

———, ed. 2011. *The Marcus Garvey and Universal Negro Improvement Association Papers.* Vol. 11 of *The Caribbean Diaspora, 1910–1920.* Durham, N.C.: Duke University Press.

Hoare, Prince. 1820. *Memoirs of Granville Sharp, Esq.* London: Henry Colburn.

Houlberg, Marilyn. 1995. "Magique Marasa: The Ritual Cosmos of Twins and Other Sacred Children." In *The Sacred Arts of Haitian Vodou,* edited by Donald Cosentino, 267–83. Los Angeles: UCLA Fowler Museum of Cultural History.

———. 1996. "Sirens and Snakes: Water Spirits in the Arts of Haitian Vodou." *African Arts* 29, no. 2: 30–35, 101.

Hurston, Zora Neale. (1935) 1990. *Mules and Men.* New York: Harper and Row.

Hutcheon, Linda. 1988. *A Poetics of Postmodernism.* New York: Routledge.

Jackson, Shona. 2012. *Creole Indigeneity: Between Myth and Nation in the Caribbean.* Minneapolis: University of Minnesota Press.

James, C. L. R. (1938) 1989. *The Black Jacobins: Toussaint L'Ouverture and the San Domingo Revolution.* 2nd ed, revised. New York: Vintage.

James, Cynthia. 2001. "Reconnecting the Caribbean-American Diaspora in Paule Marshall's 'Brown Girl, Brownstones' and Erna Brodber's 'Louisiana.'" *CLA Journal* 45, no. 2: 151–70.

James, Leslie R. 2009. "Pocomania." In *African American Religious Cultures,* 2 vols., edited by Anthony Pinn, 322–30. ABC-CLIO. http://publisher.abc-clio.com/9781576075128.

Jones, Bridget. 1995. "'The Unity Is Submarine': Aspects of a Pan-Caribbean Consciousness in the Work of Kamau Brathwaite." In *The Art of Kamau Brathwaite,* edited by Stewart Brown, 85–100. Brigend, Mid Glamorgan, Wales: Seren.

Josephs, Kelly Baker. 2013. "Beyond Geography, Past Time: Afrofuturism, *The Rainmaker's Mistake,* and Caribbean Studies." *Small Axe* 17, no. 2: 123–35.

Keizer, Arlene R. 2004. *Black Subjects: Identity Formation in the Contemporary Narrative of Slavery.* Ithaca, N.Y.: Cornell University Press.

Kempadoo, Roshini. 2016. *Creole in the Archive: Imagery, Presence and the Location of the Caribbean Figure.* London: Rowman and Littlefield.

Kincaid, Jamaica. 1988. *A Small Place.* New York: Farrar, Straus and Giroux.

Krauss, Rosalind. 1979. "Grids." *October* 9 (Summer): 50–64. doi: 10.2307/778321.

Krikler, Jeremy. 2007. "The *Zong* and the Lord Chief Justice." *History Workshop Journal* 64: 29–47.

Lamming, George. [1960] 1992. *The Pleasures of Exile.* Ann Arbor: University of Michigan Press.

Lerebours, Michel Philippe. 1989. *Haïti et ses peintres de 1804 à 1980: Souffrances et espoirs d'un people.* Vol. 1. Port-au-Prince: Bibliothèque Nationale d'Haïti.

Lewis, Andrew. 2007. "Martin Dockray and the Zong: A Tribute in the Form of a Chronology." *Journal of Legal History* 28, no. 3: 357–70.

Lowe, Lisa. 2015. *The Intimacies of Four Continents.* Durham, N.C.: Duke University Press.

Lyall, Andrew. 2017. *Granville Sharp's Cases on Slavery.* London: Hart.

Machung, Anne. 1988. "'Who Needs a Personality to Talk to a Machine?' Communication in the Automated Office." In *Technologies and Women's Voices,* edited by Cheris Kramarae, 50–65. New York: Routledge and Kegan Paul.

Mallipeddi, Ramesh. 2016. *Spectacular Suffering: Witnessing Slavery in the Eighteenth-Century British Atlantic.* Charlottesville: University of Virginia Press.

Marcelin, Milo. 1949. *Mythologie Vodou (rite arada).* Port-au-Prince: Éditions Haïtiennes.

Massumi, Brian. 2002. *Parables for the Virtual: Movement, Affect, Sensation.* Durham, N.C.: Duke University Press.

Mbembe, Achille. 2002. "The Power of the Archive and Its Limits." In *Refiguring the Archive,* edited by Carolyn Hamilton, 19–26. Cape Town: Kluwer Academic.

McCarthy Brown, Karen. 1976. "The *Vèvè* of Haitian Vodou: A Structural Analysis of Visual Imagery." Ph.D. diss., Temple University.

———. 1991. *Mama Lola: A Vodou Priestess in Brooklyn.* Berkeley: University of California Press.

———. 1995. *Tracing the Spirit: Ethnographic Essays on Haitian Art.* Seattle: University of Washington Press.

———. 2006. "Afro-Caribbean Spirituality: A Haitian Case Study." In Michel and Bellegarde-Smith, 1–26.

McKittrick, Katherine. 2017. "Commentary: Worn Out." *Southeastern Geographer* 57, no. 1: 96–100.

McNeil, Jean. 1995. "Hoodoo, Obeah and Myal." *Times Literary Supplement,* February 3.

Métraux, Alfred. (ca. 1959) 1972. *Voodoo in Haiti.* Translated by Hugo Charteris. New York: Schocken.

Michel, Claudine. 1996. "Of Worlds Seen and Unseen: The Educational Character of Haitian Vodou." *Comparative Education Review* 40, no. 3: 280–94.

———. 2012. "Mama Lola's Triplets, Haiti's Sacred Ground, and Vodou's Quintessential Lesson." *Journal of Haitian Studies* 18, no. 2 (Fall): 34–50.

Michel, Claudine, and Patrick Bellegarde-Smith, eds. 2006. *Vodou in Haitian Life and Culture: Invisible Powers.* New York: Palgrave Macmillan.

Middelanis, Carl Hermann. 2001. "'Worldpainting.' Art-vadou, et/our néo-baroque: Le peintre haïtien Edouard Duval-Carrié." *Thamyris/Intersecting* 8: 257–71.

———. 2005. "Blending with Motifs and Colors: Haitian History Interpreted by Édouard Duval-Carrié." *Small Axe* 9, no. 2: 109–23.

Mignolo, Walter D. 1992. "Putting the Americas on the Map (Geography and the Colonization of Space)." *Colonial Latin American Review* 1, no. 1–2: 25–63.

Miller, Chrislaine Pamphile. 2013. "'Blessed Are the Peacemakers': African American Emigration to Haiti, 1816–1826." Ph.D. diss., University of California, Santa Cruz.

Miller, J. Hillis. 2007. "Boundaries in *Beloved.*" *symplokē* 15, no. 1–2: 24–39.

Mills, Michael. 2004. "More at MoA: Irvin Lippman Has Helped Change the Landmark Museum." *Broward/Palm Beach New Times,* August 12. http://www.browardpalmbeach.com/2004-08-12/culture/more-at-moa/.

Moïse, Myriam. 2010. "Grasping the Ungraspable in M. NourbeSe Philip's Poetry." *Commonwealth Essays and Studies* 33, no. 1: 23–33.

Morgan, Jennifer L. 2015. "Archives and Histories of Racial Capitalism: An Afterword." *Social Text* 33, no. 4: 153–61.

Morgan, Mary E. 2001. "The Silver Feather." In *For the Geography of the Soul: Emerging Perspectives on Kamau Brathwaite,* edited by Timothy J. Reiss, 317–31. Trenton, N.J.: Africa World Press.

Morrison, Toni. [1987] 2004. *Beloved.* New York: Random House.

———. 2008. "Rootedness: The Ancestor as Foundation." In *What Moves at the Margin: Selected Nonfiction,* edited by Carolyn C. Denard, 56–64. Jackson: University Press of Mississippi.

Morrison, Toni, and Gloria Naylor. 1985. "A Conversation." *Southern Review* 21, no. 3: 567–93.

Moynagh, Maureen. 2018. "Speculative Pasts and Afro-Futures: Nalo Hopkinson's Trans-American Imaginary." *African American Review* 51, no. 3: 211–22.

Naipaul, V. S. 1973. *The Loss of El Dorado.* Harmondsworth: Penguin.

Nair, Supriya. 2000. "Creolization, Orality, Nation Language." In *A Companion to Postcolonial Studies,* edited by Henry Schwarz and Sangeeta Ray, 236–51. Oxford: Blackwell.

Newton, John. 1788. *Thoughts upon the African Slave Trade.* 2nd ed. London: J. Buckland.

Ngũgĩ wa Thiong'o. 1994. "Brathwaite: The Voice of African Presence." *World Literature Today* 68, no. 4: 677–82.

Nixon, Rob. 1987. "Caribbean and African Appropriations of *The Tempest.*" *Critical Inquiry* 13 (Spring): 557–78.

N'Zengou Tayo, Marie José. 1998. "Le vodou dans la representation littéraire de la migration des boats-people haïtiens." *Conjonction* 203: 33–45.

O'Callaghan, Evelyn. 2012. "Play It Back a *Next* Way: Teaching Brodber Teaching Us." *Small Axe* 16, no. 3: 59–71.

Oldham, James. 2007. "Insurance Litigation Involving the Zong and Other British Slave Ships, 1780–1807." *Journal of Legal History* 28, no. 3: 299–318.

Page, Kezia. 2005. "'Two Places Can Make Children:' Erna Brodber's *Louisiana.*" *Journal of West Indian Literature* 13, no. 1/2: 57–79.

Palmié, Stephan. 2002. *Wizards and Scientists: Explorations in Afro-Cuban Modernity and Tradition.* Durham, N.C.: Duke University Press.

Paravisini-Gebert, Lizabeth, and Martha Daisy Kelehan. 2008. "The 'Children of the Sea': Uncovering Images of the *Botpippel* Experience in Caribbean Art and Literature." In *Displacements and Transformations in Caribbean Cultures,* edited by Paravisini-Gebert and Ivette Romero-Cesareo, 127–61. Gainesville: University Press of Florida.

Paton, Diana. 2015. *The Cultural Politics of Obeah: Religion, Colonialism and Modernity in the Caribbean World.* Cambridge: Cambridge University Press.

Philip, Marlene Nourbese (M. NourbeSe). 1989. *She Tries Her Tongue, Her Silence Softly Breaks*. Charlottetown, Prince Edward Island: Ragweed.

———. 1991. *Looking for Livingstone: An Odyssey of Silence*. Toronto: Mercury.

———. 1996. "In the Matter of Memory." In *Fertile Ground: Memories and Vision*, edited by Kalamu ya Salaam and Kysha N. Brown, 21–28. New Orleans: Runnagate.

———. 1997. *A Genealogy of Resistance and Other Essays*. Toronto: Mercury.

———. 2003. "Interview with an Empire." In *Assembling Alternatives: Reading Postmodern Poetries Transnationally*, edited by Romana Huk, 195–206. Middleton, Ct.: Wesleyan University Press.

———. 2005. "Song Lines of Memory." *Save Cow Pastor*, October. http://tomraworth.com/nourbeSe.pdf.

———. 2008a. "A Travelogue of Sorts: Transatlantic Trafficking in Silence and Erasure." *Anthurium* 6, no. 1: article 3. https://scholarlyrepository.miami.edu/cgi/viewcontent.cgi?article=1153&context=anthurium.

———. 2008b. *Zong! As Told to the Author by Setaey Adamu Boateng*. Middletown, Ct.: Wesleyan University Press.

———. 2014. Twitter Post. November 24, 9:32 P.M. https://twitter.com/mnourbese/status/537116710999162880.

Philogene, Jerry. 2004. "Visual Narratives of Cultural Memory and Diasporic Identities: Two Contemporary Haitian American Artists." *Small Axe* 8, no. 2: 84–99.

———. 2008. "The Continental Conversations of Edouard Duval-Carrié." *Small Axe* 12, no. 2: 142–50.

Pinto, Samantha. 2013. *Difficult Diasporas: The Transnational Feminist Aesthetic of the Black Atlantic*. New York: New York University Press.

Pollard, Velma. 2009. "Writing Bridges of Sound: *Praise Song for the Widow* and *Louisiana*." *Caribbean Quarterly* 55, no. 1: 33–41.

Pressley-Sanon, Toni. 2017. *Istwa across the Water: Haitian History, Memory, and the Cultural Imagination*. Gainesville: University of Florida Press.

Puri, Shalini. 2004. *The Caribbean Postcolonial: Social Equality, Post-Nationalism, and Cultural Hybridity*. New York: Palgrave Macmillan.

Rampini, Charles. 1873. *Letters from Jamaica: The Land of Streams and Woods*. Edinburgh, Scotland: Edmonston and Douglas.

Ramsey, Kate. 2011. *The Spirits and the Law: Vodou and Power in Haiti*. Chicago: University of Chicago Press.

Rausing, Lisbet, and Peter Baldwin. 2015. Introduction to *From Dust to Digital: Ten Years of the Endangered Archives Programme*, edited by Maja Kominko, xxxvii–xxxviii. Cambridge: Open Book.

Rediker, Marcus. 2007. *The Slave Ship: A Human History*. New York: Viking.

———. 2014. "Motley Crews and the Crucible of Culture: The Art of Frantz Zéphirin." *Beacon Broadside*, 12 Aug. http://www.beaconbroadside.com/broadside/2014/08/the-art-of-frantz-zephirin.html.

———. 2018. "Vodou Surrealism." Carnegie Museum of Art. https://blog.cmoa.org/2018/03/vodou-surrealism/.

Reed, Anthony. 2014. *Freedom Time: The Poetics and Politics of Black Experimental Writing*. Baltimore: Johns Hopkins University Press.

Reiss, Timothy J., ed. 2001. *For the Geography of the Soul: Emerging Perspectives on Kamau Brathwaite*. Trenton, N.J.: Africa World Press.

Rhys, Jean. 1966. *Wide Sargasso Sea*. London: Deutsch.

Richman, Karen E. 2007. "Peasants, Migrants and the Discovery of African Traditions: Ritual and Social Change in Lowland Haiti." *Journal of Religion in Africa* 37, no. 3: 371–97.

Ricoeur, Paul. 2006. "Archives, Documents, Traces, 1978." In *The Archive*, edited by Charles Merewether, 66–69. Cambridge: MIT Press.

Rigby, Graeme. 1994. "Publishing Brathwaite: Adventures in the Video Style." *World Literature Today* 68, no. 4: 708–14.

Roach, Joseph. 1996. *Cities of the Dead: Circum-Atlantic Performance*. New York: Columbia University Press.

Roberts, June E. 2002. "Erna Brodber's *Louisiana*: An Alternative Aesthetic, or Oral Authority in the Written Text." *Literary Griot* 14, no. 1/2: 75–93.

———. 2006. *Reading Erna Brodber: Uniting the Black Diaspora through Folk Culture and Religion*. Westport, Ct.: Preager.

Rodriguez, Emilio. 1998. "Time of the Voice, Time of the Bodies." *Caribbean Quarterly* 44, no. 3/4: 122–30.

Rohlehr, Gordon. 2007. *Transgression, Transition, Transformation: Essays in Caribbean Culture*. San Juan: Lexicon Trinidad.

Rupprecht, Anita. 2007. "'A Very Uncommon Case': Representations of the *Zong* and the British Campaign to Abolish the Slave Trade." *Journal of Legal History* 28, no. 3: 329–46.

———. 2008. "'A Limited Sort of Property': History, Memory and the Slave Ship Zong." *Slavery & Abolition* 29, no. 2: 265–77.

Rushdy, Ashraf H. A. 1999. *Neo-Slave Narratives: Studies in the Social Logic of a Literary Form*. Oxford: Oxford University Press.

Ruskin, John. 1903. *The Works of John Ruskin*. Vol. 3, *Modern Painters*, edited by E. T. Cook and Alexander Wedderburn. London: George Allen.

Samatar, Sofia. 2017. "Toward a Planetary History of Afrofuturism." *Research in African Literatures* 48, no. 4: 175–91.

Saunders, Patricia. 2001. "The Project of Becoming for Marlene Nourbese-Philip and Erna Brodber." *Bucknell Review* 44, no. 2: 133–59.

———. 2008. "Defending the Dead, Confronting the Archive: A Conversation with M. NourbeSe Philip." *Small Axe* 12, no. 2: 63–79.

Schuler, Monica. 1980. *"Alas, Alas, Kongo": A Social History of Indentured African Immigration into Jamaica, 1841–1865*. Baltimore: Johns Hopkins University Press.

Scott, David. 2008. "Introduction: On the Archaeologies of Black Memory." *Small Axe* 12, no. 2: v–xvi.

Sedgwick, Eve Kosofsky. 2003. *Touching Feeling: Affect, Pedagogy, Performativity*. Durham, N.C.: Duke University Press.

Sharpe, Christina. 2016. *In the Wake: On Blackness and Being*. Durham, N.C.: Duke University Press.

Sharpe, Jenny. 2003. *Ghosts of Slavery: A Literary Archeology of Black Women's Lives*. Minneapolis: University of Minnesota Press.

———. 2018. "Thinking 'Diaspora' with Stuart Hall." *Qui Parle* 27, no. 1: 21–46.

Shepherd, Verene. 1993. *Transients to Settlers: The Experience of Indians in Jamaica 1845–1950*. Leeds: Peepal Tree, 1993.

Shockley, Evie. 2011. "Going Overboard: African American Poetic Innovation and the Middle Passage." *Contemporary Literature* 52, no. 4: 791–817.

Mansingh, Laxmi, and Ajai Mansingh. 1999. *Home Away from Home: 150 Years of Indian Presence in Jamaica, 1845–1995*. Kingston, Jamaica: Ian Randle.

Sinha, Manisha. 2016. *The Slave's Cause: A History of Abolition*. New Haven, Ct.: Yale University Press.

Smallwood, Stephanie E. 2007. *Saltwater Slavery: A Middle Passage from Africa to American Diaspora*. Cambridge: Harvard University Press.

Smith, Katherine. 2012. "Haitian Art and the Vodou Imaginary." In *Kafou: Haiti, Art and Vodou,* edited by Alex Farquharson and Leah Gordon, 36–39. Nottingham: Nottingham Contemporary.

Smith, Valerie. 2007. "Neo–Slave Narratives." In *The Cambridge Companion to the African American Slave Narrative,* edited by Audrey A. Fisch, 168–88. Cambridge: Cambridge University Press.

Steedman, Carolyn. 2002. *Dust: The Archive and Cultural History*. New Brunswick, N.J.: Rutgers University Press.

Sterne, Jonathan. 2003. *The Audible Past: Cultural Origins of Sound Reproduction*. Durham, N.C.: Duke University Press.

Stewart, Dianne M. 2005. *Three Eyes for the Journey: African Dimensions of the Jamaican Religious Experience*. Oxford: Oxford University Press.

———. 2006. "Indigenous Wisdom at Work in Jamaica: The Power of *Kumina.*" In *Indigenous Peoples' Wisdom and Power: Affirming Our Knowledge through Narratives,* edited by Julian E. Kunnie and Nomalungelo I. Goduka, 127–40. Burlington, Vt.: Ashgate.

Stoler, Ann Laura. 2009. *Along the Archival Grain: Epistemic Anxieties and Colonial Common Sense*. Princeton, N.J.: Princeton University Press.

Strongman, Roberto. 2008. "Transcorporeality in Vodou." *Journal of Haitian Studies* 14, no. 2: 4–29.

Sullivan, Edward J. 2007. *Continental Shifts: The Art of Edouard Duval-Carrié*. Miami: American Art Corp.

———. 2008. "Navigating between the Continents: Further Thoughts on Edouard Duval-Carrié's Work." *Small Axe* 12, no. 3: 165–74.

Tanna, Laura. 1983. "Anansi—Jamaica's Trickster Hero." *Jamaica Journal* 16, no. 2: 20–30.

Taylor, Diana. 2003. *The Archive and the Repertoire: Performing Cultural Memory in the Americas*. Durham, N.C.: Duke University Press.

[Thackeray, W. M.]. 1840. "A Pictorial Rhapsody by Michael Angelo Titmarsh. With an Introductory Letter to Mr. Yorke." *Fraser's Magazine* 21 (January–June): 731.

Tinsley, Omisek'eke Natasha. 2018. *Ezili's Mirrors: Imagining Black Queer*. Durham, N.C.: Duke University Press.

Tobin, Beth Fowkes. 1999. *Picturing Imperial Power: Colonial Subjects in Eigh-teenth-Century British Painting*. Durham, N.C.: Duke University Press.

Toland-Dix, Shirley. 2007. "'This Is the Horse. Will You Ride?': Zora Neale Hurston, Erna Brodber, and Rituals of Spirit Possession." In *Just Below South: Intercultural Performance in the Caribbean and the U.S. South*, edited by Jessica Adams, Michael P. Bibler, and Cécile Accilien, 191–210. Charlottesville: University of Virginia Press.

Torres-Saillant, Silvio. 1994. "The Trials of Authenticity in Kamau Brathwaite." *World Literature Today* 68, no. 4: 697–707.

———. 2006. *An Intellectual History of the Caribbean*. New York: Palgrave Macmillan.

Trouillot, Michel-Rolph. 1995. *Silencing the Past: Power and the Production of History*. Boston: Beacon.

Turks and Caicos Museum. 2016. "Runaway Slaves: Qwest for Freedom." Turks and Caicos Museum. http://tcmuseum.org/slavery/runaway-slaves/.

Valovirta, Elina. 2013. "Blowing the Love-Breath: Healing Men in Caribbean Women's Writing." *Feminist Review* 104, no. 1: 100–118.

Walcott, Derek. 1986. "The Schooner *Flight*" and "The Sea Is History." In *Collected Poems, 1948–1984*, 345–67. New York: Farrar, Straus and Giroux.

Walmsley, Anne. 1992. *The Caribbean Artists Movement, 1966–1972: A Literary and Cultural History*. London: New Beacon.

———. 1994. "Her Stem Singing: Kamau Brathwaite's Zea Mexican Diary: 7 Sept 1926–7 Sept 1986." *World Literature Today*, 68, no. 4: 747–49.

Walvin, James. 1992. *Black Ivory: A History of British Slavery*. London: HarperCollins.

———. 2011. *The Zong: A Massacre, the Law and the End of Slavery*. New Haven, Ct.: Yale University Press.

Warner-Lewis, Maureen. 2003. *Central Africa in the Caribbean: Transcending Time, Transforming Cultures*. Kingston, Jamaica: University of the West Indies Press.

Warren, Calvin. 2016. "Black Time: Slavery, Metaphysics, and the Logic of Wellness." In *The Psychic Hold of Slavery: Legacies in American Expressive Culture,* edited by Soyica Diggs Colbert, Robert J. Patterson, and Aida Levy-Hussen, 55–68. New Brunswick, N.J.: Rutgers University Press.

Weber, Elisabeth. 2005. "Deconstruction Is Justice." *SubStance* 34, no. 1: 38–43.

Weinstein, Joel. 2007. "Memory and Its Discontents." In *Continental Shifts,* edited by Edward J. Sullivan, 57–61. Miami: American Art Corp.

Wexler, Anna. 2000. "'I Am Going to See Where My Oungan Is': The Artistry of a Haitian Vodou Flagmaker." In *Sacred Possessions: Vodou, Santería, Obeah, and the Caribbean,* edited by Margarite Fernández Olmos and Lizabeth Paravisini-Gebert, 59–78. New Brunswick, N.J.: Rutgers University Press.

Williams, Emily Allen, ed. 2004. *The Critical Response to Kamau Brathwaite*. Westport, Ct.: Praeger.

Wood, Marcus. 1997. "Imaging the Unspeakable and Speaking the Unimaginable: The 'Description' of the Slave Ship *Brookes* and the Visual Interpretation of the Middle Passage." *Lumen: Selected Proceedings from the Canadian Society for Eighteenth-Century Studies* 16: 211–45.

———. 2000. *Blind Memory: Visual Representations of Slavery in England and America*. New York: Routledge.

Wynter, Sylvia. 1990. "Beyond Miranda's 'Demonic Ground' of Caliban's 'Woman.'" In *Out of the Kumbla: Caribbean Women and Literature*, edited by Carole Boyce Davies and Elaine Savory Fido, 355–72. Trenton, N.J.: Africa World Press.

———. 2013. "The Pope Must Have Been Drunk, the King of Castile a Madman: Culture as Actuality, and the Caribbean Rethinking Modernity." In *Caribbean Political Thought: Theories of the Post-Colonial State*, edited by Aaron Kamugisha, 490–507. Kingston, Jamaica: Ian Randle.

Young, James E. 1999. "Memory and Counter-Memory: The End of the Monument in Germany." *Harvard Design Magazine* 9: 1–10.

Zéphirin, Frantz. 2012. "Dominique Batraville Interviews Frantz Zéphirin." In *Kafou: Haiti, Art and Vodou*, by Dominique Batraville, 190. Nottingham: Nottingham Contemporary.

Index

abolitionism, 69, 166n11; and
Brooks diagram, 165n7; empathy
in, 52; and empire, 35; and
Haitian Revolution, 69–70; and
melancholy, 29–30; and Middle
Passage, 28–29, 67–69, 81–82;
and slave revolts, 69–70, 166n11;
slaves, representations of, 14, 29;
and *Zong* massacre, 20, 23, 25,
27–30
Abolition of the Slave Trade Act
(1807): bicentenary of, 21, 36–37,
53, 58, 67, 164n7
affect, 21–22, 43; as form of
expression, 13, 30, 41; and gender,
21; as memory, 14, 22, 33, 37–38,
54; the social in, 13, 43, 50, 52,
84–85, 100; theories of, 21–22; in
Zong!, 42–43, 50, 52
African diaspora: and culture, 13,
15, 67, 87–89, 98, 99, 127, 153,
171n10; and personhood, 20,
24–25, 45–46, 48, 54; and trauma,
10, 14, 21–22, 24, 36, 39, 52,
58–59, 62, 74, 124, 162. *See also*
cosmology
Afrofuturism, 170n5; of Brathwaite,
124, 130
afterlife: of death, 106, 167n28; of
Middle Passage, 31, 55; of slavery,
9, 38, 40, 55
agency: of black women, 17, 21, 41,
100, 116–17, 120–22, 130–31,
150; and secular humanism, 12–13
Agwe, 70–72, 76, 166n15; in *The
Slave Ship Brooks*, 70–73; *vèvè* of,
70–72, 71 fig. 2.2
Amerindians: art of, 165n1; and
Caribbean indigeneity, 152–53,
165n5; and El Dorado, 15, 75;
Warao, 125, 140, 153
Anim-Addo, Joan, 21–22
Appadurai, Arjun, 21
Apter, Andrew, 62
archive fever, 11, 131, 143, 146–49,
158. *See also* Derrida, Jacques
archives: archival turn in, 6, 149,
171n15; *arkhē*, 148–49, 156;

191

Brown, Wendy, 163n3
Butler, Judith, 52
Byrd, Jodi, 153

Caribbean Artists Movement (CAM),
 135, 152, 153, 171n8
Carrigan, Anthony, 160
Carson, Rachel L., 79, 81
Certeau, Michel de, 112, 169n14
Césaire, Aimé, 3, 133
Chakrabarty, Dipesh, 12, 96
Chevannes, Barry, 168n1
Christian, Barbara, 114, 124
Christophe, Henri, 91, 166n10
Clark, VèVè, 10, 63–64, 164n6
Clarkson, Thomas, 29, 34, 81,
 166n13; on Haitian Revolution,
 69, 166n10
Cobham-Sander, Rhonda, 133–34,
 154, 170n3, 171n16
Collingwood, Luke, 23, 25, 27
Connolly, Brian, 7
Connor, Steven, 111
Copeland, Huey, 67
Cosentino, Donald, 65
cosmology: African, 5, 79, 129–30;
 African diasporic, 11, 124, 153,
 172n19; Judeo-Christian, 85–86;
 Vodou, 5, 14, 59, 63–64, 72, 79,
 81–84
CowPastor, 159–60, 161, 172n20
creolization: of affects, 21;
 Brathwaite's theory of, 60, 152–53,
 171n12, 172n18; and Caribbean
 modernism, 132; in Duval-Carrié,
 15, 171n12; of language, 55,
 71, 133; of religion, 71, 73, 112,
 168n1
Cruikshank, Isaac, 81
Cugoano, Quobna Ottobah, 29, 31,
 69

Dabydeen, David, 36, 57
D'Aguiar, Fred, 57; Feeding the
 Ghosts, 36, 58, 59
Danticat, Edwidge, 165n4, 167n21,
 167n28

Davis, Natalie Zemon, 156
Dayan, Colin, 62–63, 93; on
 Brathwaite, 128; on lwa, 73,
 165n3, 166n14; on "possession,"
 97–98
DeGraff, Michel, 166n16
Deleuze, Gilles, 45, 165n9
DeLoughrey, Elizabeth, 130, 171n18
Derby, Lauren, 62
Derrida, Jacques, 14, 38–39, 58;
 Archive Fever, 131–32, 146–50,
 171nn14–15; and hauntology,
 10–11, 112–13; on memory, 147
Dery, Mark, 170n5
Dockray, Martin, 157
Donnell, Alison, 99
Dowling, Sarah, 46
drapos, 61; in Duval-Carrié, 81, 91,
 93; Lasirèn in, 73
dreamstories, 17, 139, 171n18; black
 women's agency in, 150; "Dream
 Chad" as, 141–46; as prophetic,
 150; temporality of, 141, 150. See
 also Brathwaite, Kamau
Dunham, Katherine, 62
Duval-Carrié, Edouard, 5, 15–16,
 59–60; as artiste philosophe, 82;
 drapos in, 81, 91, 93; lwa in, 78–79,
 84–85, 87, 89, 90 fig. 2.6, 91, 122,
 167nn26–27; and naïve style, 5,
 77; Rétable des neuf esclaves, 77,
 86; Vodou aesthetics of, 63, 76–77,
 167n18. See also Indigo Room or
 Is Memory Water Soluble? The,
 (Duval-Carrié); La vraie histoire des
 Ambaglos (Duval-Carrié)

Edwards, Bryan, 89
Eichorn, Kate, 32, 50
Emancipation Act (Slavery Abolition
 Act of 1834), 25, 34, 70, 115, 168n2
empathy: as antislavery trope, 14, 52
Equiano, Olaudah (Gustavus Vassa),
 25, 27, 164n5
Ezili Dantò, 73–74; in The Indigo
 Room, 87, 89, 90 fig. 2.6, 91, 122,
 167n27

Pressley-Sanon, Toni, 130
Puri, Shalini, 101
pwen, 60, 165n2; in *La vraie histoire*,
81; in *The Slave Ship Brooks*, 68, 72

race: in Britain, 35–37; and
colonization, 165n5; and diaspora,
119; and *Gregson v. Gilbert*, 32,
45; mixed-race people, 53–54, 83,
125, 166n11; and slavery, 8–9, 37;
and trauma, 58
racism: countering of, 10, 36,
52, 113, 116, 120; "end of,"
113; internalized, 169n11; and
regrammaring, 120; and slavery,
59, 113, 114
Rainsford, Thomas, 81
Raleigh, Walter, 75–76
Ramchand, Kenneth, 153
Rastafarianism, 99, 117, 124; and
Brathwaite, 11, 124; Brodber, 99,
168n3
Rediker, Marcus, 65, 67, 165n5
Reid, Beverley, 139, 160
Revival Zion, 103, 117, 118, 124
Rhys, Jean, 171n12; *Wide Sargasso
Sea*, 144–45
Richman, Karen E., 95, 165n4
Ricoeur, Paul, 164n8
Rigaud, Milo, 164n6
Rigby, Graeme, 170n3
Roberts, June, 100, 124, 160
Rohlehr, Gordon, 125–26, 142, 144,
146
Rupprecht, Anita, 24, 28–29, 37
Rushdy, Ashraf H. A., 164n1
Ruskin, John, 34–36, 164n6

Saar, Alison, 91
Saar, Betye, 58
Salkey, Andrew, 171n8
Samatar, Sofia, 170n5
Sargasso Sea, 79, 81; in *La vraie
histoire*, 171n12
Saunders, Patricia, 41, 101, 108, 133
Saunders, Prince, 166n10
Scott, David, 151–52

Seacole, Mary, 171n11
Sedgwick, Eve Kosofsky, 21
Sharp, Granville, 25, 27, 30–31, 157
Sharpe, Christina, 39
Shockley, Evie, 46, 56
silence, 4; archival, 6, 50; in
Brathwaite, 131, 146; as diasporic
black female space, 14; in *Gregson
v. Gilbert*, 50; and language, 40,
42, 46; and oral history, 105; in
Philip, 19–21, 40–43, 150; and
prophecy, 146; and slavery, 20,
22; and storytelling, 20–21; and
visibility, 19; and writing, 4–5
slave revolts, 166n11; Haitian
Revolution, 37, 69–70
slavery: afterlife of, 9, 31, 40, 55;
and freedom, 15; in Haitian art,
61; and haunting, 113–15; and
hauntology, 113; and humanism,
130; and lack, 7–8; and loss, 13;
and modernity, 5; and race, 9, 37;
and silence, 20, 22; social death
of, 109; and the social sciences,
17; trauma of, 59, 113–14; and
Western humanism, 130
slaves: in abolitionist accounts,
14, 29; as cargo, 14, 20, 30, 40,
164n2; humanity of, 20, 24–25,
48; invisibility of, 74; as property,
13–14, 20, 40, 46, 48, 53
Slave Ship (Turner), 20–21, 33–36,
68, 164n6; and affect, 33; as
melancholic, 79
Slave Ship Brooks, The (Zépherin),
14–15, 65–73, 66 fig. 2.1, 86;
Agwe in, 70–73; *lwa* in, 65, 68, 73;
Middle Passage in, 71–73; *pwen*
in, 68, 72; signs of death in, 72;
Vodou iconography of, 64–65
Smallwood, Stephanie E., 24, 48
Smith, Katherine, 61, 166n15
Soulouque, Faustin, 91; in *The Indigo
Room*, 92 fig. 2.8
Spiritism. *See* spiritualism
spirit possession, 10, 62, 168n6;
and "Dream Chad," 142–43; in

FLASHPOINTS